CLYMER®

HONDA

CB750 DOHC FOURS • 1979-1982

The world's finest publisher of mechanical how-to manuals

INTERTEC PUBLISHING
P.O. Box 12901, Overland Park, Kansas 66282-2901

Copyright ©1985 Intertec Publishing

FIRST EDITION
First Printing June, 1980
Second Printing September, 1980
Third Printing January, 1981
Fourth Printing July, 1981

SECOND EDITION
First Printing February, 1982

THIRD EDITION
Revised by Ed Scott to include 1982 models
First Printing September, 1985
Second Printing July, 1986
Third Printing June, 1987
Fourth Printing April, 1988
Fifth Printing November, 1988
Sixth Printing December, 1989
Seventh Printing October, 1990
Eighth Printing August, 1991
Ninth Printing May, 1992
Tenth Printing August, 1993
Eleventh Printing January, 1995
Twelfth Printing November, 1996
Thirteenth Printing December, 1997
Fourteenth Printing October, 1999
Fifteenth Printing June, 2001

Printed in U.S.A.

CLYMER and colophon are registered trademarks of Intertec Publishing.

ISBN: 0-89287-304-3

Technical illustrations by Mitzi McCarthy.

COVER: Photographed by Michael Brown Photographic Productions, Los Angeles, California. Team Honda CB750 ridden by Roberto Pietri at the Daytona Superbike Race, 1980. Simpson RX helmet by Simpson Helmets, Torrance, California.

CONTENTS

CLYMER®

HONDA

CB750 DOHC FOURS • 1979-1982

QUICK REFERENCE DATA

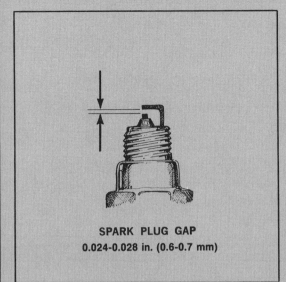

SPARK PLUG GAP

0.024-0.028 in. (0.6-0.7 mm)

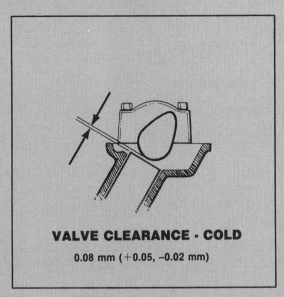

VALVE CLEARANCE - COLD

0.08 mm (+0.05, –0.02 mm)

TIMING MARK (No. 1 and No. 4 Cylinder)

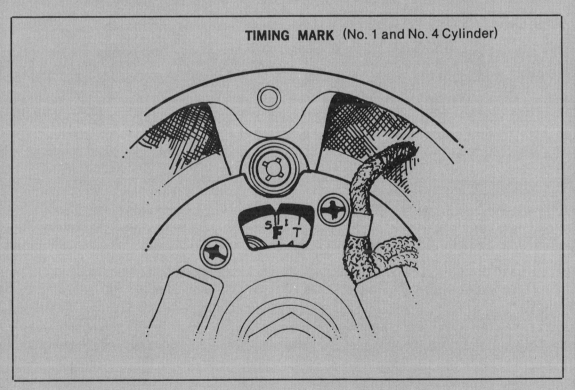

FREE PLAY ADJUSTMENTS

Clutch lever	3/8-3/4 in. (10-20 mm)
Rear brake pedal (drum type only)	3/4-1 1/4 in. (20-30 mm)
Drive chain	5/8-1 in. (15-25 mm)

FRAME TORQUE SPECIFICATIONS

Item	N·m	ft.-lb.
Front axle clamp nuts	18-25	13-18
Front axle nut	55-65	40-47
Handlebar holder/fuse panel bolts	18-25	13-18
Fork bridge bolts		
Upper	9-13	7-9
Lower	30-40	22-29
Steering stem nut	80-100	58-87
Fork 6 mm Allen bolt (bottom of slider)	8-12	6-9
Fork cap bolt	20-30	15-22
Wheel spokes	2.5-5.0	22-43 in.-lb.
Rear axle nut	80-100	58-72
Rear swing arm pivot nut	55-70	40-51
Shock absorbers		
Upper mounting nut	20-30	14-22
Lower mounting bolt	30-40	22-29
Drive sprocket nuts		
Model CB750F	55-65	40-47
Model CB750K and K-LTD	80-100	58-72
Brake torque link bolt and nut	18-25	13-18
Brake hose union bolts	25-35	18-25
Caliper mounting bolt		
1979-1981	30-40	22-29
1982		
Kokiko calipers	18-23	13-17
Nisshin calipers	20-25	14-18
Caliper shaft nut—Kokiko (1982)	30-36	22-26
Caliper shaft—Nisshin (1982)	25-30	18-22
Brake disc mounting bolts and nuts	27-33	20-24

ELECTRICAL SYSTEM

Fuse		
Main (fusible link)	30 amp	
Headlight	10 amp	
Turn signal/stoplight	10 amp	
Indicator lights	10 amp	
Meter illumination, taillight	10 amp	
Battery	12 volt, 14 amp hour	
Replacement bulbs	U.S. and Canada	U.K.
Headlight	12V, 50/65	12V 50/65
Tail/stop	12V 8/27W	12V 7/23
	(SAE 1157)	
Directionals	12V 23W	12V 24W
	(SAE) 1034/1073	
Instrument/indicators	12V 3.4W	12V 3W
	(SAE 57)	
Pilot (city)	—	12V 6W

TUNE-UP SPECIFICATIONS

Cylinder head cap nuts	26-29 ft.-lb. (36-40 N•m)
Valve clearance	
(cold below 35° C/95° F)	
Intake and exhaust	0.08 mm (+0.05/−0.02 mm)
Compression pressure	
Cold @ sea level	170 ±14 psi (12 ±1.0 kg/cm²)
Spark plug type	
1979-1981	
Standard heat range	ND X24ES-U or NGK D8EA
Cold weather*	ND X22ES-U or NGK D7EA
Extended high-speed riding	ND X27ES-U or NGK D9EA
Canadian models (all)	ND X24ESR-U or NGK DR8ESL
1982 (U.S. and Canadian)	
Standard heat range	ND X24EPR-U9 or NGK DPR8EA-9
Cold weather*	ND X22EPR-U9 or NGK DPR7EA-9
Extended high-speed riding	ND X27EPR-U9 or NGK DPR9EA-9
Spark plug gap	0.024-0.028 in. (0.6-0.7 mm)
Idle speed	1,000 ±100 rpm
Firing order	1-2-4-3

* Cold weather climate—below 5° C (41° F).

ENGINE TORQUE SPECIFICATIONS

Item	Foot Pounds (Ft.-lb.)	Newton Meters (N•m)
Cylinder head cap nuts	26-29	36-40
Camshaft bearing cap bolts	9-12	12-16
Alternator rotor bolt	58-72	80-100

TIRES

Load	Pressure (cold)
Up to 200 lb. (90 kg)	
Front - all models	29 psi (2.0 kg/cm²)
Rear	
Models CB750K, F	32 psi (2.25 kg/cm²)
Model CB750K-LTD	28 psi (2.0 kg/cm²)
Model CB750K (1980)	28 psi (2.0 kg/cm²)
Maximum load limit*	
Front - all models	28 psi (2.0 kg/cm²)
Rear - all models	40 psi (2.8 kg/cm²)

*Maximum load includes total weight of motorcycle with accessories, rider(s) and luggage.

FLUIDS

Item	Type	Quantity
Engine oil		
Above 59°F (15°C)	SAE 30	3.7 U.S. qt.
		(3.5 liters, 3.1 Imp. qt.)
32°-59°F (0°-15°C)	SAE 20 or 20W	
Below 32°F (0°C)	SAE 10W	
All purpose	10W-40	
Fork oil	ATF or SAE 10W fork oil	5.2 oz. (155cc)
Brake fluid	DOT-3	Upper level line
Fuel		
CB750K, K-LTD, F	Regular	5.3 U.S. gal.
		(20.0 liters, 4.4 Imp. gal.)
CB750C		4.5 U.S. gal.
		(16.9 liters, 3.7 Imp. gal.)

—NOTES—

INTRODUCTION

This detailed, comprehensive manual covers the Honda CB750, Models K, K Limited Edition, C and F. The expert text gives complete information on maintenance, repair, and overhaul. Hundreds of photos and drawings guide you through every step. The book includes all you need to know to keep your Honda running right.

Where repairs are practical for the owner/mechanic, complete procedures are given. Equally important, difficult jobs are pointed out. Such operations are usually more economically performed by a dealer or independent garage.

A shop manual is a reference. You want to be able to find information fast. As in all Clymer books, this one is designed with this in mind. All chapters are thumb tabbed. Important items are indexed at the rear of the book. Finally, all the most frequently used specifications and capacities are summarized on the *Quick Reference* pages at the front of the book.

Keep the book handy. It will help you to better understand your Honda, lower repair and maintenance costs, and generally improve your satisfaction with your bike.

CHAPTER ONE

GENERAL INFORMATION

The troubleshooting, maintenance, tune-up, and step-by-step repair procedures in this book are written specifically for the owner and home mechanic. The text is accompanied by helpful photos and diagrams to make the job as clear and correct as possible.

Troubleshooting, maintenance, tune-up, and repair are not difficult if you know what to do and what tools and equipment to use. Anyone of average intelligence, with some mechanical ability, and not afraid to get their hands dirty can perform most of the procedures in this book.

In some cases, a repair job may require tools or skills not reasonably expected of the home mechanic. These procedures are noted in each chapter and it is recommended that you take the job to your dealer, a competent mechanic, or a machine shop.

MANUAL ORGANIZATION

This chapter provides general information, safety and service hints. Also included are lists of recommended shop and emergency tools as well as a brief description of troubleshooting and tune-up equipment.

Chapter Two provides methods and suggestions for quick and accurate diagnosis and repair of problems. Troubleshooting procedures discuss typical symptoms and logical methods to pinpoint the trouble.

Chapter Three explains all periodic lubrication and routine maintenance necessary to keep your motorcycle running well. Chapter Three also includes recommended tune-up procedures, eliminating the need to constantly consult chapters on the various subassemblies.

Subsequent chapters cover specific systems such as the engine, transmission, and electrical system. Each of these chapters provides disassembly, inspection, repair, and assembly procedures in a simple step-by-step format. If a repair is impractical for the home mechanic it is indicated. In these cases it is usually faster and less expensive to have the repairs made by a dealer or competent repair shop. Essential specifications are included in the appropriate chapters.

When special tools are required to perform a task included in this manual, the tools are illustrated. It may be possible to borrow or rent these tools. The inventive mechanic may also be able to find a suitable substitute in his tool box, or to fabricate one.

The terms NOTE, CAUTION, and WARNING have specific meanings in this manual. A NOTE provides additional or explanatory information. A

CAUTION is used to emphasize areas where equipment damage could result if proper precautions are not taken. A WARNING is used to stress those areas where personal injury or death could result from negligence, in addition to possible mechanical damage.

SERVICE HINTS

Time, effort, and frustration will be saved and possible injury will be prevented if you observe the following practices.

Most of the service procedures covered are straightforward and can be performed by anyone reasonably handy with tools. It is suggested, however, that you consider your own capabilities carefully before attempting any operation involving major disassembly of the engine.

Some operations, for example, require the use of a press. It would be wiser to have these performed by a shop equipped for such work, rather than to try to do the job yourself with makeshift equipment. Other procedures require precision measurements. Unless you have the skills and equipment required, it would be better to have a qualified repair shop make the measurements for you.

Repairs go much faster and easier if the parts that will be worked on are clean before you begin. There are special cleaners for washing the engine and related parts. Brush or spray on the cleaning solution, let stand, then rinse it away with a garden hose. Clean all oily or greasy parts with cleaning solvent as you remove them.

WARNING
Never use gasoline as a cleaning agent. It presents an extreme fire hazard. Be sure to work in a well-ventilated area when using cleaning solvent. Keep a fire extinguisher, rated for gasoline fires, handy in any case.

Much of the labor charge for repairs made by dealers is for the removal and disassembly of other parts to reach the defective unit. It is frequently possible to perform the preliminary operations yourself and then take the defective unit in to the dealer for repair, at considerable savings.

Once you have decided to tackle the job yourself, make sure you locate the appropriate section in this manual, and read it entirely. Study the illustrations and text until you have a good idea of what is involved in completing the job satisfactorily. If special tools are required, make arrangements to get them before you start. Also, purchase any known defective parts prior to starting on the procedure. It is frustrating and time-consuming to get partially into a job and then be unable to complete it.

Simple wiring checks can be easily made at home, but knowledge of electronics is almost a necessity for performing tests with complicated electronic testing gear.

During disassembly of parts keep a few general cautions in mind. Force is rarely needed to get things apart. If parts are a tight fit, like a bearing in a case, there is usually a tool designed to separate them. Never use a screwdriver to pry apart parts with machined surfaces such as cylinder head or crankcase halves. You will mar the surfaces and end up with leaks.

Make diagrams wherever similar-appearing parts are found. You may think you can remember where everything came from — but mistakes are costly. There is also the possibility you may get sidetracked and not return to work for days or even weeks — in which interval, carefully laid out parts may have become disturbed.

Tag all similar internal parts for location, and mark all mating parts for position. Record number and thickness of any shims as they are removed. Small parts such as bolts can be identified by placing them in plastic sandwich bags that are sealed and labeled with masking tape.

Wiring should be tagged with masking tape and marked as each wire is removed. Again, do not rely on memory alone.

Disconnect battery ground cable before working near electrical connections and before disconnecting wires. Never run the engine with the battery disconnected; the alternator could be seriously damaged.

Protect finished surfaces from physical damage or corrosion. Keep gasoline and brake fluid off painted surfaces.

Frozen or very tight bolts and screws can often be loosened by soaking with penetrating oil like Liquid Wrench or WD-40, then sharply striking the bolt head a few times with a hammer and punch (or screwdriver for screws). Avoid heat unless absolutely necessary, since it may melt, warp, or remove the temper from many parts.

Avoid flames or sparks when working near a charging battery or flammable liquids, such as gasoline.

No parts, except those assembled with a press fit, require unusual force during assembly. If a part is hard to remove or install, find out why before proceeding.

Cover all openings after removing parts to keep dirt, small tools, etc., from falling in.

When assembling two parts, start all fasteners, then tighten evenly.

Wiring connections and brake shoes, drums, pads, and discs and contact surfaces in dry clutches should be kept clean and free of grease and oil.

When assembling parts, be sure all shims and washers are replaced exactly as they came out.

Whenever a rotating part butts against a stationary part, look for a shim or washer. Use new gaskets if there is any doubt about the condition of old ones. Generally, you should apply gasket cement to one mating surface only, so the parts may be easily disassembled in the future. A thin coat of oil on gaskets helps them seal effectively.

Heavy grease can be used to hold small parts in place if they tend to fall out during assembly. However, keep grease and oil away from electrical, clutch, and brake components.

High spots may be sanded off a piston with sandpaper, but emery cloth and oil do a much more professional job.

Carburetors are best cleaned by disassembling them and soaking the parts in a commercial carburetor cleaner. Never soak gaskets and rubber parts in these cleaners. Never use wire to clean out jets and air passages; they are easily damaged. Use compressed air to blow out the carburetor, but only if the float has been removed first.

Take your time and do the job right. Do not forget that a newly rebuilt engine must be broken in the same as a new one. Refer to your owner's manual for the proper break-in procedures.

SAFETY FIRST

Professional mechanics can work for years and never sustain a serious injury. If you observe a few rules of common sense and safety, you can enjoy many safe hours servicing your motorcycle. You could hurt yourself or damage the motorcycle if you ignore these rules.

1. Never use gasoline as a cleaning solvent.

2. Never smoke or use a torch in the vicinity of flammable liquids such as cleaning solvent in open containers.

3. Never smoke or use a torch in an area where batteries are being charged. Highly explosive hydrogen gas is formed during the charging process.

4. Use the proper sized wrenches to avoid damage to nuts and injury to yourself.

5. When loosening a tight or stuck nut, be guided by what would happen if the wrench should slip. Protect yourself accordingly.

6. Keep your work area clean and uncluttered.

7. Wear safety goggles during all operations involving drilling, grinding, or use of a cold chisel.

8. Never use worn tools.

9. Keep a fire extinguisher handy and be sure it is rated for gasoline (Class B) and electrical (Class C) fires.

EXPENDABLE SUPPLIES

Certain expendable supplies are necessary. These include grease, oil, gasket cement, wiping rags, cleaning solvent, and distilled water. Also, special locking compounds, silicone lubricants, and engine and carburetor cleaners may be useful. Cleaning solvent is available at most service stations and distilled water for the battery is available at supermarkets.

SHOP TOOLS

For complete servicing and repair you will need an assortment of ordinary hand tools **(Figure 1)**.

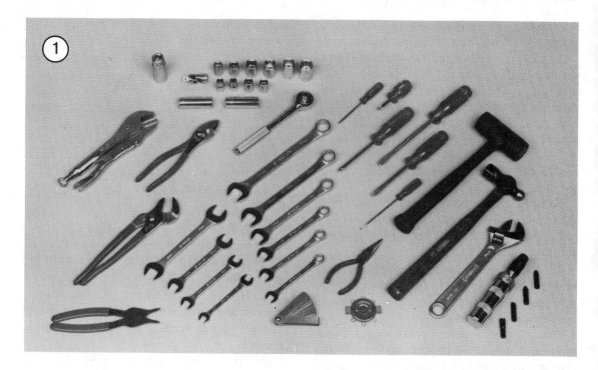

As a minimum, these include:

a. Combination wrenches

b. Sockets

c. Plastic mallet

d. Small hammer

e. Impact driver

f. Snap ring pliers

g. Gas pliers

h. Phillips screwdrivers

i. Slot (common) screwdrivers

j. Feeler gauges

k. Spark plug gauge

l. Spark plug wrench

Special tools required are shown in the chapters covering the particular repair in which they are used.

Engine tune-up and troubleshooting procedures require other special tools and equipment. These are described in detail in the following sections.

EMERGENCY TOOL KITS

Highway

A small emergency tool kit kept on the bike is handy for road emergencies which otherwise could leave you stranded. The tools and spares listed below and shown in **Figure 2** will let you handle most roadside repairs.

a. Motorcycle tool kit (original equipment)

b. Impact driver

c. Silver waterproof sealing tape (duct tape)

d. Hose-clamps (3 sizes)

e. Silicone sealer

f. Lock 'N' Seal

g. Flashlight

h. Tire patch kit

i. Tire irons

j. Plastic pint bottle (for oil)

k. Waterless hand cleaner

l. Rags for clean up

Off-Road

A few simple tools and aids carried on the motorcycle can mean the difference between walking or riding back to camp or to where repairs can be made. See **Figure 3**.

A few essential spare parts carried in your truck or van can prevent a day or weekend of trail riding from being spoiled. See **Figure 4**.

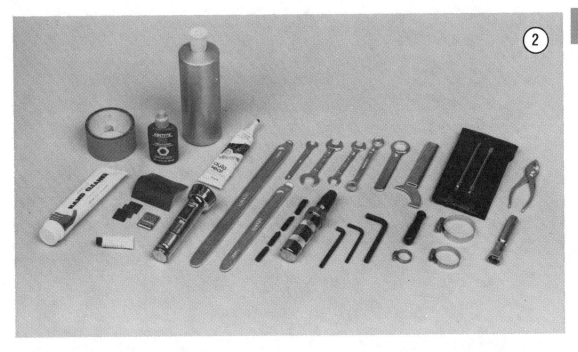

On the Motorcycle

a. Motorcycle tool kit (original equipment)
b. Drive chain master link
c. Tow line
d. Spark plug
e. Spark plug wrench
f. Shifter lever
g. Clutch/brake lever
h. Silver waterproof sealing tape (duct tape)
i. Loctite Lock 'N' Seal

In the Truck

a. Control cables (throttle, clutch, brake)
b. Silicone sealer
c. Tire patch kit
d. Tire irons
e. Tire pump
f. Impact driver
g. Oil

> WARNING
> *Tools and spares should be carried on the motorcycle — not in clothing where a simple fall could result in serious injury from a sharp tool.*

TROUBLESHOOTING AND TUNE-UP EQUIPMENT

Voltmeter, Ohmmeter, and Ammeter

For testing the ignition or electrical system, a good voltmeter is required. For motorcycle use, an instrument covering 0-20 volts is satisfactory. One which also has a 0-2 volt scale is necessary for testing relays, points, or individual contacts where voltage drops are much smaller. Accuracy should be ± ½ volt.

An ohmmeter measures electrical resistance. This instrument is useful for checking continuity (open and short circuits), and testing fuses and lights.

The ammeter measures electrical current. Ammeters for motorcycle use should cover 0-50 amperes and 0-250 amperes. These are useful for checking battery charging and starting current.

Several inexpensive VOM's (volt-ohm-milli-ammeter) combine all three instruments into one which fits easily in any tool box. See **Figure 5**. However, the ammeter ranges are usually too small for motorcycle work.

Hydrometer

The hydrometer gives a useful indication of battery condition and charge by measuring the

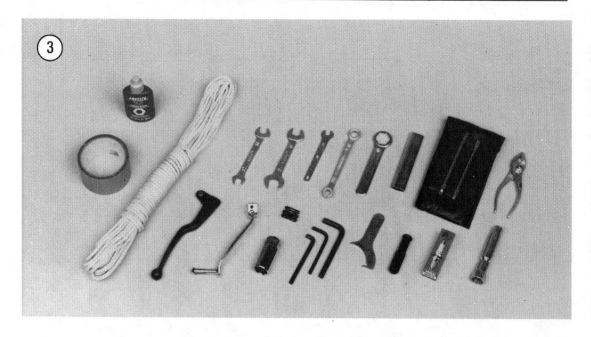

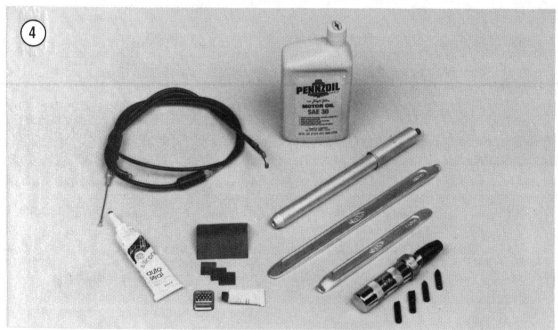

specific gravity of the electrolyte in each cell. See **Figure 6**. Complete details on use and interpretation of readings are provided in the electrical chapter.

Compression Tester

The compression tester measures the compression pressure built up in each cylinder. The results, when properly interpreted, can indicate general cylinder, ring, and valve condition. See **Figure 7**. Extension lines are available for hard-to-reach cylinders.

Dwell Meter (Contact Breaker Point Ignition Only)

A dwell meter measures the distance in degrees of cam rotation that the breaker points remain closed while the engine is running. Since

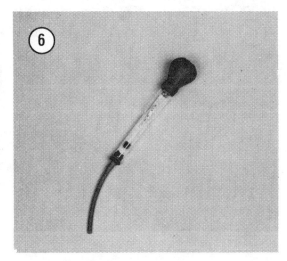

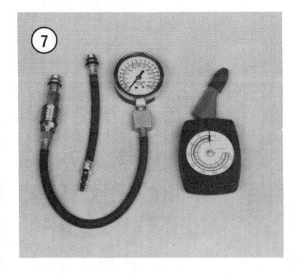

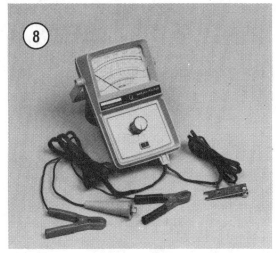

this angle is determined by breaker point gap, dwell angle is an accurate indication of breaker point gap.

Many tachometers intended for tuning and testing incorporate a dwell meter as well. See **Figure 8**. Follow the manufacturer's instructions to measure dwell.

Tachometer

A tachometer is necessary for tuning. See **Figure 8**. Ignition timing and carburetor adjustments must be performed at the specified idle speed. The best instrument for this purpose is one with a low range of 0-1,000 or 0-2,000 rpm for setting idle, and a high range of 0-4,000 or more for setting ignition timing at 3,000 rpm. Extended range (0-6,000 or 0-8,000 rpm) instruments lack accuracy at lower speeds. The instrument should be capable of detecting changes of 25 rpm on the low range.

> NOTE: *The motorcycle's tachometer is not accurate enough for correct idle adjustment.*

Strobe Timing Light

This instrument is necessary for tuning, as it permits very accurate ignition timing. The light flashes at precisely the same instant that No. 1 cylinder fires, at which time the timing marks on the engine should align. Refer to Chapter Three for exact location of the timing marks for your engine.

Suitable lights range from inexpensive neon bulb types ($2-3) to powerful xenon strobe lights ($20-40). See **Figure 9**. Neon timing lights are difficult to see and must be used in dimly lit areas. Xenon strobe timing lights can be used outside in bright sunlight.

Tune-up Kits

Many manufacturers offer kits that combine several useful instruments. Some come in a convenient carry case and are usually less expensive than purchasing one instrument at a time. **Figure 10** shows one of the kits that is available. The prices vary with the number of instruments included in the kit.

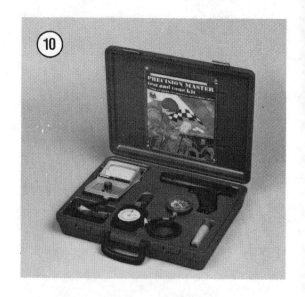

Manometer (Carburetor Synchronizer)

A manometer is essential for accurately synchronizing carburetors on multi-cylinder engines. The instrument detects intake pressure differences between carburetors and permits them to be adjusted equally. A suitable manometer costs about $25 and comes with detailed instructions for use. See **Figure 11**.

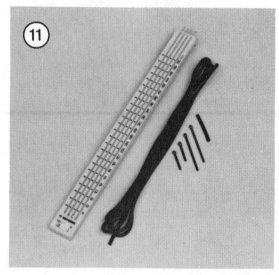

Fire Extinguisher

A fire extinguisher is a necessity when working on a vehicle. It should be rated for both *Class B* (flammable liquids — gasoline, oil, paint, etc.) and *Class C* (electrical — wiring, etc.) type fires. It should always be kept within reach. See **Figure 12**.

CHAPTER TWO

TROUBLESHOOTING

Troubleshooting motorcycle problems is relatively simple. To be effective and efficient, however, it must be done in a logical step-by-step manner. If it is not, a great deal of time may be wasted, good parts may be replaced unnecessarily, and the true problem may never be uncovered.

Always begin by defining the symptoms as closely as possible. Then, analyze the symptoms carefully so that you can make an intelligent guess at the probable cause. Next, test the probable cause and attempt to verify it; if it's not at fault, analyze the symptoms once again, this time eliminating the first probable cause. Continue on in this manner, a step at a time, until the problem is solved.

At first, this approach may seem to be time consuming, but you will soon discover that it's not nearly so wasteful as a hit-or-miss method that may never solve the problem. And just as important, the methodical approach to troubleshooting ensures that only those parts that are defective will be replaced.

The troubleshooting procedures in this chapter analyze typical symptoms and show logical methods for isolating and correcting trouble. They are not, however, the only methods; there may be several approaches to a given problem, but all good troubleshooting methods have one thing in common — a logical, systematic approach.

ENGINE

The entire engine must be considered when trouble arises that is experienced as poor performance or failure to start. The engine is more than a combustion chamber, piston, and crankshaft; it also includes a fuel delivery system, an ignition system, and an exhaust system.

Before beginning to troubleshoot any engine problems, it's important to understand an engine's operating requirements. First, it must have a correctly metered mixture of gasoline and air (**Figure 1**). Second, it must have an airtight combustion chamber in which the mixture can be compressed. And finally, it requires a precisely timed spark to ignite the compressed mixture. If one or more is missing, the engine won't run, and if just one is deficient, the engine will run poorly at best.

Of the three requirements, the precisely timed spark — provided by the ignition system — is most likely to be the culprit, with gas/air mixture (carburetion) second, and poor compression the least likely.

STARTING DIFFICULTIES

Hard starting is probably the most common motorcycle ailment, with a wide range of problems likely. Before delving into a reluctant or non-starter, first determine what has changed

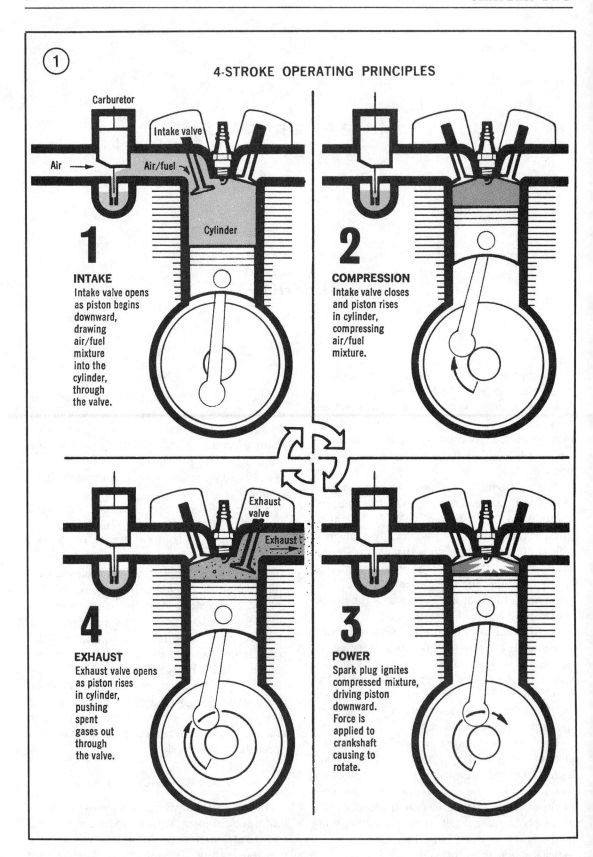

① 4-STROKE OPERATING PRINCIPLES

1 INTAKE
Intake valve opens as piston begins downward, drawing air/fuel mixture into the cylinder, through the valve.

2 COMPRESSION
Intake valve closes and piston rises in cylinder, compressing air/fuel mixture.

4 EXHAUST
Exhaust valve opens as piston rises in cylinder, pushing spent gases out through the valve.

3 POWER
Spark plug ignites compressed mixture, driving piston downward. Force is applied to crankshaft causing to rotate.

Carburetor
Intake valve
Air
Air/fuel
Cylinder
Exhaust valve
Exhaust

since the motorcycle last started easily. For instance, was the weather dry then and is it wet now? Has the motorcycle been sitting in the garage for a long time? Has it been ridden many miles since it was last fueled?

Has starting become increasingly more difficult? This alone could indicate a number of things that may be wrong but is usually associated with normal wear of ignition and engine components.

While it's not always possible to diagnose trouble simply from a change of conditions, this information can be helpful and at some future time may uncover a recurring problem.

Fuel Delivery

Although it is the second most likely cause of trouble, fuel delivery should be checked first simply because it is the easiest.

First, check the tank to make sure there is fuel in it. Then, disconnect the fuel hose at the carburetor, open the valve and check for flow (**Figure 2**). If fuel does not flow freely make sure the tank vent is clear. Next, check for blockage in the line or valve. Remove the valve and clean it as described in the fuel system chapter.

If fuel flows from the hose, reconnect it and remove the float bowl from the carburetor, open the valve and check for flow through the float needle valve. If it does not flow freely when the float is extended and then shut off when the flow is gently raised, clean the carburetor as described in the fuel system chapter.

When fuel delivery is satisfactory, go on to the ignition system.

Ignition

Remove the spark plug from the cylinder and check its condition. The appearance of the plug is a good indication of what's happening in the combustion chamber; for instance, if the plug is wet with gas, it's likely that engine is flooded. Compare the spark plug to **Figure 3**. Make certain the spark plug heat range is correct. A "cold" plug makes starting difficult.

After checking the spark plug, reconnect it to the high-tension lead and lay it on the cylinder head so it makes good contact (**Figure 4**). Then,

with the ignition switched on, crank the engine several times and watch for a spark across the plug electrodes. A fat, blue spark should be visible. If there is no spark, or if the spark is weak, substitute a good plug for the old one and check again. If the spark has improved, the old plug is faulty. If there was no change, keep looking.

Make sure the ignition switch is not shorted to ground. Remove the spark plug cap from the end of the high-tension lead and hold the exposed end of the lead about $\frac{1}{8}$ inch from the cylinder head. Crank the engine and watch for a spark arcing from the lead to the head. If it's satisfactory, the connection between the lead and the cap was faulty. If the spark hasn't improved, check the coil wire connections.

If the spark is still weak, remove the ignition cover and remove any dirt or moisture from the points or sensor. Check the point or air gap against the specifications in the *Quick Reference Data* at the beginning of the book.

If spark is still not satisfactory, a more serious problem exists than can be corrected with simple adjustments. Refer to the electrical system chapter for detailed information for correcting major ignition problems.

Compression

Compression — or the lack of it — is the least likely cause of starting trouble. However, if compression is unsatisfactory, more than a simple adjustment is required to correct it (see the engine chapter).

An accurate compression check reveals a lot about the condition of the engine. To perform this test you need a compression gauge (see Chapter One). The engine should be at operating temperature for a fully accurate test, but even a cold test will reveal if the starting problem is compression.

Remove the spark plug and screw in a compression gauge (**Figure 5**). With assistance, hold the throttle wide open and crank the engine several times, until the gauge ceases to rise. Normal compression should be 130-160 psi, but a reading as low as 100 psi is usually sufficient for the engine to start. If the reading is much lower than normal, remove the gauge and pour about a tablespoon of oil into the cylinder.

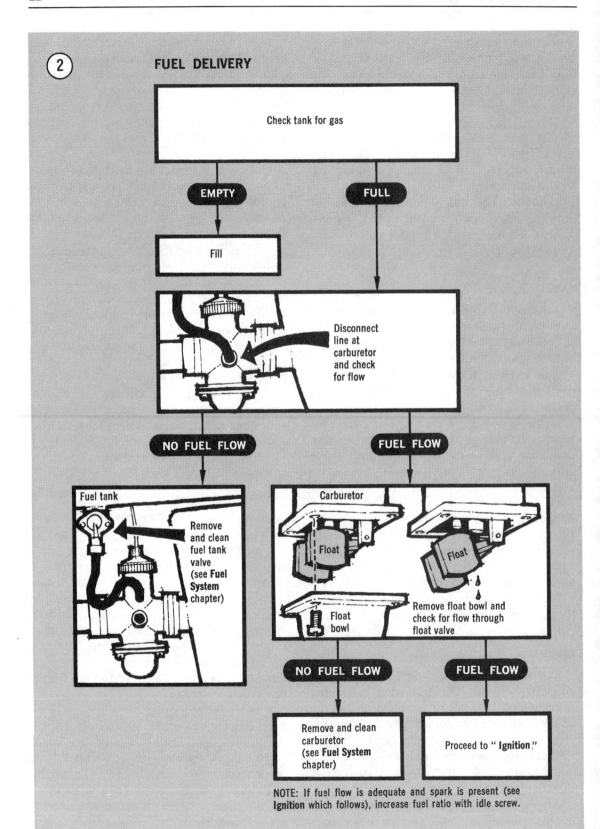

FUEL DELIVERY

Check tank for gas

EMPTY — Fill

FULL — Disconnect line at carburetor and check for flow

NO FUEL FLOW — Remove and clean fuel tank valve (see **Fuel System** chapter)

Fuel tank

FUEL FLOW — Carburetor

Float

Float

Float bowl

Remove float bowl and check for flow through float valve

NO FUEL FLOW — Remove and clean carburetor (see **Fuel System** chapter)

FUEL FLOW — Proceed to " **Ignition**,"

NOTE: If fuel flow is adequate and spark is present (see **Ignition** which follows), increase fuel ratio with idle screw.

NORMAL
- Appearance—Firing tip has deposits of light gray to light tan.
- Can be cleaned, regapped and reused.

CARBON FOULED
- Appearance—Dull, dry black with fluffy carbon deposits on the insulator tip, electrode and exposed shell.
- Caused by—Fuel/air mixture too rich, plug heat range too cold, weak ignition system, dirty air cleaner, faulty automatic choke or excessive idling.
- Can be cleaned, regapped and reused.

OIL FOULED
- Appearance—Wet black deposits on insulator and exposed shell.
- Caused by—Excessive oil entering the combustion chamber through worn rings, pistons, valve guides or bearings.
- Replace with new plugs (use a hotter plug if engine is not repaired).

LEAD FOULED
- Appearance — Yellow insulator deposits (may sometimes be dark gray, black or tan in color) on the insulator tip.
- Caused by—Highly leaded gasoline.
- Replace with new plugs.

LEAD FOULED
- Appearance—Yellow glazed deposits indicating melted lead deposits due to hard acceleration.
- Caused by—Highly leaded gasoline.
- Replace with new plugs.

OIL AND LEAD FOULED
- Appearance—Glazed yellow deposits with a slight brownish tint on the insulator tip and ground electrode.
- Replace with new plugs.

FUEL ADDITIVE RESIDUE
- Appearance — Brown colored hardened ash deposits on the insulator tip and ground electrode.
- Caused by—Fuel and/or oil additives.
- Replace with new plugs.

WORN
- Appearance — Severely worn or eroded electrodes.
- Caused by—Normal wear or unusual oil and/or fuel additives.
- Replace with new plugs.

PREIGNITION
- Appearance — Melted ground electrode.
- Caused by—Overadvanced ignition timing, inoperative ignition advance mechanism, too low of a fuel octane rating, lean fuel/air mixture or carbon deposits in combustion chamber.

PREIGNITION
- Appearance—Melted center electrode.
- Caused by—Abnormal combustion due to overadvanced ignition timing or incorrect advance, too low of a fuel octane rating, lean fuel/air mixture, or carbon deposits in combustion chamber.
- Correct engine problem and replace with new plugs.

INCORRECT HEAT RANGE
- Appearance—Melted center electrode and white blistered insulator tip.
- Caused by—Incorrect plug heat range selection.
- Replace with new plugs.

2

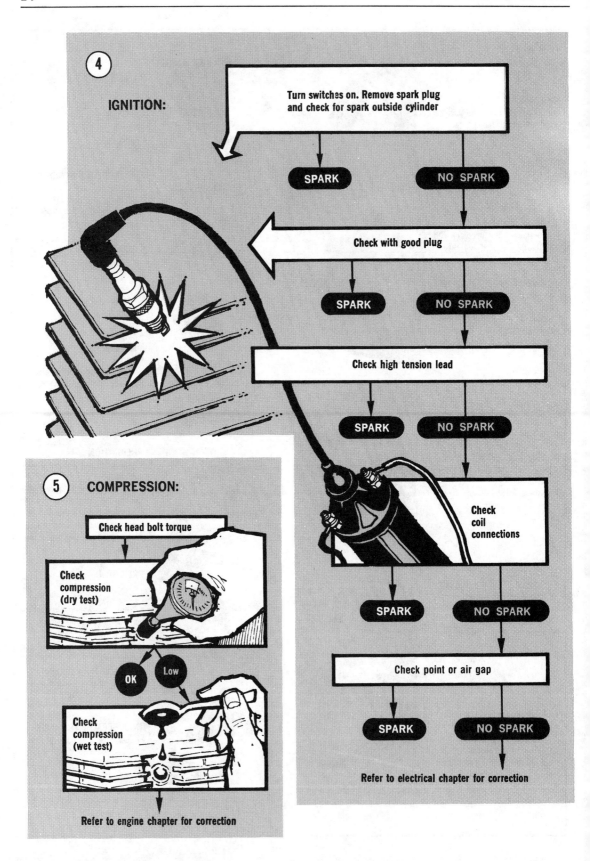

④ IGNITION:

Turn switches on. Remove spark plug and check for spark outside cylinder

SPARK   NO SPARK

Check with good plug

SPARK   NO SPARK

Check high tension lead

SPARK   NO SPARK

Check coil connections

SPARK   NO SPARK

Check point or air gap

SPARK   NO SPARK

Refer to electrical chapter for correction

⑤ COMPRESSION:

Check head bolt torque

Check compression (dry test)

OK   Low

Check compression (wet test)

Refer to engine chapter for correction

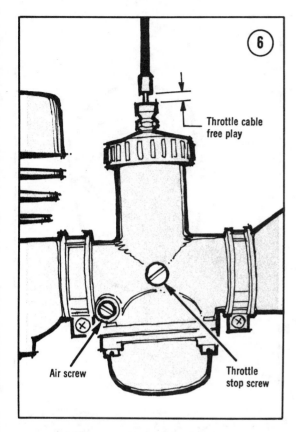

Throttle cable free play

Air screw

Throttle stop screw

6

7

Crank the engine several times to distribute the oil and test the compression once again. If it is now significantly higher, the rings and bore are worn. If the compression did not change, the valves are not seating correctly. Adjust the valves and check again. If the compression is still low, refer to the engine chapter.

> NOTE: *Low compression indicates a developing problem. The condition causing it should be corrected as soon as possible.*

POOR PERFORMANCE

Poor engine performance can be caused by any of a number of things related to carburetion, ignition, and the condition of the sliding and rotating components in the engine. In addition, components such as brakes, clutch, and transmission can cause problems that seem to be related to engine performance, even when the engine is in top running condition.

Poor Idling

Idling that is erratic, too high, or too low is most often caused by incorrect adjustment of the carburetor idle circuit. Also, a dirty air filter or an obstructed fuel tank vent can affect idle speed. Incorrect ignition timing or worn or faulty ignition components are also good possibilities.

First, make sure the air filter is clean and correctly installed. Then, adjust the throttle cable free play, the throttle stop screw, and the idle mixture air screw (**Figure 6**) as described in the routine maintenance chapter.

If idling is still poor, check the carburetor and manifold mounts for leaks; with the engine warmed up and running, spray WD-40 or a similar light lube around the flanges and joints of the carburetor and manifold (**Figure 7**). Listen for changes in engine speed. If a leak is present, the idle speed will drop as the lube "plugs" the leak and then pick up again as it is drawn into the engine. Tighten the nuts and clamps and test again. If a leak persists, check for a damaged gasket or a pinhole in the manifold. Minor leaks in manifold hoses can be repaired with silicone sealer, but if cracks or holes are extensive, the manifold should be replaced.

A worn throttle slide may cause erratic running and idling, but this is likely only after many thousands of miles of use. To check, remove the carburetor top and feel for back and forth movement of the slide in the bore; it should be barely perceptible. Inspect the slide for large worn areas and replace it if it is less than perfect (**Figure 8**).

If the fuel system is satisfactory, check ignition timing and breaker point gap (air gap in electronic ignition). Check the condition of the system components as well. Ignition-caused idling problems such as erratic running can be the fault of marginal components. See the electrical system chapter for appropriate tests.

Rough Running or Misfiring

Misfiring (see **Figure 9**) is usually caused by an ignition problem. First, check all ignition connections (**Figure 10**). They should be clean, dry, and tight. Don't forget the kill switch; a loose connection can create an intermittent short.

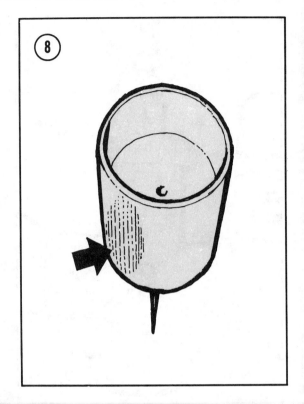

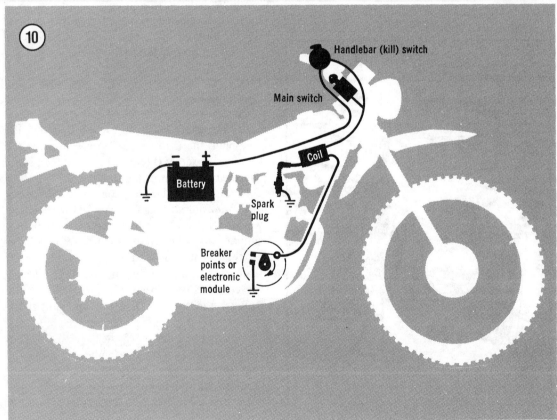

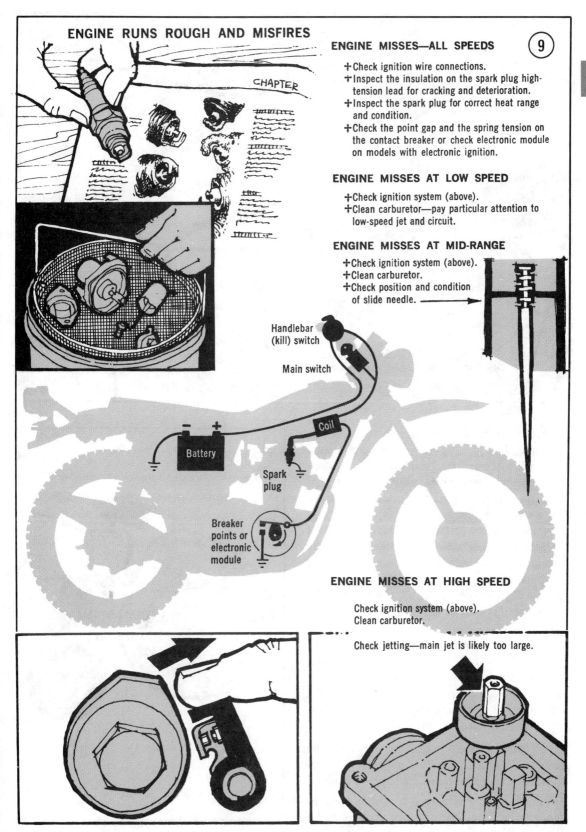

ENGINE RUNS ROUGH AND MISFIRES

ENGINE MISSES—ALL SPEEDS ⑨

✝Check ignition wire connections.
✝Inspect the insulation on the spark plug high-tension lead for cracking and deterioration.
✝Inspect the spark plug for correct heat range and condition.
✝Check the point gap and the spring tension on the contact breaker or check electronic module on models with electronic ignition.

ENGINE MISSES AT LOW SPEED

✝Check ignition system (above).
✝Clean carburetor—pay particular attention to low-speed jet and circuit.

ENGINE MISSES AT MID-RANGE

✝Check ignition system (above).
✝Clean carburetor.
✝Check position and condition of slide needle. →

CHAPTER

Handlebar (kill) switch

Main switch

Coil

Battery

Spark plug

Breaker points or electronic module

ENGINE MISSES AT HIGH SPEED

Check ignition system (above).
Clean carburetor.

Check jetting—main jet is likely too large.

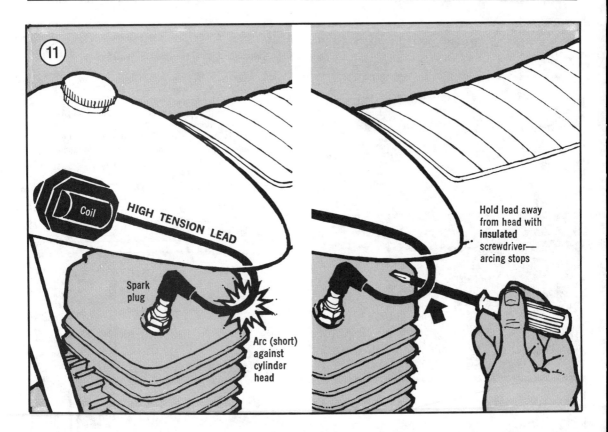

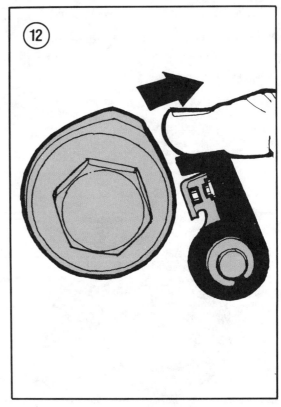

Check the insulation on the high-tension spark plug lead. If it is cracked or deteriorated it will allow the spark to short to ground when the engine is revved. This is easily seen at night. If arcing occurs, hold the affected area of the wire away from the metal to which it is arcing, using an insulated screwdriver (**Figure 11**), and see if the misfiring ceases. If it does, replace the high-tension lead. Also check the connection of the spark plug cap to the lead. If it is poor, the spark will break down at this point when the engine speed is increased.

The spark plug could also be poor. Test the system with a new plug.

Incorrect point gap or a weak contact breaker spring can cause misfiring. Check the gap and the alignment of the points. Push the moveable arm back and check for spring tension (**Figure 12**). It should feel stiff.

On models with electronic ignition, have the electronic module tested by a dealer or substitute a known good unit for a suspected one.

If misfiring occurs only at a certain point in engine speed, the problem may very likely be

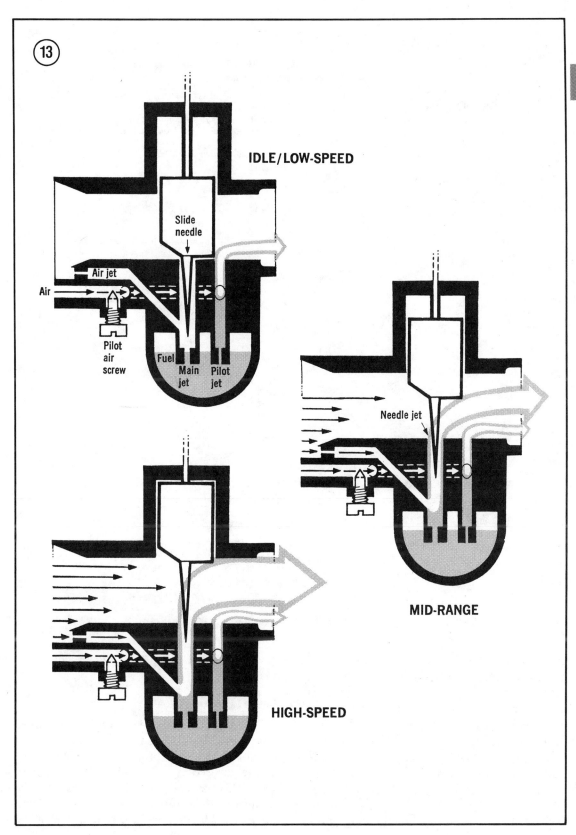

IDLE/LOW-SPEED

Slide needle

Air jet

Air

Pilot air screw

Fuel

Main jet

Pilot jet

Needle jet

MID-RANGE

HIGH-SPEED

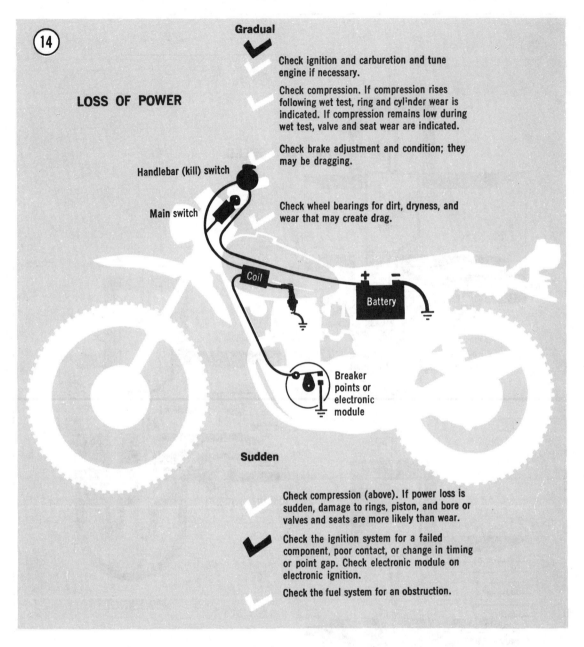

(14)

LOSS OF POWER

Gradual

Check ignition and carburetion and tune engine if necessary.

Check compression. If compression rises following wet test, ring and cylinder wear is indicated. If compression remains low during wet test, valve and seat wear are indicated.

Check brake adjustment and condition; they may be dragging.

Handlebar (kill) switch

Main switch

Check wheel bearings for dirt, dryness, and wear that may create drag.

Coil

Battery

Breaker points or electronic module

Sudden

Check compression (above). If power loss is sudden, damage to rings, piston, and bore or valves and seats are more likely than wear.

Check the ignition system for a failed component, poor contact, or change in timing or point gap. Check electronic module on electronic ignition.

Check the fuel system for an obstruction.

carburetion. Poor performance at idle is described earlier. Misfiring at low speed (just above idle) can be caused by a dirty low-speed circuit or jet (**Figure 13**). Poor midrange performance is attributable to a worn or incorrectly adjusted needle and needle jet. Misfiring at high speed (if not ignition related) is usually caused by a too-large main jet which causes the engine to run rich. Any of these carburetor-related conditions can be corrected by first cleaning the carburetor and then adjusting it as

described in the tune-up and maintenance chapter.

Loss of Power

First determine how the power loss developed (**Figure 14**). Did it decline over a long period of time or did it drop abruptly? A gradual loss is normal, caused by deterioration of the engine's state of tune and the normal wear of the cylinder and piston rings and the valves and seats. In such case, check the condition of the

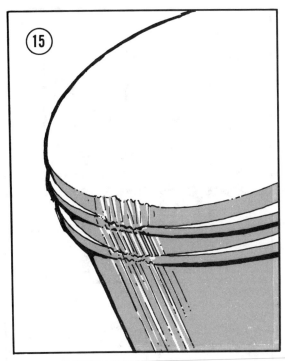

ignition and carburetion and measure the compression as described earlier.

A sudden power loss may be caused by a failed ignition component, obstruction in the fuel system, damaged valve or seat, or a broken piston ring or damaged piston (**Figure 15**).

If the engine is in good shape and tune, check the brake adjustment. If the brakes are dragging, they will consume considerable power. Also check the wheel bearings. If they are dry, extremely dirty, or badly worn they can create considerable drag.

Engine Runs Hot

A modern motorcycle engine, in good mechanical condition, correctly tuned, and operated as it was intended, will rarely experience overheating problems. However, out-of-spec conditions can create severe overheating that may result in serious engine damage. Refer to **Figure 16**.

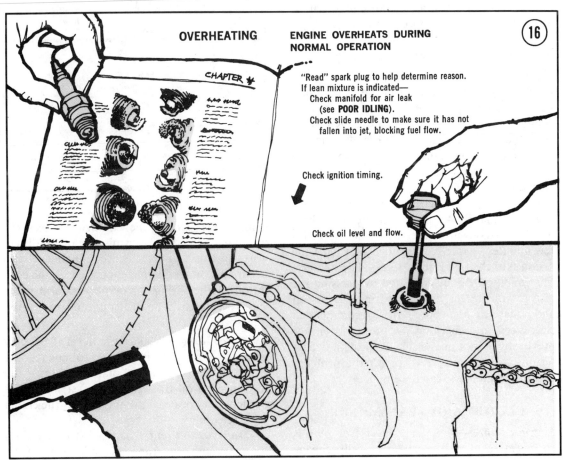

OVERHEATING   ENGINE OVERHEATS DURING NORMAL OPERATION

CHAPTER #

"Read" spark plug to help determine reason.
If lean mixture is indicated—
    Check manifold for air leak
        (see **POOR IDLING**).
    Check slide needle to make sure it has not
        fallen into jet, blocking fuel flow.

Check ignition timing.

Check oil level and flow.

Overheating is difficult to detect unless it is extreme, in which case it will usually be apparent as excessive heat radiating from the engine, accompanied by the smell of hot oil and sharp, snapping noises when the engine is first shut off and begins to cool.

Unless the motorcycle is operated under sustained high load or is allowed to idle for long periods of time, overheating is usually the result of an internal problem. Most often it's caused by a too-lean fuel mixture.

Remove the spark plug and compare it to **Figure 3**. If a too-lean condition is indicated, check for leaks in the intake manifold (see *Poor Idling*). The carburetor jetting may be incorrect but this is unlikely if the overheating problem has just developed (unless, of course, the engine was jetted for high altitude and is now being run near sea level). Check the slide needle in the carburetor to make sure it hasn't come loose and is restricting the flow of gas through the main jet and needle jet (**Figure 17**).

Check the ignition timing; extremes of either advance or retard can cause overheating.

Piston Seizure and Damage

Piston seizure is a common result of overheating (see above) because an aluminum piston expands at a greater rate than a steel cylinder. Seizure can also be caused by piston-to-cylinder clearance that is too small; ring end gap that is too small; insufficient oil; spark plug heat range too hot; and broken piston ring or ring land.

A major piston seizure can cause severe engine damage. A minor seizure — which usually subsides after the engine has cooled a few minutes — rarely does more than scuff the piston skirt the first time it occurs. Fortunately, this condition can be corrected by dressing the piston with crocus cloth, refitting the piston and rings to the bore with recommended clearances, and checking the timing to ensure overheating does not occur. Regard that first seizure as a warning and correct the problem before continuing to run the engine.

CLUTCH AND TRANSMISSION

1. *Clutch slips*—Make sure lever free play is sufficient to allow the clutch to fully engage

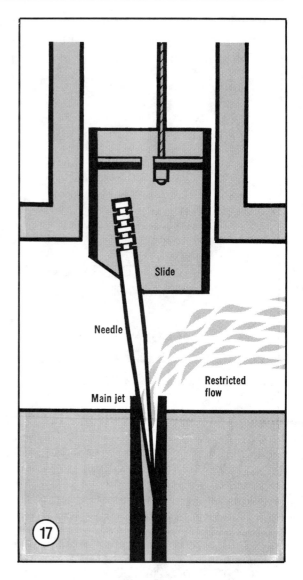
Slide

Needle

Main jet

Restricted flow

(17)

(**Figure 18**). Check the contact surfaces for wear and glazing. Transmission oil additives also can cause slippage in wet clutches. If slip occurs only under extreme load, check the condition of the springs or diaphragm and make sure the clutch bolts are snug and uniformly tightened.

2. *Clutch drags*—Make sure lever free play isn't so great that it fails to disengage the clutch. Check for warped plates or disc. If the transmission oil (in wet clutch systems) is extremely dirty or heavy, it may inhibit the clutch from releasing.

3. *Transmission shifts hard*—Extremely dirty oil can cause the transmission to shift hard.

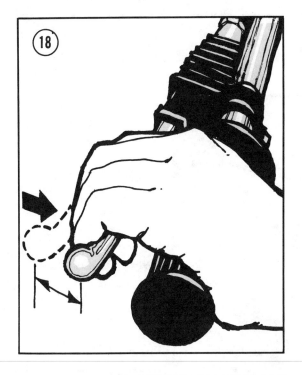

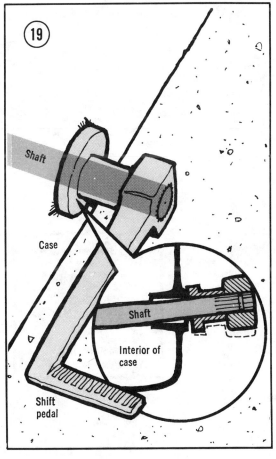

Check the selector shaft for bending (**Figure 19**). Inspect the shifter and gearsets for wear and damage.

4. *Transmission slips out of gear*—This can be caused by worn engagement dogs or a worn or damaged shifter (**Figure 20**). The overshift travel on the selector may be misadjusted.

5. *Transmission is noisy*—Noises usually indicate the absence of lubrication or wear and damage to gears, bearings, or shims. It's a good idea to disassemble the transmission and carefully inspect it when noise first occurs.

DRIVE TRAIN

Drive train problems (outlined in **Figure 21**) arise from normal wear and incorrect maintenance.

CHASSIS

Chassis problems are outlined in **Figure 22**.

1. *Motorcycle pulls to one side*—Check for loose suspension components, axles, steering

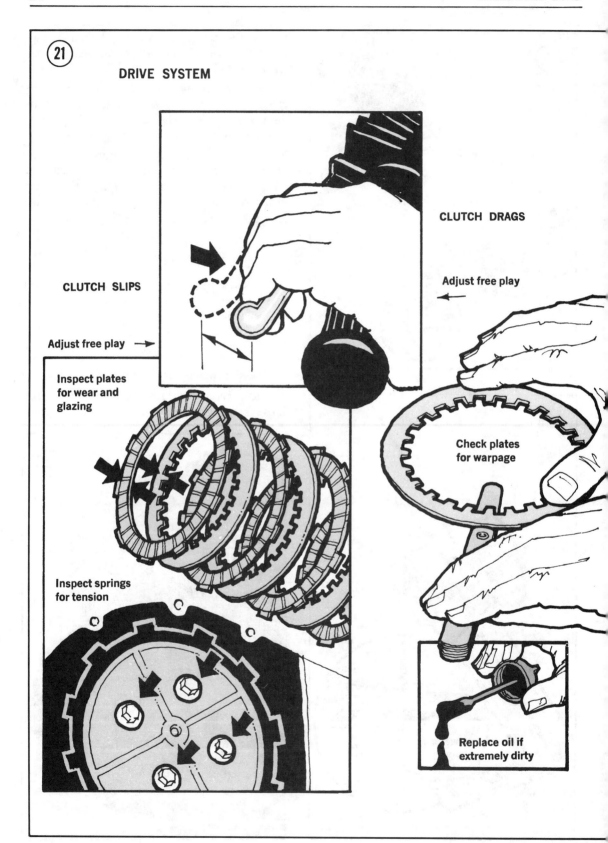

TRANSMISSION SLIPS OUT OF GEAR

TRANSMISSION SHIFTS HARD

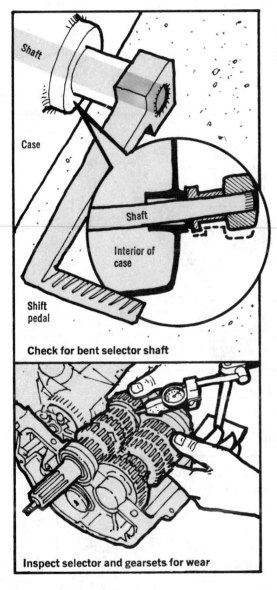

Check for bent selector shaft

Inspect selector and gearsets for wear

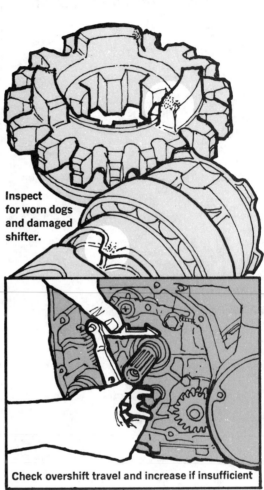

Inspect for worn dogs and damaged shifter.

Check overshift travel and increase if insufficient

TRANSMISSION IS NOISY

Check oil level

Disassemble and inspect (see Transmission chapter)

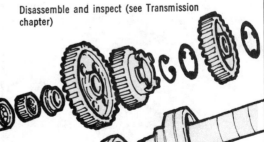

㉒

SUSPENSION AND HANDLING

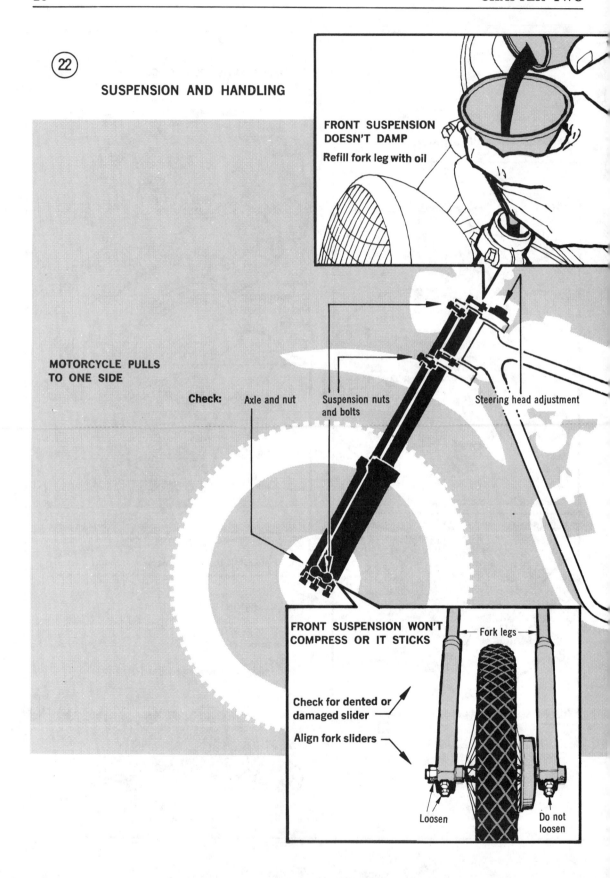

FRONT SUSPENSION
DOESN'T DAMP

Refill fork leg with oil

MOTORCYCLE PULLS
TO ONE SIDE

Check: Axle and nut   Suspension nuts   Steering head adjustment
                              and bolts

FRONT SUSPENSION WON'T
COMPRESS OR IT STICKS

Fork legs

Check for dented or
damaged slider

Align fork sliders

Loosen   Do not
                                              loosen

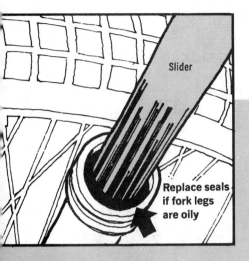

Slider

Replace seals if fork legs are oily

SUSPENSION AND HANDLING CONTINUED ➡ 2

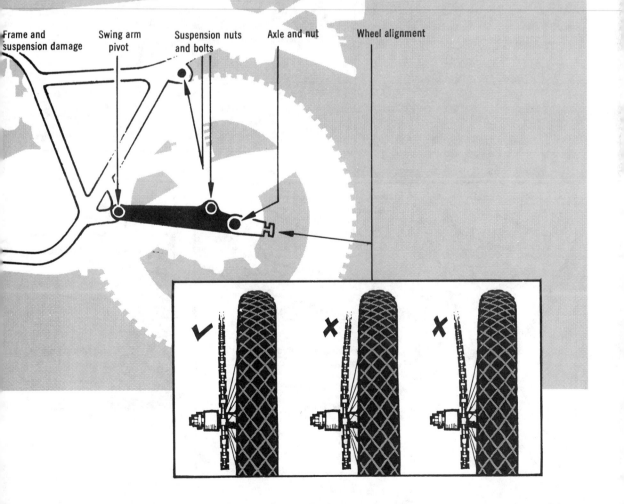

Frame and suspension damage

Swing arm pivot

Suspension nuts and bolts

Axle and nut

Wheel alignment

SUSPENSION AND HANDLING CONTINUED

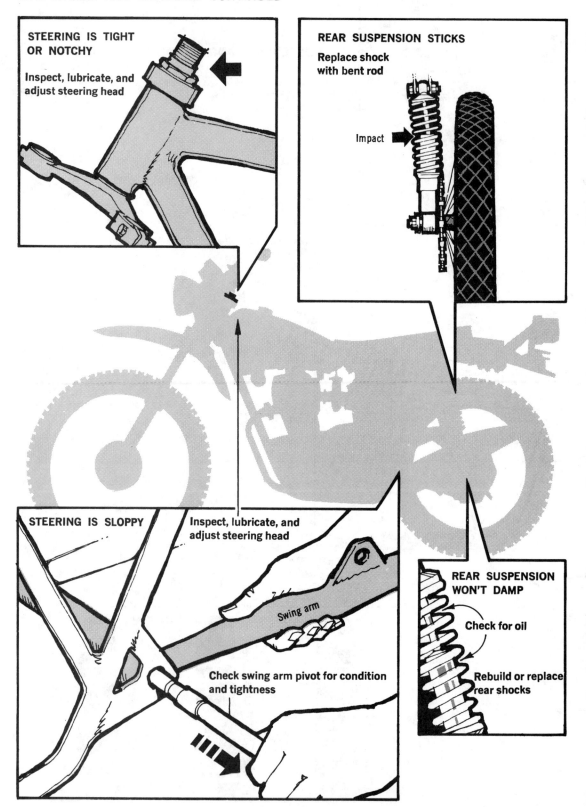

STEERING IS TIGHT OR NOTCHY

Inspect, lubricate, and adjust steering head

REAR SUSPENSION STICKS

Replace shock with bent rod

Impact

STEERING IS SLOPPY   Inspect, lubricate, and adjust steering head

Swing arm

Check swing arm pivot for condition and tightness

REAR SUSPENSION WON'T DAMP

Check for oil

Rebuild or replace rear shocks

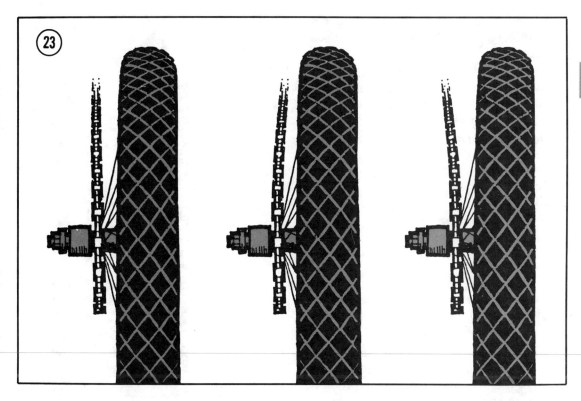

head, swing arm pivot. Check wheel alignment (**Figure 23**). Check for damage to the frame and suspension components.

2. *Front suspension doesn't damp*—This is most often caused by a lack of damping oil in the fork legs. If the upper fork tubes are exceptionally oily, it's likely that the seals are worn out and should be replaced.

3. *Front suspension sticks or won't fully compress*—Misalignment of the forks when the wheel is installed can cause this. Loosen the axle nut and the pinch bolt on the nut end of the axle (**Figure 24**). Lock the front wheel with the brake and compress the front suspension several times to align the fork legs. Then, tighten the pinch bolt and then the axle nut.

The trouble may also be caused by a bent or dented fork slider (**Figure 25**). The distortion required to lock up a fork tube is so slight that it is often impossible to visually detect. If this type of damage is suspected, remove the fork leg and remove the spring from it. Attempt to operate the fork leg. If it still binds, replace the slider; it's not practical to repair it.

4. *Rear suspension does not damp*—This is usually caused by damping oil leaking past

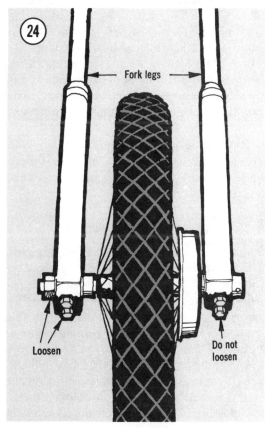

worn seals. Rebuildable shocks should be refitted with complete service kits and fresh oil. Non-rebuildable units should be replaced.

5. *Rear suspension sticks*—This is commonly caused by a bent shock absorber piston rod (**Figure 26**). Replace the shock; the rod can't be satisfactorily straightened.

6. *Steering is tight or "notchy"*—Steering head bearings may be dry, dirty, or worn. Adjustment of the steering head bearing pre-load may be too tight.

7. *Steering is sloppy*—Steering head adjustment may be too loose. Also check the swing arm pivot; looseness or extreme wear at this point translate to the steering.

BRAKES

Brake problems arise from wear, lack of maintenance, and from sustained or repeated exposure to dirt and water.

1. *Brakes are ineffective*—Ineffective brakes are most likely caused by incorrect adjustment. If adjustment will not correct the problem, remove the wheels and check for worn or glazed linings. If the linings are worn beyond the service limit, replace them. If they are simply glazed, rough them up with light sandpaper.

In hydraulic brake systems, low fluid levels can cause a loss of braking effectiveness, as can worn brake cylinder pistons and bores. Also check the pads to see if they are worn beyond the service limit.

2. *Brakes lock or drag*—This may be caused by incorrect adjustment. Check also for foreign matter embedded in the lining and for dirty and dry wheel bearings.

ELECTRICAL SYSTEM

Many electrical system problems can be easily solved by ensuring that the affected connections are clean, dry, and tight. In battery equipped motorcycles, a neglected battery is the source of a great number of difficulties that could be prevented by simple, regular service to the battery.

A multimeter, like the volt/ohm/milliammeter described in Chapter One, is invaluable for efficient electrical system troubleshooting.

See **Figures 27 and 28** for schematics showing

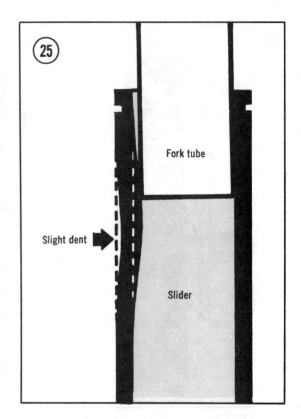

Fork tube

Slight dent

Slider

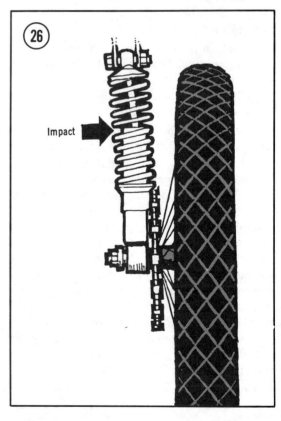

Impact

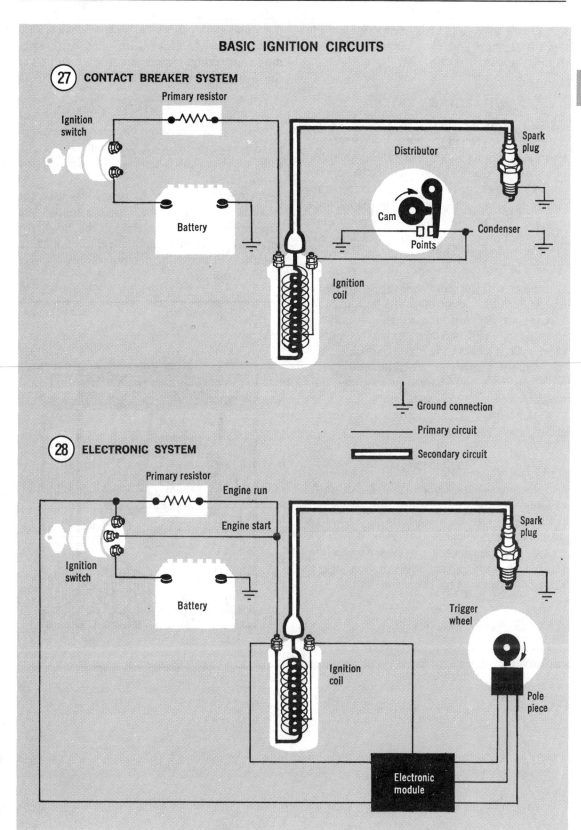

BASIC IGNITION CIRCUITS

27 CONTACT BREAKER SYSTEM

Primary resistor

Ignition switch

Battery

Distributor

Cam

Points

Condenser

Spark plug

Ignition coil

28 ELECTRONIC SYSTEM

Primary resistor

Engine run

Engine start

Ignition switch

Battery

Ground connection

Primary circuit

Secondary circuit

Spark plug

Trigger wheel

Ignition coil

Pole piece

Electronic module

simplified conventional and electronic ignition systems. Typical and most common electrical troubles are also described.

CHARGING SYSTEM

1. *Battery will not accept a charge*—Make sure the electrolyte level in the battery is correct and that the terminal connections are tight and free of corrosion. Check for fuses in the battery circuit. If the battery is satisfactory, refer to the electrical system chapter for alternator tests. Finally, keep in mind that even a good alternator is not capable of restoring the charge to a severely discharged battery; it must first be charged by an external source.

2. *Battery will not hold a charge*—Check the battery for sulfate deposits in the bottom of the case (**Figure 29**). Sulfation occurs naturally and the deposits will accumulate and eventually come in contact with the plates and short them out. Sulfation can be greatly retarded by keeping the battery well charged at all times. Test the battery to assess its condition.

If the battery is satisfactory, look for excessive draw, such as a short.

LIGHTING

Bulbs burn out frequently—All bulbs will eventually burn out, but if the bulb in one particular light burns out frequently check the light assembly for looseness that may permit excessive vibration; check for loose connections that could cause current surges; check also to make sure the bulb is of the correct rating.

FUSES

Fuse blows—When a fuse blows, don't just replace it; try to find the cause. Consider a fuse

a warning device as well as a safety device. And never replace a fuse with one of greater amperage rating. It probably won't melt before the insulation on the wiring does.

WIRING

Wiring problems should be corrected as soon as they arise — before a short can cause a fire that may seriously damage or destroy the motorcycle.

A circuit tester of some type is essential for locating shorts and opens. Use the appropriate wiring diagram at the end of the book for reference. If a wire must be replaced make a notation on the wiring diagram of any changes in color coding.

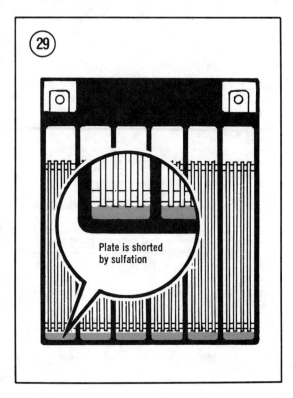

Plate is shorted by sulfation

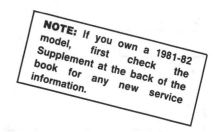

NOTE: If you own a 1981-82 model, first check the Supplement at the back of the book for any new service information.

CHAPTER THREE

LUBRICATION, MAINTENANCE, AND TUNE-UP

A motorcycle, even in normal use, is subjected to tremendous heat, stress and vibration. When neglected, any bike becomes unreliable and actually dangerous to ride. When properly maintained, the Honda CB750 is one of the most reliable bikes available and will give many miles and years of reliable, fast and safe riding. An afternoon spent now, cleaning and adjusting, can prevent costly mechanical problems in the future and unexpected breakdowns on the road.

The procedures presented in this chapter can be easily carried out by anyone with average mechanical skills. The operations are presented step-by-step; if they are followed, it is difficult to go wrong.

Tables 1-6 are located at the end of this chapter.

ROUTINE CHECKS

The following simple checks should be performed at each stop at a service station for gas.

Engine Oil Level

Refer to *Checking Engine Oil Level* under *Periodic Lubrication* in this chapter.

General Inspection

1. Quickly examine the engine for signs of oil or fuel leakage.

2. Check the tires for imbedded stones. Pry them out with your ignition key.
3. Make sure all lights work.

NOTE
At least check the brake light. It can burn out any time. Motorists cannot stop as quickly as you and need all the warning you can give.

Tire Pressure

Tire pressure must be checked with the tires cold. Correct tire pressure depends a lot on the load you are carrying. See **Table 1**.

Lights and Horn

With the engine running, check the following:
1. Pull the front brake lever and check that the brake light comes on.
2. Push the rear brake pedal and check that the brake light comes on soon after you have begun depressing the pedal.
3. Turn the headlight switch to the ON position. Check to see that headlight and taillight are on.
4. Move the dimmer switch up and down between the high and low positions and check to see that both headlight elements are working.

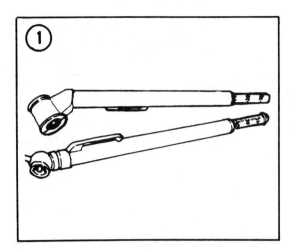

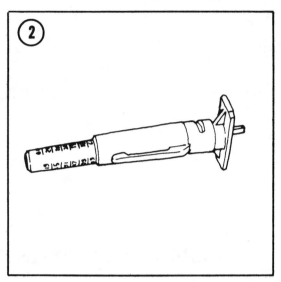

5. Push the turn signal switch to the left position and the right position and check that all 4 turn signal lights are working.

6. Push the horn button and note that the horn blows loudly.

7. If, during the tests, the rear brake pedal traveled too far before the brake light came on, adjust the rear brake light switch. Refer to *Rear Brake Light Switch Adjustment* in Chapter Seven. If the horn or any light failed to work properly, refer to Chapter Seven.

SERVICE INTERVALS

The services and intervals shown in **Table 2** are recommended by the factory. Strict adherence to these recommendations will go a long way toward ensuring long service from your Honda CB750.

For convenient maintenance of your motorcycle, most of the services shown in the table are described in this chapter. However, some procedures which require more than minor disassembly or adjustment are covered elsewhere in the appropriate chapter.

TIRES

Pressure

Tire pressure should be checked and adjusted to accomodate rider and luggage weight. A simple, accurate gauge (**Figure 1**) can be purchased for a few dollars and should be carried in your motorcycle tool kit. The appropriate tire pressures are shown in **Table 1**.

Inspection

Check tread for excessive wear, deep cuts, and imbedded objects such as stones, nails, etc. If you find a nail in a tire, mark its location with a light crayon before pulling it out. This will help locate the hole in the inner tube. Refer to *Tire Changing* in Chapter Eight.

Check local traffic regulations concerning minimum tread depth. Measure with a tread depth gauge (**Figure 2**) or small ruler. Honda recommends replacement when the front tread depth is 1/16 in. (1.5 mm) or less and rear tread depth is 3/32 in. (2.0 mm) or less. Tread wear indicators appear across the tire when tread reaches minimum safe depth. Replace the tire at this point.

Wheel Spoke Tension

1. Tap each spoke with a wrench. The higher the pitch of sound it makes, the tighter the spoke. The lower the sound frequency, the looser the spoke. A "ping" is good; a "klunk" says the spoke is too loose.

2. If one or more spokes are loose, tighten them as described under *Wheels* in Chapter Eight.

CRANKCASE BREATHER HOSE (U.S. MODELS ONLY)

Raise the seat and inspect the hose for cracks and deterioration. Make sure that the hose clamps are tight (**Figure 3**).

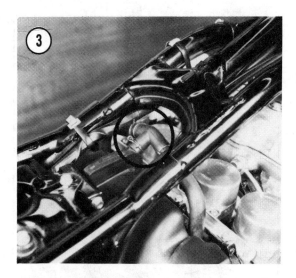

3

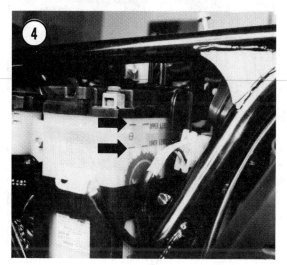

BATTERY

Electrolyte Level Check

The battery is the heart of the electrical system. It should be checked and serviced as indicated. The majority of electrical system troubles can be attributed to neglect of this vital component.

In order to correctly check the electrolyte level it is necessary to remove the battery from the frame. The electrolyte level should be maintained between the two marks on the battery case (**Figure 4**). If the electrolyte level is low, it's a good idea to completely remove the battery so that it can be thoroughly cleaned, serviced and checked.

1. Remove the right- and left-hand side covers.
2. Disconnect the battery negative cable from the battery (A, **Figure 5**).
3. Disconnect the battery positive cable from the starter solenoid terminal (**Figure 6**).
4. Remove the holder plate bolt (B, **Figure 5**) and pivot it out of the way. Disconnect the vent tube (C, **Figure 5**).
5. Slide the battery and holder tray out of the frame (**Figure 7**) and remove it.

CAUTION
Be careful not to spill battery electrolyte acid on painted or polished surfaces. The liquid is highly corrosive and will damage

the finish. If it is spilled, wash it off immediately with soapy water and thoroughly rinse with clean water.

6. Remove the caps from the battery cells and add distilled water to correct the level. Never add electrolyte (acid) to correct the level.

7. After the level has been corrected and the battery allowed to stand for a few minutes, check the specific gravity of the electrolyte in each cell with a hydrometer (**Figure 8**). Follow the manufacturer's instructions for reading the instrument.

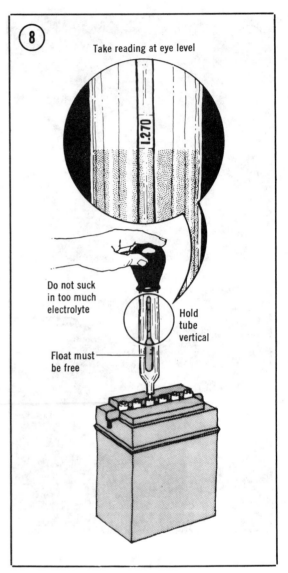

Testing

Hydrometer testing is the best way to check battery condition. Use a hydrometer with numbered graduations from 1.100 to 1.300 rather than one with color-coded bands. To use the hydrometer, squeeze the rubber ball, insert the tip into the cell and release the ball. Draw enough electrolyte to float the weighted float inside the hydrometer. Note the number in line with the surface of the electrolyte; this is the specific gravity for this cell. Return the electrolyte to the cell from which it came. The specific gravity of the electrolyte in each battery cell is an excellent indication of that cell's condition. A fully charged cell will read 1.260-1.280, while a cell in good condition reads from 1.230-1.250 and anything below 1.140 is discharged.

Specific gravity varies with temperature. For each 10° that electrolyte temperature exceeds 80° F (27° C), add 0.004 to the reading indicated on hydrometer. Subtract 0.004 for each 10° below 80° F (27° C).

If the cells test in the poor range, the battery requires recharging. The hydrometer is useful for checking the progress of the charging operation. **Table 3** shows approximate state of charge.

Charging

WARNING
During charging, highly explosive hydrogen gas is released from the battery.

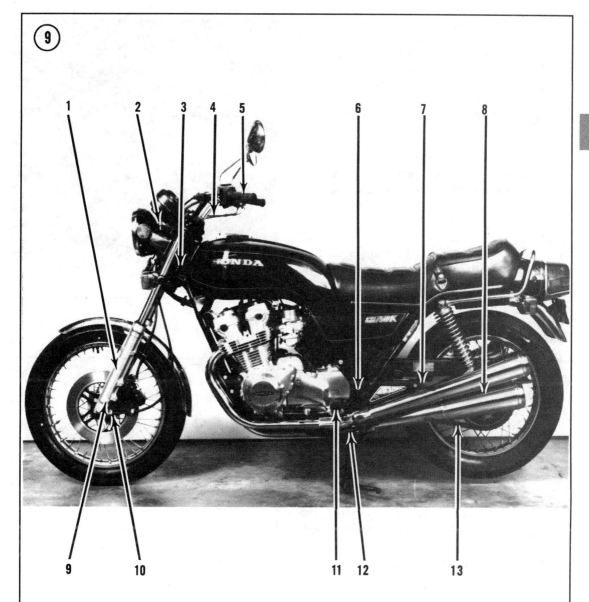

LUBRICATION POINTS

1. Front forks
2. Speedometer and tachometer cables
3. Steering head bearings
4. Clutch, throttle and choke cables
5. Throttle grip, clutch and brake lever pivots
6. Rear swing arm
7. Rear foot pegs
8. Rear wheel bearings
9. Front wheel bearings
10. Speedometer drive gear
11. Front foot pegs
12. Side and center stand pivots
13. Drive chain

The battery should be charged only in a well-ventilated area away from open flames (including pilot lights on home gas appliances). Do not allow any smoking in the area. Never check the charge of the battery by arcing across the terminals; the resulting spark can ignite the hydrogen gas.

> CAUTION
> *Always remove the battery from the motorcycle before connecting charging equipment.*

1. Connect the positive (+) charger lead to the positive battery terminal and the negative (-) charger lead to the negative battery terminal.

2. Remove all vent caps from the battery, set the charger at 12 volts and switch it on. If the output of the charger is variable, it is best to select a low setting—1 1/2 to 2 amps.

3. After battery has been charged for about 8 hours, turn the charger off, disconnect the leads and check the specific gravity. It should be within the limits specified in **Table 3**.

If it is, and remains stable for one hour, the battery is charged.

4. Clean the battery terminals, case and tray and reinstall them in the bike, reversing the removal steps. Coat the terminals with Vaseline or silicone spray to retard decomposition of the terminals.

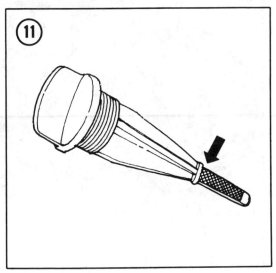

Checking Engine Oil Level

Engine oil level is checked with the dipstick, located on the top of the crankcase on the left-hand side (**Figure 10**).

1. Place the bike on the centerstand. Start the engine and let it reach normal operating temperature.

2. Stop the engine and allow the oil to settle. Remove the dipstick, wipe it clean and rest it on the case threads; do not screw it in. Remove it and check the level. The motorcycle must be level for the correct reading.

3. The level should be between the 2 lines but not above the upper one (**Figure 11**). If

New Battery Installation

When replacing the old battery with a new one, be sure to charge it completely (specific gravity of 1.260-1.280) before installing it in the bike. Failure to do so, or using the battery with a low electrolyte level, will permanently damage the battery.

PERIODIC LUBRICATION

Refer to **Figure 9** for lubrication points.

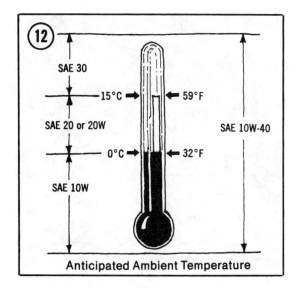

Anticipated Ambient Temperature

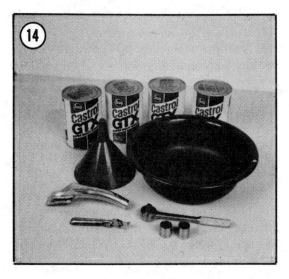

necessary, add the recommended weight of oil (**Figure 12**) to correct the level; do not overfill. Install the dipstick and tighten it securely.

Changing Engine Oil and Filter

The factory-recommended oil and filter change interval is every 4,000 miles (6,400 km). This assumes that the motorcycle is operated in moderate climates. In extremely cold climates, oil should be changed every 30 days. The time interval is more important than the mileage interval because acids formed (by gasoline and water vapor from combustion) will contaminate the oil even if the motorcycle is not run for several months. If the motorcycle is operated under dusty conditions, the oil will get dirty more quickly and should be changed more frequently than recommended.

Use only a detergent oil with an API classification of SE or SF. The classification is stamped on top of the can (**Figure 13**). Try always to use the same brand of oil. Refer to **Figure 12** for correct weight of oil to use under different ambient temperatures.

> *NOTE*
> *Never dispose of motor oil in the trash, on the ground, or down a storm drain. Many service stations accept used motor oil and waste haulers provide curbside used motor oil collection. Do not combine other fluids with motor oil to be recycled. To locate a recycler, contact the American Petroleum Institute (API) at www.recycleoil.org.*

To change the engine oil and filter you will need the following (**Figure 14**):

   a. Drain pan

   b. Funnel

   c. Can opener or pour spout

   d. 17 mm wrench (drain plug), 12 mm wrench (filter bolt)

   e. 4 quarts of oil

   f. Oil filter element

NOTE
Some service stations and oil retailers will accept your used oil for recycling; some may even give you money for it. Check local regulations before discarding the oil in your household trash.

1. Place the motorcycle on the centerstand.
2. Start the engine and run it until it is at normal operating temperature, then turn it off.
3. Place a drain pan under the crankcase and remove the drain plug (**Figure 15**). Remove the dipstick (**Figure 10**); this will speed up the flow of oil.
4. Let it drain for at least 15-20 minutes. During this time, push the starter button a couple of times to help drain any remaining oil.

CAUTION
Do not let the engine start and run without oil in the crankcase.

NOTE
Before removing filter cover, thoroughly clean off all road dirt and oil around it.

5. Move the drain pan under the filter and unscrew the bolt securing the filter cover (**Figure 16**) to the crankcase.
6. Remove the cover and the filter. Discard the old filter and clean out the cover and the bolt with cleaning solvent. Dry parts thoroughly.
7. Inspect the O-ring on the cover (**Figure 17**). Replace if necessary.

NOTE
Prior to installing the cover, clean off the mating surface of the crankcase—do not allow any road dirt to enter into the oil system.

8. Insert the bolt into the cover and install the spring and washer (**Figure 18**). Insert the filter and reinstall the filter assembly onto the crankcase.
9. Tighten the filter cover bolt to 20-23 ft.-lb. (27-31 N•m). Install the drain plug and tighten to 25-29 ft.-lb. (34-39 N•m).
10. Fill the crankcase with the correct weight and quantity of oil.

NOTE
The capacity is approximately 3.7 U.S. qt. (3.5 liters).

11. Screw in the dipstick securely.
12. Start the engine; the oil light should go off within 5 seconds. If it stays on, shut off the engine immediately and locate the problem. Do not run the engine with the light on.
13. Let the engine idle at moderate speed and check for leaks.
14. Turn the engine off and check for correct oil level; adjust if necessary.

Front Fork Oil Change

There is no factory recommended fork oil change interval but it's good practice to change it every 6,000 miles (10,000 km) or when it becomes contaminated.

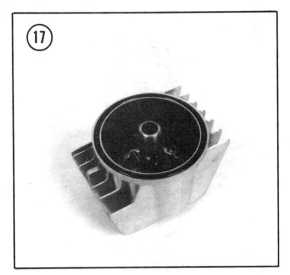

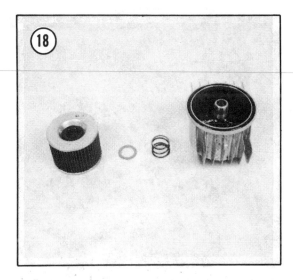

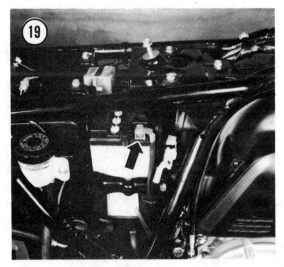

To gain access to the fork top cap bolts it is necessary to partially remove the handlebar assembly.

1. Place the bike on the centerstand and disconnect the battery negative lead (**Figure 19**). Remove the rear view mirrors.

2. Remove the screws (A, **Figure 20**) securing the fuse cover and remove it.

3. Remove the Allen bolts (**Figure 21**) securing the fuse holder.

> *CAUTION*
> *Cover the fuel tank with a heavy cloth or plastic tarp to protect it from accidental spilling of brake fluid. Wash any brake fluid off of any painted or plated surface immediately, as it will destroy the finish. Use soapy water and rinse thoroughly.*

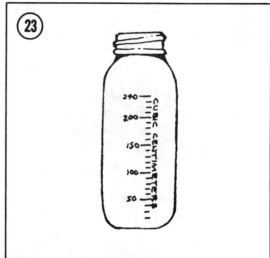

4. Pull the handlebar assembly up and slightly to the rear. Rest it on the fuel tank; do not pull too strongly as the electrical cables may be damaged.

5. Remove the black protective cap and top cap bolt (B, **Figure 20**).

6. Place a drain pan under the fork and remove the drain screw (**Figure 22**). Allow the oil to drain for at least 5 minutes.

> *CAUTION*
> *Do not allow the fork oil to come in contact with any of the brake components.*

> *NOTE*
> *Hold onto the handlebar assembly so it will not slide off the fuel tank during the next step.*

7. With both of the bike's wheels on the ground and the rear brake applied, push down on the upper fork bridge to work the forks up and down. Continue until all oil is expelled.

8. Install the drain screw.

9. Repeat for the other fork.

10. Fill each fork tube with 5.2 oz. (155 cc) of Dexron ATF (automatic transmission fluid) or fork oil.

> *NOTE*
> *In order to measure the correct amount of fluid, use a plastic baby bottle. These have measurements in fluid ounces (oz.) and cubic centimeters (cc) on the side (Figure 23).*

11. After filling both fork tubes, pump the fork tubes several times to expel air from the upper and lower fork chambers.

12. Install the cap bolts and tighten to 15-20 ft.-lb. (20-27 N•m).

13. Install the handlebar assembly and tighten the Allen bolts (**Figure 21**) to 13-18 ft.-lb. (18-25 N•m). Tighten the front bolts first, then the rear.

> *NOTE*
> *Be sure to align the punch mark on the handlebar with the top surface of the fork bridge (Figure 24).*

14. Road test the bike and check for leaks.

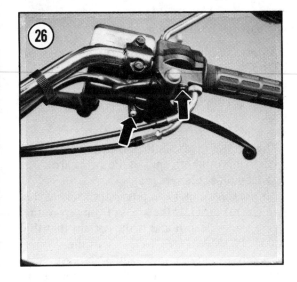

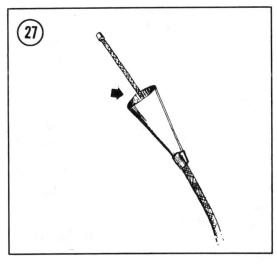

Drive Chain Lubrication

Oil the drive chain every 300 miles (500 km) or sooner if it becomes dry.

1. Place the bike on the centerstand.

CAUTION
Models since 1980 are equipped with an O-ring type chain. Do not use engine oil as a lubricant as the O-rings will be damaged. Use PJ1 Blue Label chain lubricant, or equivalent, specifically designed for this type of chain.

2. Oil the bottom chain run with a commercial chain lubricant. Concentrate on getting the oil down between the side plates of the chain links.

3. Rotate the wheel to bring the unoiled portion of the chain within reach. Continue until all the chain is lubricated.

Control Cables

Every 4,000 miles (6,400 km) the control cables should be lubricated. Also, they should be inspected at this time for fraying and the cable sheath should be checked for chafing. The cables are relatively inexpensive and should be replaced when found to be faulty.

The control cables can be lubricated either with oil or with any of the popular cable lubricants and a cable lubricator. The first method requires more time and the complete lubrication of the entire cable is less certain.

Examine the exposed end of the inner cable. If it is dirty, or the cable feels gritty when moved up and down in its housing, first spray it with a lubricant/solvent such as LPS-25 or WD-40. Let this solvent drain out, then proceed with the following steps.

Oil method

1. Disconnect the cable from the clutch lever (**Figure 25**) and the throttle grip assembly.

NOTE
*On the throttle cable it is necessary to remove the screws (**Figure 26**) that clamp the housing together to gain access to the cable ends.*

2. Make a cone of stiff paper and tape it to the end of the cable sheath (**Figure 27**).

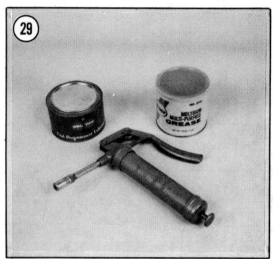

3. Hold the cable upright and pour a small amount of light oil (SAE 10W/30) into the cone. Work the cable in and out of the sheath for several minutes to help the oil work its way down to the end of the cable.

NOTE
To avoid a mess at the end of the cable, place a shop cloth to catch the oil as it runs out the end.

4. Remove the cone, reconnect the cable and adjust the cable(s) as described in this chapter.

NOTE
While the throttle housing is separated, apply a light coat of grease to the metal surfaces of the grip assembly.

Lubricator method

1. Disconnect the cable(s) as previously described.
2. Attach the lubricator following the manufacturer's instructions.
3. Insert the nozzle of the lubricant can in the lubricator, press the button on the can and hold it down until the lubricant begins to flow out of the other end of the cable.

NOTE
Place a shop cloth at the end of the cable(s) to catch all excess lubricant that will flow out.

4. Remove the lubricator, reconnect the cable(s) and adjust as described in this chapter.

Rear Swing Arm Bushings or Bearings Lubrication

Lubricate the rear swing arm bushings or bearings every 4,000 miles (6,400 km) using the grease fitting (**Figure 28**) located on the bottom of the swing arm. Use a good grade multi-purpose grease and apply with a small hand-held grease gun (**Figure 29**).
1. Force the grease into the fitting until the grease runs out both ends of the swing arm.
2. Clean off excess grease.
3. If grease will not run out of the ends of the swing arm, unscrew the grease fitting from the swing arm. Clean it and make certain that the ball check valve is free. Reinstall fitting.
4. Apply the grease gun again. If grease does not run out both ends of the swing arm, remove the swing arm as described under *Rear Swing Arm Removal/Installation* in Chapter Nine. Disassemble the swing arm, thoroughly clean and repack with grease.

Rear Brake Cam Lubrication (Drum Brake Models)

Lubricate the brake cam every 12,000 miles (19,200 km), 2 years or whenever the rear wheel is removed.
1. Remove the rear wheel as described under *Rear Wheel Removal/Installation* in Chapter Nine.
2. Take out the brake backing plate.
3. Wipe away the old grease, being careful not to get any of it on the brake shoes.

3

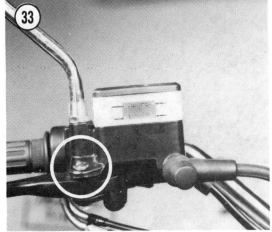

4. Sparingly apply high-temperature grease to the camming surfaces of the camshaft, the camshaft groove, the brake shoe pivots and the ends of the springs (**Figure 30**). Do not get any grease on the brake shoes.

5. Reassemble the rear wheel and install it.

Speedometer and Tachometer Cable Lubrication

Lubricate both cables every year or whenever needle operation is erratic. The procedure is the same for either instrument.

1. Remove the cable from the instrument cluster (**Figure 31**).

2. Pull the cable from its sheath.

3. If the grease is contaminated, thoroughly clean off all old grease.

4. Thoroughly coat the cable with a good grade of multi-purpose grease and reinstall it into the sheath.

5. Make sure the cable is correctly seated into the drive unit.

Miscellaneous Lubrication Points

Lubricate the clutch lever (**Figure 32**); front brake lever (**Figure 33**); rear brake lever (**Figure 34**); center and side stand pivot points (**Figure 35**); and footrest pivot points. Use SAE 10W/30 motor oil.

PERIODIC MAINTENANCE

Drive Chain Adjustment

The drive chain should be checked and adjusted every 600 miles (1,000 km). It

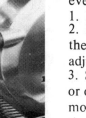

should be removed, cleaned and lubricated every 2,000 miles (3,200 km).

1. Place the transmission in NEUTRAL.

2. Remove the axle nut cotter pin. Loosen the axle nut (A, **Figure 36**) and the axle adjusting locknuts (B, **Figure 36**).

3. Screw the adjusters (C, **Figure 36**) either in or out as required, in equal amounts. With the motorcycle on a support block or centerstand, the free movement of the chain, pushed up midway between the sprockets, should be between 5/8-1 in. (15-25 mm). See **Figure 37**. Rotate the rear wheel to move the chain to another position and recheck the adjustment; chains rarely wear or stretch evenly and, as a result, the free play will not remain constant over the entire chain. If the chain can not be adjusted within these limits, it is excessively

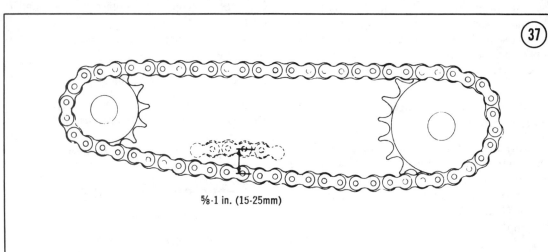

5/8-1 in. (15-25mm)

worn and stretched and should be replaced. Replace the drive chain when the red zone (**Figure 38**) on the label aligns with the rear of the swing arm or when free play exceeds 3/4 in. (20 mm).

WARNING
Excessive free play can result in chain breakage which could cause a serious accident.

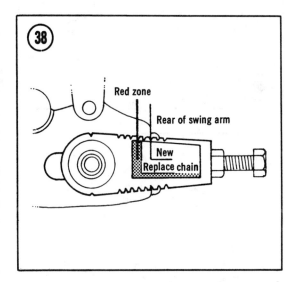

NOTE
Replacement chain is as follows: all 1979 models—No. 630 by 90 links; 1980 model CB750C—No. 530 by 90 links; CB750F and CB750K—No. 530 by 108 links.

4. When the adjustment is correct, sight along the chain from the rear sprocket to see that it is correctly aligned. It should leave the top of the rear sprocket in a straight line. If it is cocked to one side or the other (**Figure 39**), the rear wheel is incorrectly aligned and must be corrected by turning the adjusters counter to one another until the chain and sprocket are correctly aligned. When the alignment is correct, readjust the free play as described above and tighten the adjuster locknuts and axle nut securely. Torque the axle nut to 58-72 ft.-lb. (80-100 N•m) and install a new cotter pin.

NOTE
Always install a new cotter pin and bend it over completely. Never reuse an old one as it may break and fall out.

5. After adjusting the drive chain, adjust the rear brake pedal free play as described under *Rear Brake Adjustment* in this chapter.

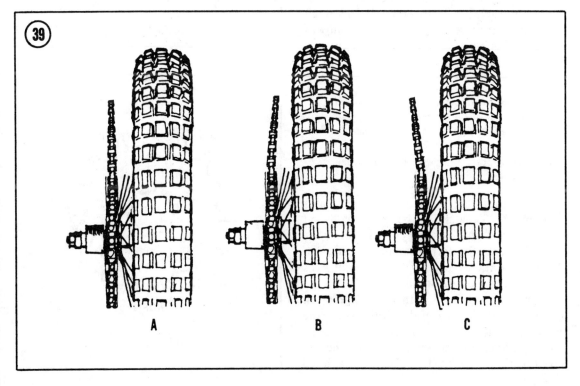

Drive Chain Cleaning, Inspection and Lubrication (1979 Models Only)

Every 2,000 miles (3,200 km) remove, thoroughly clean and lubricate the chain.

CAUTION
Do not clean the O-ring chain (models since 1980) as the rubber O-rings will be damaged.

1. Remove the drive chain as described under *Drive Chain Removal/Installation* in Chapter Nine.
2. Immerse the chain in a pan of cleaning solvent and allow it to soak for about half an hour. Move it around and flex it during this period so that dirt between the pins and rollers may work its way out.
3. Scrub the rollers and side plates with a stiff brush and rinse away loosened grit. Rinse it a couple of times to make sure all dirt is washed out. Hang up the chain and allow it to thoroughly dry.
4. After cleaning the chain, examine it carefully for wear or damage. If any signs are visible, replace the chain.
5. Lay the chain alongside a ruler (**Figure 40**) and compress the links together. Then stretch them apart. If more than 1/4 in. (0.6 mm) of movement is possible, replace the chain; it is too worn to be used again.

CAUTION
*Always check both sprockets (**Figure 41**) every time the drive chain is removed. If any wear is visible on the teeth, replace the sprocket. Never install a new chain over worn sprockets or a worn chain over new sprockets.*

6. Check the inner faces of the inner plates (**Figure 42**). They should be lightly polished on both sides. If they show considerable wear on both sides, the sprockets are not aligned. Adjust alignment as described in Step 4 of *Drive Chain Adjustment* in this chapter.
7. Lubricate the chain with a good grade of chain lubricant, carefully following the manufacturer's instructions. As an alternative, lubricate by soaking in a pan of heated all-purpose grease such as Castrol Graphited

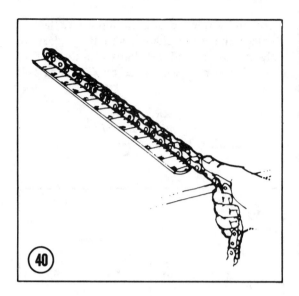

40

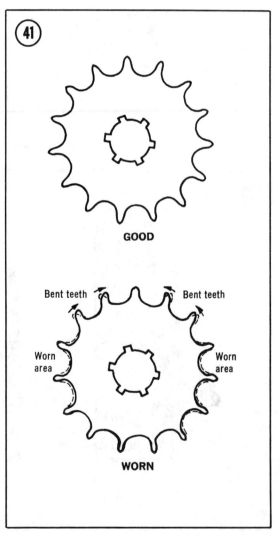

41

GOOD

Bent teeth | Bent teeth

Worn area | Worn area

WORN

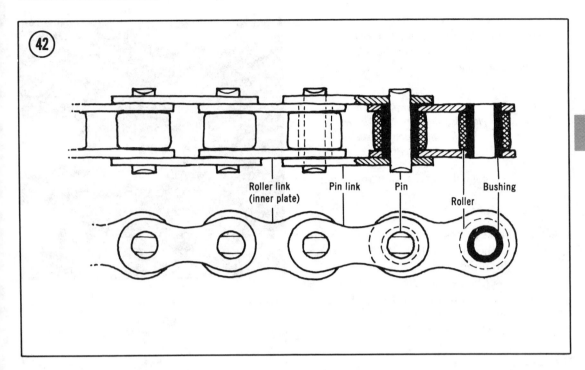

Roller link (inner plate)   Pin link   Pin   Bushing   Roller

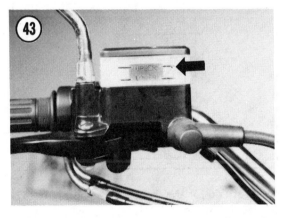

Grease, Shell Retinex A or DC, Mobilgrease MP or Marfax All-Purpose Grease. Heating permits the grease to penetrate the rollers and pins, but extreme care must be taken.

WARNING
If the grease is heated excessively, it may reach its flash point, resulting in a dangerous and difficult fire to extinguish. Never heat the grease with an open flame or a hot plate. Heat it only by placing the grease pan in a larger pan containing about an inch of boiling water and only after the water has been removed from the heat source.

After the chain has soaked in the grease for about half an hour, remove it from the pan and wipe off all excess grease with a clean rag.

8. Reinstall the chain as described under *Drive Chain Removal/Installation* in Chapter Nine.

9. Adjust chain free play as described under *Drive Chain Adjustment* in this chapter.

Disc Brake Fluid Level

NOTE
The rear brake on some models is drum type.

The hydraulic brake fluid in the disc brake master cylinders should be checked every month or 4,000 miles (6,400 km), whichever comes first. The brake pads should also be checked for wear at the same time. Bleeding the hydraulic system, servicing brake components and replacing the brake pads are covered in Chapter Ten.

1. The fluid level in the reservoir should be up to the upper level line. See **Figure 43** for the front brake and **Figure 44** for the rear brake. If necessary, correct the level. Remove the cover, gasket and diaphragm and add fresh brake fluid.

WARNING
Use brake fluid clearly marked DOT 3 only and specified for disc brakes. Others may vaporize and cause brake failure.

CAUTION
Be careful not to spill brake fluid on painted or plated surfaces as it will destroy the surface. Wash immediately with soapy water and thoroughly rinse it off.

2. Reinstall the diaphragm, gasket and cover.

Disc Brake Lines

Check brake lines between the master cylinder and the brake caliper. If there is any leakage, tighten the connections and bleed the brakes as described under *Bleeding the System* in Chapter Ten. If this does not stop the leak, or if a line is obviously damaged, cracked or chafed, replace the line and bleed the brake.

Disc Brake Pad Wear

Inspect the brake pads for excessive or uneven wear, scoring and oil or grease on the friction surface. If pads are worn to the red line (**Figure 45**), they must be replaced.

NOTE
Always replace both pads at the same time.

If any of these conditions exist, replace the pads as described under *Brake Pad Replacement* in Chapter Ten.

Disc Brake Fluid Change

Every time you remove the reservoir cap a small amount of dirt and moisture enters the brake fluid. The same thing happens if a leak occurs or if any part of the hydraulic system is loosened or disconnected. Dirt can clog the system and cause unnecessary wear. Water in the fluid vaporizes at high temperatures, impairing the hydraulic action and reducing brake performance.

To maintain peak performance, change the brake fluid every 10,000 miles (16,000 km) or 2 years.

1. Remove dust cap from the caliper bleeder valve. Connect a small clear hose to the valve and place the free end into a container. Refer

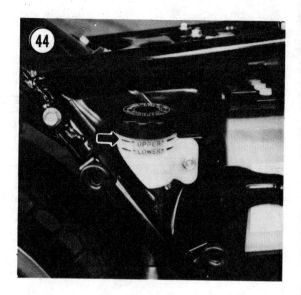

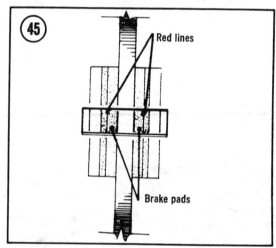

to **Figure 46** for the front wheel and **Figure 47** for the rear wheel.

2. Open the bleeder valve with a wrench about 1/2 turn.

3. Squeeze the brake lever several times to force out as much brake fluid as possible. Close the bleeder valve.

WARNING
Do not reuse brake fluid which has been drained from a brake system. Contaminated fluid can cause brake failure.

4. Fill the reservoir with new brake fluid, install the cap and bleed the system as described under *Bleeding the System* in Chapter Ten.

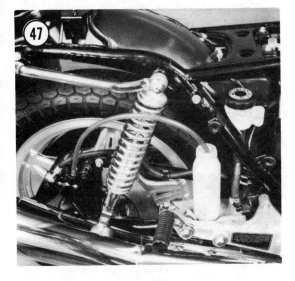

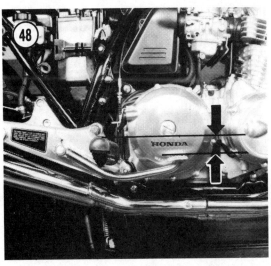

WARNING
Use brake fluid clearly marked DOT 3 only. Others may vaporize and cause brake failure.

Rear Brake Pedal Height Adjustment

The rear brake pedal height should be adjusted every 4,000 miles (6,400 km).

1. Place the motorcycle on the centerstand.

2. Check to be sure the brake pedal is in the at-rest position.

3. The correct height position below the top of the foot peg (**Figure 48**) is as follows:

    a. Models CB750K, K-LTD and C—3/8 in. (10 mm)

    b. Model CB750F—1/4 in. (7 mm)

4A. On drum brake models, loosen the locknut (A, **Figure 49**) and turn the adjusting bolt (B, **Figure 49**) to achieve the correct height. Tighten the locknut securely and adjust the free play and brake light switch as described in this chapter and Chapter Seven.

4B. On disc brake models, loosen the locknut and turn the adjuster (**Figure 50**) to achieve the correct height. Tighten the locknut securely and adjust the brake light switch as described in Chapter Seven.

Rear Brake Pedal Free Play
(Drum Type)

Adjust the brake pedal to the correct height as described in this chapter. Turn the adjustment nut on the end of the brake rod

(**Figure 51**) until the brake pedal has 3/4 to 1 1/4 in. (20-30 mm) free play. Free play is the distance the pedal travels from the at-rest position to the applied position when the pedal is depressed lightly by hand.

Rotate the rear wheel and check for brake drag. Also operate the pedal several times to make sure it returns to the at-rest position immediately after release.

Adjust the rear brake light switch as described under *Rear Brake Light Switch Adjustment* in Chapter Seven.

Clutch Adjustment

The clutch free play should be checked every 4,000 miles (6,400 km).

There are 2 different clutch adjustment areas, the clutch cable and the mechanism adjustment on the engine. The cable adjustment takes up slack caused by cable stretching. The mechanism adjustment takes up slack due to clutch component wear.

Cable adjustment

At the hand lever, loosen the locknut (A, **Figure 52**) and rotate the adjuster (B, **Figure 52**) until 3/8-3/4 in. (10-20 mm) of free play is obtained. Tighten the locknut.

If sufficient free play cannot be obtained at the hand lever, additional adjustment can be made at the cable length adjuster and at the clutch mechanism.

Mechanism adjustment

1. Loosen the locknut (C, **Figure 53**) and turn the adjuster barrel (D, **Figure 53**) all the way out to obtain maximum cable free play.

2. Remove the clutch lifter cap (**Figure 54**). Loosen the clutch lifter locknut (A, **Figure 55**) and turn the adjuster (B, **Figure 55**) clockwise until a slight resistance is felt, then *stop.* Back out the adjuster counterclockwise 3/4 turn and tighten the locknut. Install the lifter cap.

NOTE
Make sure the adjuster does not turn while tightening the locknut.

3

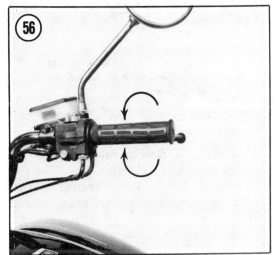

3. At the cable length adjuster, turn the adjuster barrel (D, **Figure 53**) until the correct amount of free play is achieved at the hand lever. Tighten the locknut (C, **Figure 53**).

Additional fine tuning can be made at the hand lever if necessary.

> *NOTE*
> *When making adjustments at the hand lever, do not expose the threads on the adjuster more than 15/16 in. (8 mm); refer to* ***Figure 52***.

If proper amount of free play cannot be achieved by using these 2 adjustment procedures, the cable has stretched to the point that it needs replacing. Refer to *Clutch*

Cable Removal/Installation in Chapter Five for the complete procedure.

Throttle Operation/Adjustment

The throttle grip should have 0.08-0.24 in. (2-6 mm) rotational play (**Figure 56**). If adjustment is necessary, loosen the cable locknut (A, **Figure 57**) and turn the adjuster (B, **Figure 57**) in or out to achieve the proper free play. Tighten the locknut (A).

Check the throttle cables from grip to carburetors. Make sure they are not kinked or chafed. Replace them if necessary.

Make sure that the throttle grip rotates smoothly from fully closed to fully open. Check at center, full left and full right position of the steering.

Camshaft Chain Tensioner Adjustment

In time, the camshaft chain and guide will wear and develop slack. This will cause engine noise and if neglected too long will cause engine damage. The chain tension should be adjusted every 4,000 miles (6,400 km).

1. Place the bike on the centerstand, start the engine and let it idle.

2. At the front adjuster, loosen the locknut (A, **Figure 58**) and loosen the tensioner bolt (B, **Figure 58**) 1/2 turn. Tighten the bolt and locknut.

3. At the rear adjuster, loosen the upper and lower locknuts (**Figure 59**) 1/2 turn, then tighten them. The engine is shown partially disassembled in this figure for clarity only; it is not necessary to remove any components for this adjustment.

> *NOTE*
> *By making these 2 adjustments, the cam chain tensioner will automatically adjust to the correct tension.*

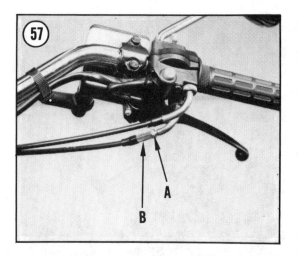

Air Cleaner
Removal/Installation

A clogged air cleaner can decrease the efficiency and life of the engine. Never run the bike without the air cleaner installed; even minute particles of dust can cause severe internal wear.

Clean the air cleaner element every 4,000 miles (6,400 km), and more often if ridden in dusty areas. Replace the element every 8,000 miles (12,800 km).

1. Remove the left-hand side cover (**Figure 60**).

2. Remove the screws (**Figure 61**) securing the air cleaner cover and remove the cover.

3. Pull out the set spring (**Figure 62**) and slide out the air cleaner element (**Figure 63**).

4. Tap the element lightly to remove most of the dirt and dust; then apply compressed air to the inside surface of the element.

5. Inspect the element and make sure it is in good condition. Replace if necessary.

6. Clean out the interior of the housing with a shop rag and cleaning solvent. Remove any foreign matter that may have passed through a broken cleaner element.

7. Install by reversing these removal steps.

Fuel Shutoff Valve and Filter Removal/Installation

The fuel filter removes particles which might otherwise enter the carburetors and cause the float needle to stay in the open position.

1. Turn the valve to the OFF position (**Figure 64**).

2. Remove the fuel line from the valve.

3. Install a longer piece of fuel line to the valve and place the loose end into a clean, sealable, metal container. If the fuel is kept clean, it can be reused.

4. Turn the valve to the RES position and open the fuel filler cap. This will speed up the flow of fuel. Drain the tank completely.

5. Remove the fuel shutoff valve by unscrewing the locknut from the tank (A, **Figure 65**).

6. After removing the valve, insert a corner of a clean shop rag into the opening in the tank to stop the dribbling of fuel onto the engine and frame.

7. Remove the fuel filter (B, **Figure 65**) from the shutoff valve. Clean it with a medium soft toothbrush and blow out with compressed air. Replace it if defective.

8. Install by reversing these removal steps. Do not forget the gasket (C, **Figure 65**) between the valve and the tank. Check for any leakage after installation is completed.

Fuel Line Inspection

Inspect the condition of the fuel line for cracks or deterioration; replace if necessary. Make sure the hose clamps are in place and holding securely.

Wheel Bearings

There is no factory-recommended mileage interval for cleaning and repacking wheel bearings. They should be serviced whenever they are removed from the wheel hub, or whenever there is a likelihood of water contamination. The correct service procedures are covered in Chapters Eight and Nine.

Steering Play

Check steering play every 8,000 miles (12,800 km).

1. Prop up the motorcycle so that the front tire clears the ground.

2. Center the front wheel. Push lightly against the left handlebar grip to start the wheel turning to the right, then let go. The wheel should continue turning under its own momentum until the forks hit their stop.

3. Center the wheel and push lightly against the right handlebar grip.

4. If, with a light push in either direction, the front wheel will turn all the way to the stop, the steering adjustment is not too tight.

5. Center the front wheel and kneel in front of it. Grasp the bottoms of the 2 front fork slider legs. Try to pull the forks toward you

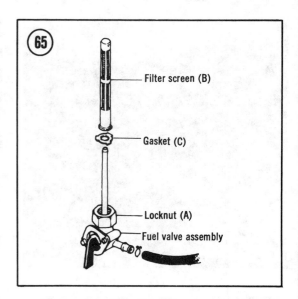

Filter screen (B)

Gasket (C)

Locknut (A)

Fuel valve assembly

and then try to push them toward the engine. If no play is felt, the steering adjustment is not too loose.

6. If the steering adjustment is too tight or too loose, readjust it as described under *Steering Stem Adjustment* in Chapter Eight.

Wheel Balance and Rim Trueness

Both wheels should be checked for balance and rim trueness every 4,000 miles (6,400 km). Check wheel hubs and rims for bends and other signs of damage. Refer to Chapter Eight.

**Wheel Spoke Inspection
(Wire Wheel Models)**

Check both wheels for bent or broken spokes. Replace damaged or broken spokes as described under *Wheels* in Chapter Eight. Pluck each spoke with your finger like a guitar string or tap each lightly with a small hammer or wrench. All spokes should emit the same sound. A spoke that is too tight will have a higher pitch than the others; one that is too loose will have a lower pitch. If only one or two spokes are slightly out of adjustment, adjust them with a spoke wrench made for this purpose (**Figure 66**). If more are affected, the wheel should be removed and trued. Refer to *Spoke Adjustment* in Chapter Eight.

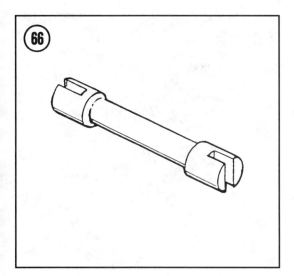

3

Front Suspension Check

1. Apply the front brake and pump the forks up and down as vigorously as possible. Check for smooth operation and check for any oil leaks.

2. Make sure the upper and lower fork bridge bolts (**Figure 67**) are tight.

3. Check the tightness of the 4 Allen bolts (**Figure 68**) securing the handlebar.

4. Check that the nuts (2 on each side) securing the front axle holder (**Figure 69**) are tight.

CAUTION
If any of the previously mentioned bolts and nuts are loose, refer to Chapter Eight for correct procedures and torque specifications.

Rear Suspension Check

1. Place the bike on the centerstand.

2. Push hard sideways on the rear wheel to check for side play in the rear swing arm bushings or bearings.

3. Check the tightness of the upper and lower shock absorber mounting nuts and bolts (**Figure 70**).

4. Make sure the rear axle nut is tight and the cotter pin is still in place (**Figure 71**).

5. On models with a drum type rear brake, check the tightness of the rear brake torque arm bolts (**Figure 72**).

CAUTION
If any of the previously mentioned nuts or bolts are loose, refer to Chapter Nine for correct procedures and torque specifications.

Nuts, Bolts and Other Fasteners

Constant vibration can loosen many fasteners on a motorcycle. Check the tightness of all fasteners, especially those on:

a. Engine mounting hardware
b. Engine crankcase covers
c. Handlebar and front forks
d. Gearshift lever
e. Brake pedal and lever
f. Exhaust system
g. Lighting equipment

Side Stand Rubber

The rubber tip of the side stand kicks the stand up if you should forget. If it wears down to the molded line (**Figure 73**), replace the rubber as it will no longer be effective.

TUNE-UP

A complete tune-up should be performed every 4,000 miles (6,400 km) of normal riding. More frequent tune-ups may be required if the bike is ridden primarily in stop-and-go traffic. The purpose of the tune-up is to restore the performance lost due to normal wear and deterioration of parts.

Table 4 summarizes tune-up specifications.

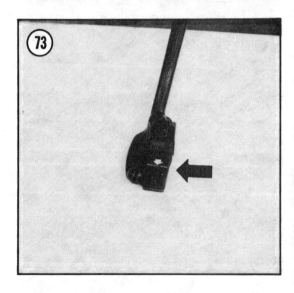

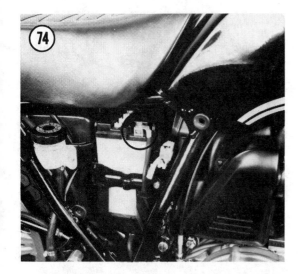

The spark plugs should be routinely replaced at every other tune-up or if the electrodes show signs of erosion. In addition, this is a good time to clean the air cleaner element. Have the new parts on hand before you begin.

Because different systems in an engine interact, the procedure should be done in the following order:

a. Tighten the cylinder head nuts.
b. Adjust the valve clearances.
c. Run a compression test.
d. Check and adjust the ignition components and timing.
e. Synchronize carburetors and set idle speed.

To perform a tune-up on your Honda, you will need the following tools:

a. 18 mm spark plug wrench
b. Socket wrench and assorted sockets
c. Flat feeler gauge
d. Special tool for changing valve lifter shims (Honda Valve Lifter Holder part No. 07964-4220001)
e. Compression gauge
f. Spark plug wire feeler gauge and gapper tool
g. Ignition timing light
h. Carburetor synchronization tool (to measure manifold vacuum)

Cylinder Head Nuts

The engine must be at room temperature for this procedure (95° F/35°C or cooler).

1. Place the bike on the centerstand.
2. Remove the right- and left-hand side covers and disconnect the battery negative lead (**Figure 74**).
3. Hinge up the seat and remove it.
4. Turn the fuel shutoff valve to the OFF position (**Figure 75**) and remove the fuel line to the carburetor.
5. Remove the bolt securing the fuel tank to the frame (**Figure 76**). Pull the tank to the rear and remove it.
6. Loosen the bolt (**Figure 77**) securing the tachometer drive cable to the cam cover and withdraw it. Disconnect the spark plug caps (A, **Figure 78**) and leads and tie them up out of the way.

7. Loosen the bolts (B, **Figure 78**) securing the cam cover in place and carefully remove the cover from the cylinder head. Do not damage the gasket while removing it.

NOTE
The bolts will stay in place on the cam cover as they are trapped within the rubber gasket/holders.

8. Tighten the cylinder head cap nuts (**Figure 79**) to 26-29 ft.-lb. (36-40 N•m) in the torque pattern indicated in **Figure 80**.
9. Leave the cam cover off for the following procedures.

Camshaft Chain Adjustment

Adjust the camshaft chain as described under *Camshaft Chain Tensioner Adjustment* in this chapter.

Valve Clearance Measurement

Valve clearance measurement must be made with the engine cool, at room temperature (95° F/35° C). All components removed for the preceding procedure must be left off for this measurement.
1. Take the bike off the centerstand.
2. Lean the bike to the right and then to the left to drain residual oil out of the pockets within the cylinder head surrounding the valve lifters. Place the bike back on the centerstand.

3. Remove the bolts (**Figure 81**) securing the alternator cover and remove the cover and the gasket.
4. Remove all 4 spark plugs (this will make it easier to turn the engine over by hand).
5. The correct valve clearance for both the intake and the exhaust valves is 0.08 mm (+0.05/−0.02 mm). For best performance, adjust to the smallest dimension.

NOTE
The cylinders are numbered 1-4 starting with the No. 1 cylinder on the left-hand side and working across from left to right with the No. 2, 3 and 4. The left-hand side refers to a rider sitting on the seat facing

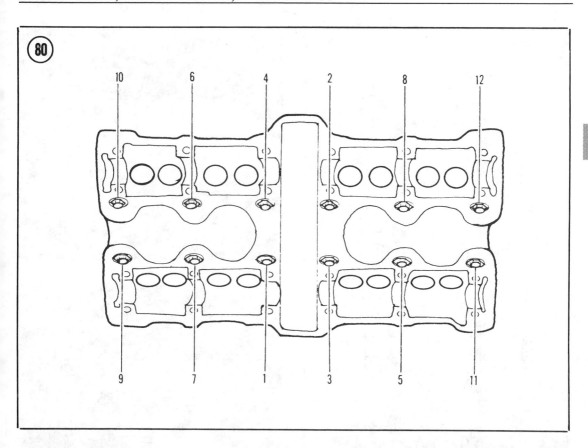

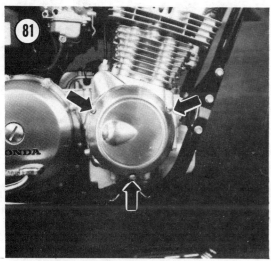

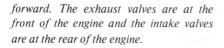

forward. The exhaust valves are at the front of the engine and the intake valves are at the rear of the engine.

6. Insert a flat feeler gauge between the cam and lifter surface (**Figure 82**). The clearance is measured correctly when there is a slight drag on the feeler gauge when it is inserted and withdrawn. Measure the valve clearance with a *metric* feeler gauge as it will be easier to calculate shim replacement, described later in this section. Measure all valves and record the clearance; they must be measured very accurately and recorded correctly.

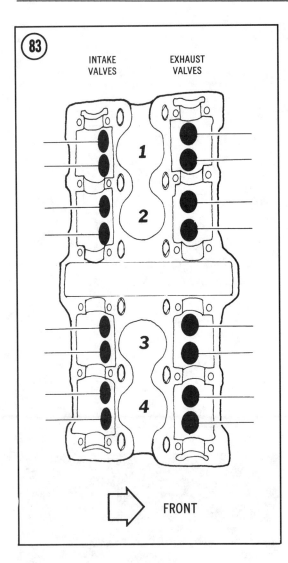

INTAKE VALVES   EXHAUST VALVES

1

2

3

4

FRONT

NOTE
Due to the number of valves and the complexity of valve clearance adjustment, use **Figure 83** *to record the valve clearance dimensions. Be sure to record the clearance dimension adjacent to the correct lifter on the drawing. Use a soft pencil (No. 2) and after the procedure is complete, carefully erase the dimensions so the page may be used the next time.*

7. Rotate the crankshaft by turning the bolt on the alternator (**Figure 84**) with a 17 mm wrench. Rotate the crankshaft *clockwise* (as viewed from the right-hand side) until the index mark on the right-hand end of the exhaust camshaft aligns with the top surface of the cylinder head. Refer to **Figure 85** and to

A, **Figure 86**. Measure the clearance of both exhaust valves on No. 1 and 3 cylinders. Record the clearance dimensions onto **Figure 83**.

8. Rotate the crankshaft clockwise 180° (this will rotate the camshaft 90°); refer to B, **Figure 86**. Measure the clearance dimension for both intake valves on No. 1 and 3 cylinders; record the dimensions.

9. Rotate the crankshaft clockwise 180°; refer to C, **Figure 86**. Measure the clearance dimension for both exhaust valves on No. 2 and 4 cylinders; record the dimensions.

10. Rotate the crankshaft clockwise 180°; refer to D, **Figure 86**. Measure the clearance dimension for both intake valves on No. 2 and 4 cylinders; record the dimensions.

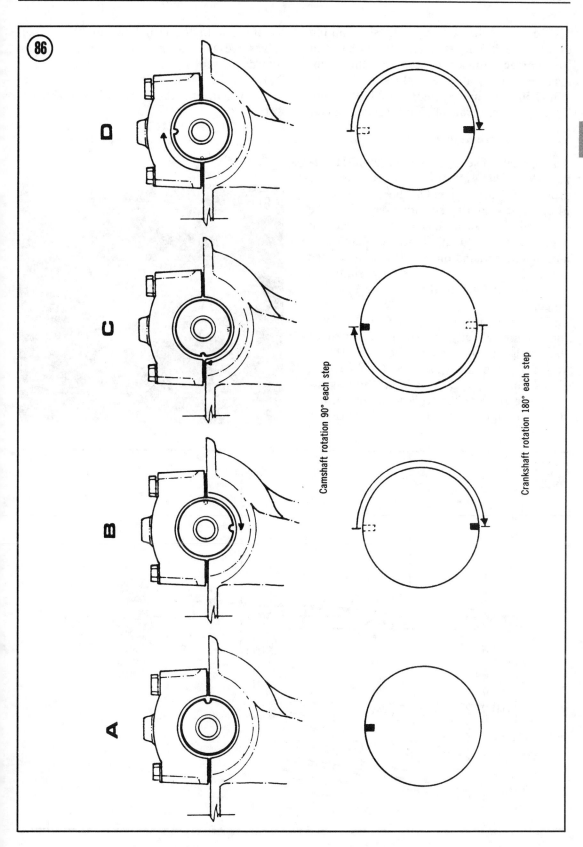

Camshaft rotation 90° each step

Crankshaft rotation 180° each step

11. To correct the clearance, the shim on top of the valve lifter must be replaced with one of the correct thickness. These shims are available in 25 different thicknesses from 2.30-3.50 mm in increments of 0.05 mm. These shims are available from Honda dealers.

Valve Clearance Adjustment

A special valve lifter holder tool (Honda part No. 07964-425001) is necessary for this procedure. This tool holds the pair of valve lifters down so the adjusting shim can be removed and replaced. This tool retails for approximately $20 at Honda dealers. This adjustment pertains only to valves that need adjustment. Do not change any shims on valves that fall within the specified tolerance range.

1. The top of the valve lifter has a notch. With the cam lobe directly opposite the lifter, rotate the lifter so that the notch is facing up. If both valves (of the same set) are to have their shims removed, rotate both lifters this way.

2. Rotate the crankshaft *clockwise* by turning the 17 mm bolt on the alternator (**Figure 87**).

Rotate it until the cam lobes on that set of valves are at maximum lift, with the valves fully depressed.

3. Insert the valve lifter holder tool between the camshaft and the 2 valve lifters (**Figure 88**).

> *CAUTION*
> *Be sure to install the tool as indicated in* ***Figure 88***.

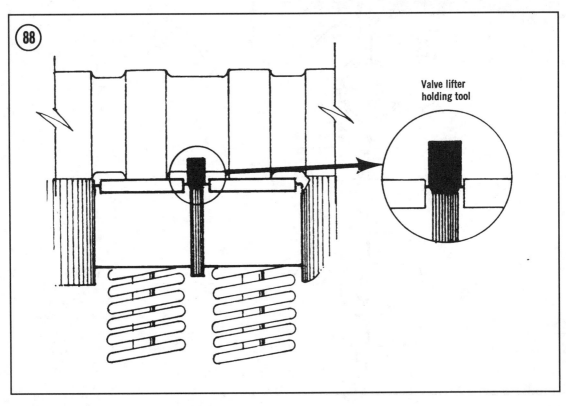

Valve lifter holding tool

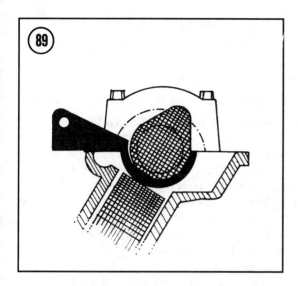

CAUTION
After the lifter holder tool has been installed, it holds this set of valves completely open. The next steps involve rotating the crankshaft and camshafts— remember this set of valves is open and protruding in the cylinder. When rotating the crankshaft watch the other set of valves on the same cylinder. Do not rotate the crankshaft so that the cam also opens the opposite set of valves. If this happens, the 4 valves will meet in the center of the cylinder and be bent or damaged.

4. Rotate the crankshaft one full turn (360°) *counterclockwise* until the cam lobes are turned away from the valve lifter holder (**Figure 89**).

CAUTION
Refer to the preceding CAUTION to avoid valve damage.

5. Remove the shim with a pair of tweezers or needlenose pliers.

NOTE
If the shims on both valves are to be replaced, do one valve at a time—this will avoid any interchange of shims and any mix up that may occur in the measuring.

NOTE
Because of the tachometer drive housing, the shim on the No. 2 cylinder exhaust valve must be removed from the front.

6. Measure the thickness of the removed shim with a micrometer. The original thickness will be marked on the lifter side of the shim. Do not rely on the marked thickness as the shim will have worn some, depending on the mileage, and will no longer be accurate.
7. For correct shim selection, proceed as follows:

NOTE
For calculations, use the mid-point of the specified clearance tolerance, e.g., for 0.06-0.13 mm use 0.09 mm.

NOTE
The following numbers are for example only.

Example:

Actual measured clearance	0.41mm
Subtract specified clearance	−0.09
Equals excess clearance	0.32
Existing shim thickness	2.75mm
Add excess clearance	+0.32
Equals new shim thickness	3.07
(round off to the nearest	
shim thickness)	3.05

8. Install new shim. Make sure it is positioned correctly within the lifter.
9. Repeat Steps 5-8 for other valve in the same set, if necessary.
10. Carefully rotate the crankshaft *clockwise* (opposite direction of that used in Step 4), one full turn until the cam lobes are at maximum lift, with the valves fully depressed.

CAUTION
See the 2nd CAUTION after Step 3—do not let the valves come in contact with each other in the cylinder.

11. Remove the valve lifter holder tool.
12. Rotate the crankshaft *clockwise* 2-3 full revolutions to make sure the shim has properly seated into the valve lifter. While rotating the crankshaft, continually observe the lifter and shim to make sure all is okay.
13. Recheck the valve clearance as described under *Valve Clearance Measurement*. If clearance is incorrect, repeat these steps until proper clearance is obtained.

NOTE
*If thickest shim (3.50 mm) will not bring the valve into the specified clearance, there is an excess of carbon buildup on the valve seat or there is damage to the valve or valve seat. If the thinnest shim (2.30 mm) will not sufficiently increase valve clearance, the valve seat is probably worn. Refer to **Valves** in Chapter Four.*

14. Discard old shims as they are worn and no longer accurate.

15. Repeat this procedure for all valves that need adjustment.

16. Install the cam cover (make sure the gasket is in good condition and replace if necessary). Tighten the bolts to 6-9 ft.-lb. (8-12 N•m). Tighten evenly in a crisscross pattern.

17. Install the tachometer drive cable and secure it with the bolt (**Figure 77**).

18. Install the alternator cover and gasket.

19. Install the fuel tank and seat, attach the battery negative lead and install the 2 side covers.

20. Install the spark plugs.

Compression Test

Every 4,000 miles (6,400 km) check cylinder compression. Record the results and compare them at the next 4,000 mile (6,400 km) check. A running record will show trends in deterioration so that corrective action can be taken before complete failure. The results, when properly interpreted, can indicate general cylinder, piston ring and valve condition.

1. Warm the engine to normal operating temperature. Ensure that the choke valves and throttle valves are completely open.

2. Remove the spark plugs.

3. Connect the compression tester to one cylinder following manufacturer's instructions (**Figure 90**).

4. Have an assistant crank the engine over until there is no further rise in pressure.

NOTE
Do not turn the engine over more than absolutely necessary. When spark plug leads are disconnected the electronic ignition will produce the highest voltage

possible and the coil may overheat and be damaged.

5. Remove the tester and record the reading.

6. Repeat Steps 3-5 for the other cylinders.

When interpreting the results, actual readings are not as important as the difference between the readings. Readings should be from about 170 ± 14 psi (12 ± 1.0 kg/cm^2). A maximum difference of 57 psi (4 kg/cm^2) between any 2 cylinders is acceptable. Greater differences indicate worn or broken rings, leaky or sticky valves, blown head gasket or a combination of all.

If compression reading does not differ between cylinders by more than 10%, the rings and valves are in good condition.

If a low reading (10% or more) is obtained on one of the cylinders, it indicates valve or ring trouble. To determine which, pour about a teaspoon of engine oil through the spark plug hole onto the top of the piston. Turn the engine over once to clear some of the excess oil, then take another compression test and record the reading. If the compression increases significantly, the valves are good but the rings are defective on that cylinder. If compression does not increase, the valves require servicing. A valve could be hanging open but not burned or a piece of carbon could be on a valve seat.

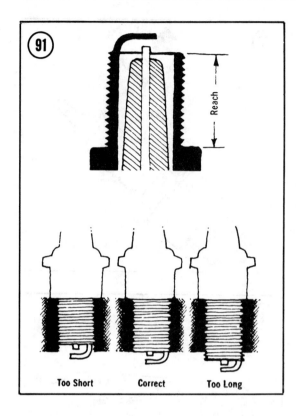

Too Short   Correct   Too Long

Correct Spark Plug Heat Range

Spark plugs are available in various heat ranges, hotter or colder than plugs originally installed at the factory.

Select plugs of a heat range designed for the loads and temperature conditions under which the bike will be run. The use of incorrect heat ranges can cause seized pistons, scored cylinder walls or damaged piston crowns.

In general, use a hot plug for low speeds, low loads and low temperatures. Use a cold plug for high speeds, high engine loads and high temperatures.

In areas where seasonal temperature variations are great, the factory recommends a "2-plug system"—a cold plug for hard summer riding and a hot plug for slower winter operation.

The reach (length) of a plug is also important. A longer than normal plug could interfere with the valves and pistons, causing permanent and severe damage. Refer to **Figure 91**.

The standard heat range spark plugs are given in **Table 5**.

Spark Plug Removal/Cleaning

1. Grasp the spark plug leads (**Figure 92**) as near to the plug as possible and pull them off the plugs. If the boot is stuck to the plug, twist it slightly to break it loose.
2. Blow away any dirt that has accumulated in the spark plug wells.

CAUTION
The dirt could fall into the cylinders when the plugs are removed, causing serious engine damage.

3. Remove spark plugs with an 18 mm spark plug wrench.

NOTE
If plugs are difficult to remove, apply penetrating oil, like WD-40 or Liquid Wrench, around base of plugs and let it soak in about 10-20 minutes.

4. Inspect spark plugs carefully. Look for plugs with broken center porcelain, excessively eroded electrodes and excessive carbon or oil fouling. Replace such plugs. If deposits are light, plugs may be cleaned in solvent with a wire brush or cleaned in a special spark plug sandblast cleaner.

Gapping and Installing the Plugs

New plugs should be carefully gapped to ensure a reliable, consistent spark. You must use a special spark plug gapping tool with a round gauge.

1. Remove the new plugs from the box. Do not screw in the small piece that is loose in each box (**Figure 93**); it is not used.

2. Insert a round gauge between the center and the side electrode of each plug (**Figure 94**). The correct gap is 0.024-0.028 in. (0.6-0.7 mm). If the gap is correct, you will feel a slight drag as you pull the gauge through. If there is no drag, or the gauge won't pass through, bend the side electrode with the gapping tool (**Figure 95**) to set the proper gap.

3. Put a small drop of oil on the threads of each spark plug.

4. Screw each spark plug in by hand until it seats. Very little effort is rquired. If force is necessary, you have a plug cross-threaded; unscrew it and try again.

5. Tighten the spark plugs to 9-12 ft.-lb. (12-16 N•m). If you don't have a torque wrench, an additional 1/4 to 1/2 turn is sufficient after the gasket has made contact with the head. If you are reinstalling old, regapped plugs and are reusing the old gasket, only tighten an additional 1/4 turn.

NOTE
Do not overtighten. This will only squash the gasket and destroy its sealing ability.

6. Install each spark plug wire. Make sure it goes to the correct spark plug.

Reading Spark Plugs

Much information about engine and spark plug performance can be determined by careful examination of the spark plugs. This information is more valid after performing the following steps.

1. Ride the bike a short distance at full throttle in any gear.

2. Turn off the engine kill switch before closing the throttle and simultaneously pull in clutch or shift to neutral; coast and brake to a stop.

3. Remove the spark plugs and examine them. Compare them to **Figure 96**.

If the insulator is white or burned, the plug is too hot and should be replaced with a colder one.

A too-cold plug will have sooty deposits ranging in color from dark brown to black.

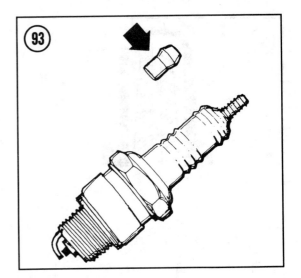

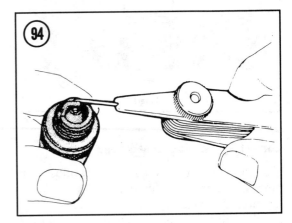

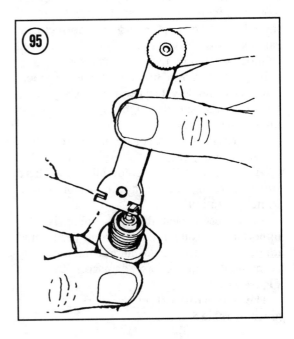

SPARK PLUG CONDITION

(96)

NORMAL
- Identified by light tan or gray deposits on the firing tip.
- Can be cleaned.

GAP BRIDGED
- Identified by deposit buildup closing gap between electrodes.
- Caused by oil or carbon fouling. If deposits are not excessive, the plug can be cleaned.

OIL FOULED
- Identified by wet black deposits on the insulator shell bore and electrodes.
- Caused by excessive oil entering combustion chamber through worn rings and pistons, excessive clearance between valve guides and stems, or worn or loose bearings. Can be cleaned. If engine is not repaired, use a hotter plug.

CARBON FOULED
- Identified by black, dry fluffy carbon deposits on insulator tips, exposed shell surfaces and electrodes.
- Caused by too cold a plug, weak ignition, dirty air cleaner, too rich a fuel mixture, or excessive idling. Can be cleaned.

LEAD FOULED
- Identified by dark gray, black, yellow, or tan deposits or a fused glazed coating on the insulator tip.
- Caused by highly leaded gasoline. Can be cleaned.

WORN
- Identified by severely eroded or worn electrodes.
- Caused by normal wear. Should be replaced.

FUSED SPOT DEPOSIT
- Identified by melted or spotty deposits resembling bubbles or blisters.
- Caused by sudden acceleration. Can be cleaned.

OVERHEATING
- Identified by a white or light gray insulator with small black or gray brown spots and with bluish-burnt appearance of electrodes.
- Caused by engine overheating, wrong type of fuel, loose spark plugs, too hot a plug, or incorrect ignition timing. Replace the plug.

PREIGNITION
- Identified by melted electrodes and possibly blistered insulator. Metallic deposits on insulator indicate engine damage.
- Caused by wrong type of fuel, incorrect ignition timing or advance, too hot a plug, burned valves, or engine overheating. Replace the plug.

3

Replace with a hotter plug and check for too-rich carburetion or evidence of oil blow-by at the piston rings.

If any one plug is found unsatisfactory, discard and replace all 4 of them.

Ignition Timing

The Honda CB750 is equipped with a capacitor discharge ignition system (CDI). This system uses no breaker points, but timing does have to be checked as the base plate may move and alter timing.

Incorrect ignition timing can cause a drastic loss of engine performance and efficiency. It may also cause overheating.

There are 2 methods to check ignition timing: static (engine not running) and dynamic (engine running). It is only necessary to check and adjust the timing on the No. 1 cylinder. Once it is adjusted correctly, the other 3 cylinders will automatically be correct.

Before starting on this procedure, check all electrical connections related to the ignition system. Make sure all connections are tight and free of corrosion and that all ground connections are tight.

> *NOTE*
> *On all models, if you have experienced a general lack of performance and some surging problems, check the air gap of both pulse generators. Insert a flat non-magnetic feeler gauge between the pulse generator and the projection on the rotor. The factory recommended clearance is 0.016-0.027 in. (0.4-0.7 mm). Try decreasing this dimension to 0.012-0.016 in. (0.3-0.4 mm). To adjust the clearance, loosen either or both screws and carefully move the pulse generator to achieve the correct clearance. Perform this adjustment on both pulse generators so that they both have the same clearance.*

Static timing

1. Place the bike on the centerstand.
2. Remove the screws (**Figure 97**) securing the ignition cover and remove the cover and the gasket.

3. Rotate the crankshaft *counterclockwise* with the outer 24 mm hex spacer (**Figure 98**). Use a 24 mm box end wrench (**Figure 99**).
4. Rotate it until the timing mark (1.4 S-F) aligns with the fixed pointer (**Figure 100**).

> *NOTE*
> *In this position, either the No. 1 or 4 cylinder will be at top dead center (TDC) on the compression stroke.*

5. Timing is correct if the narrow projection on the left-hand pulser generator (No. 1 and 4 cylinder) aligns with the projection on the rotor; refer to **Figure 101**.

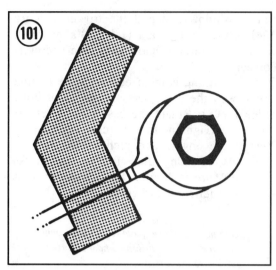

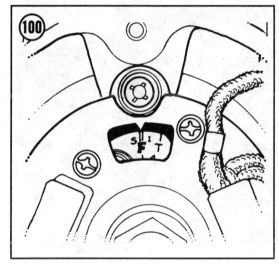

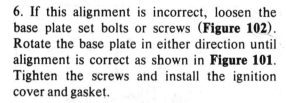

6. If this alignment is incorrect, loosen the base plate set bolts or screws (**Figure 102**). Rotate the base plate in either direction until alignment is correct as shown in **Figure 101**. Tighten the screws and install the ignition cover and gasket.

NOTE
*Rotating the base plate **clockwise** will advance the ignition and **counterclockwise** will retard it.*

Dynamic timing

1. Start the engine and let it reach normal operating temperature. Shut the engine off.
2. Place it on the centerstand.

3. Remove the screws (**Figure 97**) securing the ignition cover and remove the cover and the gasket.
4. Connect a portable tachometer following the manufacturer's instructions. The bike's tach is not accurate enough in the low rpm range for this adjustment.
5. Connect a timing light to the No. 1 cylinder (left-hand side) following the manufacturer's instructions.

NOTE
***Figure 103** shows typical connections if you have no instructions.*

6. Start the engine and let it idle (1,000 +/-100 rpm); aim the timing light at the

timing window and pull the trigger (**Figure 104**). If the timing mark (1.4 F-1) aligns with the fixed pointer (**Figure 100**), the timing is correct.

7. If the timing is incorrect, stop the engine and loosen the base plate set screws or bolts (**Figure 102**). Rotate the base plate in either direction. Tighten the 2 screws or bolts. Restart the engine and recheck the timing. Continue adjusting until the timing marks align. Be sure to tighten the screws or bolts securely when timing is correct.

NOTE
*Rotating the base plate **clockwise** will advance the ignition and **counterclockwise** will retard it.*

8. Check the ignition advance alignment. Restart the engine and increase engine speed to slightly above 6,000 rpm; check alignment of the full advance marks and the fixed pointer (**Figure 105**). If the idle speed alignment is correct but the full advance is incorrect, refer to *Ignition Advance Mechanism Inspection* in Chapter Seven.

CAUTION
Do not rev the engine past 8,000 rpm for a sustained period of time with no load on it. Possible engine damage may result.

9. Shut off the engine and disconnect the timing light and portable tachometer. Install the ignition cover and gasket.

Accelerator Pump Adjustment

Refer to *Accelerator Pump Adjustment* in Chapter Six.

Carburetor Synchronization

Prior to synchronizing the carburetors, the air cleaner must be clean and the ignition timing and valve clearance must be properly adjusted.

This procedure requires a special tool to measure the manifold vacuum for all 4 carburetors simultaneously. A carburetor gauge set (**Figure 106**) can be purchased from

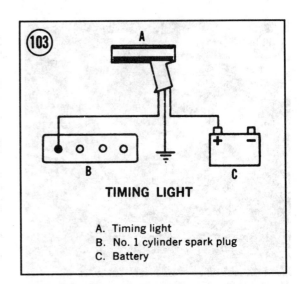

TIMING LIGHT

A. Timing light
B. No. 1 cylinder spark plug
C. Battery

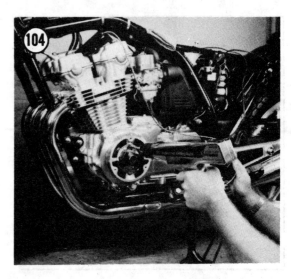

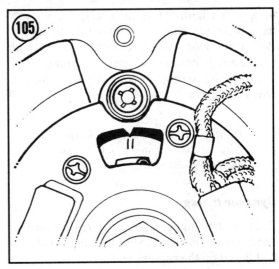

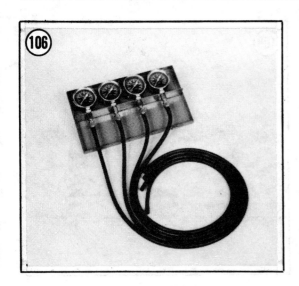

a Honda dealer, motorcycle supply store or mail order firm.

> *NOTE*
> *When purchasing this tool check that it is equipped with restrictors. These restrictors keep the mercury from being drawn into the engine when engine rpm is increased during the adjustment procedure. If the mercury is drawn into the engine the tool will have to be replaced.*

1. Place the bike on the centerstand, start the engine and let it reach normal operating temperature. Shut off the engine.

2. Remove both side covers and remove the seat.

3. Turn the fuel shutoff valve to the OFF position and remove the fuel line to the carburetors.

4. Remove the bolt securing the rear of the fuel tank, pull the tank to the rear and remove it.

5. Remove the vacuum plugs from the 4 intake ports (**Figure 107**).

6. Connect the vacuum lines from the synchronizing tool, following the manufacturer's instructions.

> *NOTE*
> *The No. 2 carburetor has no synch-ronization screw; the other 3 carburetors must be synchronized to it. The carburetors are numbered in the same manner as the cylinders with the No. 1 on*

the left-hand side and continuing with the No. 2, 3 and 4 from left to right.

7. Start the engine and let it idle (1,000 rpm). There should be enough fuel in the float bowls to run the bike for this procedure.

> *WARNING*
> *Do not rig up a temporary fuel supply as this presents a real fire danger. If you start to run out of fuel during the test, shut off the engine and momentarily install the fuel tank to refill the carburetor float bowls; remove the tank and proceed with the test.*

8. The carburetors are synchronized if all have the same gauge readings—2.4 in. Hg (60mm Hg) or less differential between any of them. If not, proceed as follows.

9. Loosen the locknut and turn the adjusting screw (**Figure 108**). Turn the adjusting screw until the reading is the same as that on the No. 2 carburetor. Tighten the locknut. Open the throttle a little and close it back down after each adjustment.

> *CAUTION*
> *If your carb-synchronizing tool is not equipped with restrictors, open and close the throttle very gently to avoid sucking mercury into the engine. If this happens, it will not harm the engine but will render the tool useless.*

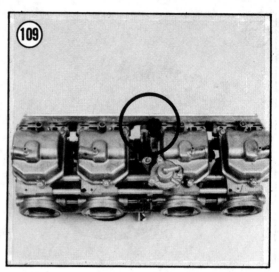

10. Perform this step on carburetors No. 1, 3 and 4 until all 4 have the same gauge reading. Make sure all locknuts are tight.

NOTE
To gain the utmost performance and efficiency from the engine, adjust the carburetors so that the gauge readings are as close to each other as possible.

11. Shut off the engine and remove the vacuum lines. Install the plugs into the vacuum ports (**Figure 107**). Make sure they are in tight to prevent a vacuum leak.
12. Install the fuel tank, seat and side covers.

Carburetor Idle Speed Adjustment

Before making this adjustment, the air cleaner must be clean, the carburetors must be synchronized and the engine must have adequate compression; refer to *Compression Test* in this chapter. Otherwise, this procedure cannot be done properly.
1. Attach a portable tachometer following the manufacturer's instructions.

NOTE
The bike's tach is not accurate enough in the low rpm range for this adjustment.

2. Start the engine and let it warm up to normal operating temperature.
3. Set the idle speed by turning the idle speed stop screw (**Figure 109**) in to increase and out to decrease idle speed.

4. The correct idle speed is 1,000 +/- 100 rpm.
5. Open and close the throttle a couple of times; check for variations in idle speed. Readjust if necessary.

WARNING
With the engine idling, move the handlebar from side to side. If idle speed increases during this movement, the throttle cables may need adjusting or they may be incorrectly routed through the frame. Correct this problem immediately. ***Do not*** *ride the bike in this unsafe condition.*

STORAGE

Several months of inactivity can cause serious problems and a general deterioration of the bike's condition. This is especially true in areas of weather extremes. During the winter months it is advisable to specially prepare the bike for lay-up.

Selecting a Storage Area

Most cyclists store their bikes in their home garages. If you do not have a home garage, facilities suitable for long-term motorcycle storage are readily available for rent or lease in most areas. In selecting a building, consider the following points.
1. The storage area must be dry, free from dampness and excessive humidity. Heating is not necessary, but the building should be well

insulated to minimize extreme temperature variations.

2. Buildings with large window areas should be avoided, or such windows should be masked (also a good security measure), if direct sunlight can fall on the bike.

3. Buildings in industrial areas, where factories are liable to emit corrosive fumes, are not desirable, nor are facilities near bodies of salt water.

4. The area should be selected to minimize the possibility of fire, theft or vandalism. The area should be fully insured, perhaps with a package covering fire, theft, vandalism, weather and liability. The advice of your insurance agent should be solicited on these matters. The building should be fireproof and items such as security of doors and windows, alarm facilities and the proximity of police should be considered.

Preparing Bike for Storage

Careful preparation will minimize deterioration and make it easier to restore the bike to service later. Use the following procedure.

1. Wash the bike completely. Make certain to remove any road salt which may have accumulated during the first weeks of winter. Wax all painted and polished surfaces, including any chromed areas. Cover all plastic, rubber and vinyl surfaces with the appropriate protective substance.

2. Run the engine for 20-30 minutes to stabilize oil temperature. Drain oil, regardless of mileage since last oil change. The old oil contains acids. These acids will corrode the engine when the bike is not in operation. Replace the oil filter and fill engine with a normal quantity of fresh oil.

3. Remove battery and coat cable terminals with petroleum jelly. If there is evidence of acid spillage in the battery box, neutralize with baking soda, wash clean and repaint the damaged area. Store the battery in a warm area and recharge it every 2 weeks.

4. Drain all gasoline from fuel tank, interconnecting hoses and carburetors. Leave fuel shutoff valve in the RESERVE position. As an alternative, a fuel preservative may be added to the fuel. This perservative is available from many motorcycle shops and marine equipment suppliers. If a preservative is used, run the engine so it is distributed through the fuel lines and carburetors.

5. Lubricate the drive chain and control cables.

6. Remove spark plugs (**Figure 110**) and add two tablespoons of fresh engine oil to each cylinder. Turn the engine a few revolutions by hand to distribute the oil and install the spark plugs. There are also specific antirust preservatives available. Follow the manufacturer's instructions for their use.

NOTE
Since the CB750 has no kickstarter, place the transmission in gear and spin the rear wheel by hand.

CAUTION
Do not turn the engine over with the starter with the spark plugs removed as the ignition system may be damaged.

7. Tie or tape a heavy plastic bag over the outlet of the mufflers and air filter openings to prevent the entry of moisture.

8. Check tire pressure, inflate to the proper pressure and move the bike to the storage area. Place it on the centerstand. If possible, securely support the motor-

cycle under the frame so that the weight is off both tires.

9. Cover the bike with a cover designed for motorcycle storage or a blanket. Place this cover over the bike mainly as a dust cover–do not wrap it tightly. Do not use a plastic cover, as it may trap moisture causing condensation. Leave room for air to circulate around the bike.

Inspection During Storage

Try to inspect the bike weekly while in storage. Any deterioration should be corrected as soon as possible. For example, if corrosion of bright metal parts is observed, cover them with a light film of grease or silicone spray.

Turn the engine over a couple of times–don't start it. Pump the front forks to keep the seals lubricated.

Restoring to Service

A bike that has been properly prepared and stored in a suitable area requires only light maintenance to restore it to service. It is advisable, however, to perform a spring tune-up.

1. Before removing the bike from the storage area, re-inflate tires to the correct pressures. Air loss during the storage period may have nearly flattened the tires and moving the bike can cause damage to tires, tubes or rims.

2. When the bike is brought to the work area, immediately install the battery (fully charged) and fill the fuel tank. The fuel shutoff valve should be on the RESERVE position; do not move it yet.

3. Check the fuel system for leaks. Open the drain screws (**Figure 111**) on all 4 carburetors and allow several cups of fuel to pass through the system (drain completely if fuel preservative was used). Move the fuel shutoff valve to the OFF position.

> *WARNING*
> *Place a metal container under the drain tubes to catch the expelled fuel–this presents a real fire danger if allowed to drain onto the floor. Dispose of fuel properly.*

4. Remove the cylinder protectors (if installed) or spark plugs and squirt a small amount of fuel into each cylinder to help remove the oil coating.

5. Install a fresh set of spark plugs and start up the engine.

6. Perform the normal tune-up as described earlier in this chapter.

7. Check safety items such as lights, horn, etc., as oxidation of switch contacts and/or sockets during storage may make one or more of these critical devices inoperative.

8. Clean and test ride the motorcycle.

> *WARNING*
> *If any type of perservative (Armor-All or equivalent) has been applied to the tire treads, be sure the tires are well "scrubbed-in" prior to any fast riding or cornering. If not, they will slip right out from under you.*

GENERAL SPECIFICATIONS

This section includes **Table 6** which gives general information and specifications. Also included are figures showing where serial numbers are located. Refer to **Figure 112A** and **Figure 112B** for location of all major controls.

MAJOR CONTROLS AND COMPONENTS

1. Rear foot pegs
2. Front foot pegs
3. Front brake lever
4. Front turn signal (amber)
5. Speedometer, tachometer and indicator lights
6. Headlight
7. Horn(s)
8. Rear brake pedal
9. Clutch
10. Alternator

MAJOR CONTROLS AND COMPONENTS

11. Clutch lever
12. Headlight, turn signal switches
13. Start button, engine stop switch
14. Throttle grip
15. Starter motor
16. Seat
17. Rear turn signal (amber)
18. Tail/brake light and
    rear reflex reflector (red)

19. Fuse panel
20. Fuel shutoff valve
21. Ignition timing cover
22. Side stand
23. Shift lever
24. Main fusible link panel
25. Centerstand
26. Shock absorber adjustment
27. Drive chain

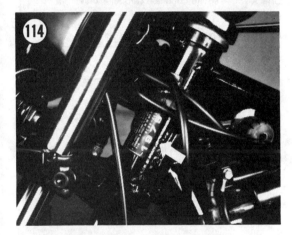

3

113). The vehicle identification number (VIN) is on the left-hand side of the steering head (**Figure 114**). The engine serial number is located on the top, right-hand side of the upper crankcase (**Figure 115**). Carburetor identification numbers are located on the left-hand side of each carburetor body as shown in **Figure 116**.

Honda makes frequent changes during a model year—some minor, some relatively major. When you order parts from the dealer or other parts distributor, always order by engine and chassis number. Write the numbers down and carry them with you. Compare new parts to old before purchasing them. If they are not alike, have the parts manager explain the difference to you.

Serial Numbers

You must know the model serial numbers and VIN number for registration purposes and when ordering replacement parts.

The frame serial number is stamped on the right-hand side of the steering head (**Figure**

TABLE 1 TIRE PRESSURES (COLD)

Load	Pressure
Up to 200 lb. (90 kg)	
Front—all models	28 psi (2.0 kg/cm^2)
Rear	
Models CB750K, F	32 psi (2.25 kg/cm^2)
Model CB750K-LTD	28 psi (2.0 kg/cm^2)
Model CB750K (1980)	28 psi (2.0 kg/cm^2)
Maximum load limit*	
Front—all models	28 psi (2.0 kg/cm^2)
Rear—all models	40 psi (2.8 kg/cm^2)
*Maximum load includes total weight of motorcycle with accessories, rider(s) and luggage.	

TABLE 2 SERVICE INTERVALS

Every 600 miles (1,000km) or 6 months	• Check engine oil. • Lubricate rear brake pedal and shift arm. • Lubricate side and center stand pivot point(s). • Inspect front steering assembly for looseness. • Lubricate and adjust the drive chain. • Check wheel bearings for smooth operation. • Check battery condition. • Check ignition timing. • Check and adjust engine idle speed. • Check clutch lever free play. • Clean fuel shutoff valve and filter. • Check wheel spoke condition (Model K only). • Check wheel runout. • Inspect brake pads and shoes for wear.
Every 1,800 miles (3,000km)	• Change engine oil and filter.
Every 4,000 miles (6,400km)	• Clean air filter element. • Inspect spark plugs, regap if necessary. • Check and adjust valve clearance. • Check and adjust clutch free play. • Adjust cam chain tension. • Inspect fuel line for chafed, cracked or swollen ends. • Lubricate control cables. • Inspect crankcase ventilation hoses for cracks, or loose hose clamps—drain out residue. • Check engine mounting bolts for tightness. • Check steering for free play. • Check all suspension components. • Adjust rear brake lever height and free play.
Every 6,000 miles (10,000km)	• Complete engine tune-up. • Dismantle and clean the carburetors. • Change oil in front forks. • Inspect and repack rear swing arm bushings. • Inspect and repack wheel bearings. • Lubricate speedometer housing. • Inspect and repack steering head bearings.
Every 8,000 miles (12,800km)	• Replace spark plugs. • Replace air filter element.
Every 12,000 miles (19,000km)	• Lubricate rear brake camshaft (Model K only). • Replace disc brake hydraulic fluid.
Every 4 years	• Replace all hydraulic brake hoses.

Table 3   STATE OF CHARGE

Specific Gravity	State of Charge
1.110 - 1.130	Discharged
1.140 - 1.160	Almost discharged
1.170 - 1.190	One-quarter charged
1.200 - 1.220	One-half charged
1.230 - 1.250	Three-quarters charged
1.260 - 1.280	Fully charged

TABLE 5 SPARK PLUGS

Standard	NGK D8EA, ND X24ES-U
Cold weather	NGK D7EA, ND X22ES-U
Extended high speed riding	NGK D9EA, ND X27ES-U
Canadian models (all)	NGK DR8ESL, ND X24ESR-U
Gap	0.024–0.028 in. (0.6–0.7mm)
Torque specification	9–12 ft.-lb. (12–16 N•m)

TABLE 4 TUNE-UP SPECIFICATIONS

Cylinder head nut torque	26–29 ft.-lb. (36–40 N•m)
Valve clearance intake and exhaust	0.08mm (+0.05 / −0.02mm)
Compression pressure (at sea level)	170 ± 14 psi (12 ± 1.0 kg/cm^2)
Spark plug type	
Standard	NGK D8EA. ND X24ES-U
Cold weather	NGK D7EA. ND X22ES-U
Extended high speed riding	NGK D9EA. ND X27ES-U
Canadian models (all)	NGK DR8ESL. ND X24ESR-U
Spark plug gap	0.024–0.028 in. (0.6–0.7mm)
Ignition timing	Timing mark "1.4 S-F" at 1,000 ± 100 rpm Advance timing mark "II" at 6,000 + rpm
Idle speed	1,000 ± 100 rpm

TABLE 6   GENERAL SPECIFICATIONS

Engine type	Air-cooled, 4-stroke, DOHC, transverse-mounted inline four
Bore and stroke	2.44 × 2.44 in. (62.0 × 62.0mm)
Displacement	45.7 cu.in. (749cc)
Compression ratio	9.0 to 1
Carburetion	4 Keihin, constant velocity with accelerator pump in No. 2 carburetor only
Models CB750K & C	VB42A or VB42C
Model CB750K-LTD	VB42A
Model CB750F	VB42C
Ignition	Capacitor discharge ignition (CDI)
Lubrication	Wet-sump, filter, oil pump
Clutch	Wet, multi-plate (7)
Transmission	5-speed, constant velocity
Transmission ratios	
1st	2.533
2nd	1.789
3rd	1.391
4th	1.160
5th	0.964

(continued)

Table 6 GENERAL SPECIFICATIONS (continued)

Final reduction ratio	2.533
Drive chain	
1979 models	No.630 90 links
1980 models	
Model C	No. 530 by 106 links
Model F, K	No 530 by 108 links
Starting system	Electric starter
Battery	12 Volt, 14 amp/hour
Alternator	Three phase AC, 0.26 kw/5,000 rpm
Firing order	1—2—4—3
Wheelbase	
Models CB750K, K-LTD, F	59.8 in. (1,520mm)
Model CB750C	60.1 (1,527mm)
Steering head angle	27° 30'
Trail	4.8 in. (121mm)
Front suspension	Telescopic fork, 6.3 in. (160mm) travel
Rear suspension	Swing arm, adjustable shock absorbers
Travel	
Models CB750K, K-LTD, C	4.4 in. (112mm)
Model CB750F	4.3 in. (110mm)
Front tire	
Model CB750K, K-LTD	3.50 H19—4PR
Model CB750F	3.25 H19—4PR tubeless
Model CB750C	110/90 19—4PR tubeless
Rear tire	
Model CB750K, K-LTD	4.50 H17—4PR (1979 models)
Model CB750K	4.25 H18—4PR (1980 models)
Model CB750F	4.00 H18—4PR tubeless
Model CB750C	130/90 16—4PR tubeless
Ground clearance	
Model CB750K	5.9 in. (150mm)
Model CB750K-LTD, C	5.7 in. (145mm)
Model CB750F	5.5 in. (140mm)
Overall height	
Models CB750K, K-LTD, C	45.7 in. (1,160mm)
Model CB750F	44.9 in. (1,140mm)
Overall width (handlebar)	
Models CB750K, K-LTD	34.6 in. (880mm)
Model CB750F	34.1 in. (865mm)
Overall length	
Models CB750K, K-LTD	87.4 in. (2,200mm)
Model CB750F	86.4 in. (2,195mm)
Fuel capacity	
Models CB750K, K-LTD, F	5.3 U.S.gal. (20.0 liters, 4.4 Imp.gal.)
Model CB750C	4.5 U.S.gal. (16.9 liters, 3.7 Imp.gal.)
Oil capacity	
Oil and filter change	3.7 qt. (3.5 liter , 3.1 Imp. qt.)
Fork oil capacity	
Oil change interval	5.2 oz. (155cc)
At overhaul	5.8–6.0 oz. (172.5–177.5cc)
Weight (dry)	
Models CB750K, C	512 lb. (233 kg)
Model CB750K-LTD	516 lb. (234 kg)
Model CB750F	507 lb. (230 kg)

ENGINE

The CB750 engine is an air-cooled, 4-stroke, 4-cylinder engine with double overhead camshafts. The crankshaft is supported by 5 main bearings and power is delivered to the primary shaft via a Hy-Vo chain within the crankcase. The camshafts are chain driven from the timing sprockets on the crankshaft and directly operate the valve lifters that are fitted to the top of the valve stems.

Engine lubrication is by wet sump, with the oil supply housed in the crankcase. The oil pump supplies oil under pressure throughout the engine and is gear driven.

The starter motor is located in the upper crankcase half on the left-hand side just behind the cylinder block.

This chapter provides complete service and overhaul procedures for Honda CB750 models built since 1979. **Tables 1-6** at the end of this chapter provide complete specifications for the engine. Although the clutch and transmission are located within the engine, they are covered separately in Chapter Five to simplify the presentation of this material.

Service procedures for all models are virtually the same. Where differences occur, they are identified.

Prior to removing the engine or any major assembly, clean the entire engine and frame with a good grade commercial degreaser, like Gunk Cycle Degreaser, or equivalent. It is easier to work on a clean engine and you will do a better job. Make certain that you have all the necessary tools available, especially any special tools, and purchase replacements for any known faulty parts prior to disassembly. Make sure you have a clean place to work.

It is a good idea to identify and mark parts as they are removed so that errors will be avoided during assembly and installation. Clean all parts thoroughly upon removal, then place them in trays or boxes with their associated mounting hardware. Make certain all parts related to a particular cylinder, piston, connecting rod or valve assembly are identifed for installation in the proper place. Do not rely on memory alone as it may be days or weeks before you complete the job.

ENGINE PRINCIPLES

Figure 1 explains how the engine works. This will be helpful when troubleshooting or repairing your engine.

SERVICING ENGINE IN FRAME

Many components can be serviced while the engine is mounted in the frame:
  a. Camshafts
  b. Clutch assembly
  c. Alternator

4-STROKE OPERATING PRINCIPLES

①

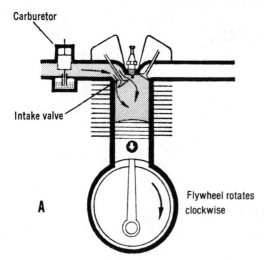

Carburetor

Intake valve

A

Flywheel rotates clockwise

As the piston travels downward, the exhaust valve is closed and the intake valve opens, allowing the new fuel/air mixture from the **carburetor** to be drawn into the cylinder. When the piston reaches the bottom of its travel (BDC), the **intake valve** closes and remains closed for the next revolution-and-a-half of the crankshaft.

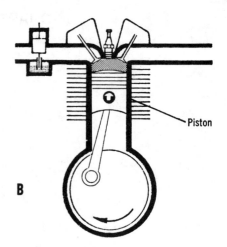

Piston

B

While the crankshaft continues to rotate, the **piston** moves upward, compressing the fuel/air mixture.

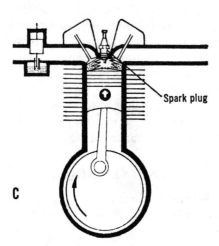

Spark plug

C

As the piston almost reaches the top of its travel, the **spark plug** fires, igniting the compressed fuel/air mixture. The piston continues to top dead center (TDC) and is pushed downward by the expanding gases.

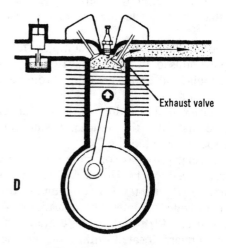

Exhaust valve

D

When the piston almost reaches BDC, the **exhaust valve** opens and remains open until the piston is near TDC. The upward travel of the piston causes the exhaust gases to be pushed out of the cylinder. After the piston has reached TDC, the exhaust valve closes and the cycle starts all over again.

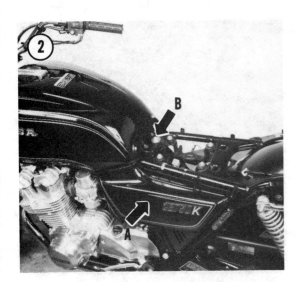

4

d. Carburetor assembly
e. Shifting mechanism

NOTE
*The cylinder head **cannot be removed** with the engine in the frame, not even by removing all but the rear lower engine mounting bolt and pivoting the engine down and forward. There is still an additional 1/2 in. (13 mm) needed to clear the cylinder studs and the frame.*

ENGINE

Removal/Installation

1. Place the bike on the centerstand and remove the seat and the side covers (A, **Figure 2**).

2. Disconnect the battery negative lead (**Figure 3**).

3. Turn the fuel shutoff valve to the OFF position (**Figure 4**) and remove the fuel line to the carburetor assembly.

4. Remove the bolt (B, **Figure 2**) securing the fuel tank; pull the tank to the rear and remove it.

5. Drain the engine oil as described under *Changing Engine Oil and Filter* in Chapter Three.

6. Disconnect the spark plug wires (**Figure 5**) and tie them up out of the way.

7. Remove the exhaust system as described under *Exhaust System Removal/Installation* in Chapter Six.

8. Remove the carburetor assembly as described under *Carburetor Removal/Installation* in Chapter Six.

9. Remove the alternator as described under *Alternator Removal/Installation* in this chapter.

10. Remove the shift lever and the left-hand rear crankcase cover (**Figure 6**).

11. Remove the rear axle nut cotter pin and loosen the axle nut (A, **Figure 7**).

12. Loosen the locknuts, then loosen the drive chain adjusters (B, **Figure 7**) to allow slack in the drive chain.

13. Have an assistant apply the rear brake to keep the drive chain taut, which keeps the drive sprocket from turning. Remove the bolt, washer and O-ring (**Figure 8**).

14. Move the wheel slightly forward and remove the drive chain from the sprocket (**Figure 9**) and remove the drive sprocket.

> *WARNING*
> *The drive chain is manufactured as a continuous closed loop with no master link. Do not cut it with a chain cutter as it will result in future chain failure and possible loss of control under riding condition.*

15. Disconnect the starter cable from the starter solenoid (**Figure 10**).

16. Loosen the bolt (**Figure 11**) securing the tachometer drive cable to the cam cover and withdraw it.

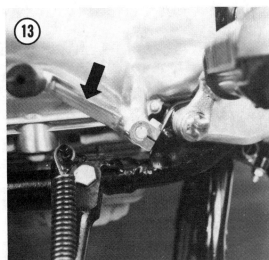

4

17. Disconnect the clutch cable at the clutch arm (A, **Figure 12**).

18. Loosen the bolt securing the rear brake lever (B, **Figure 12**) and remove the brake lever.

19. Remove the gearshift lever (**Figure 13**).

20. Take a final look all over the engine to make sure everything has been disconnected.

21. Loosen, but do not remove, all engine mounting bolts and nuts.

22. Remove the front bolts, nuts and brackets (A, **Figure 14**)

23. Remove the lower forward through bolt (B, **Figure 14**).

24. Remove the 2 lower rear bolts (A, **Figure 15**) securing the removable frame tube.

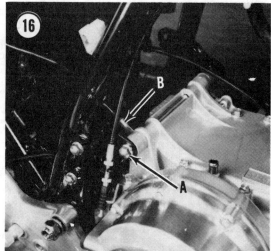

25. Place a suitable size jack, with a piece of wood to protect the crankcase, under the engine. Apply a *small amount* of jack pressure up on the engine.

26. Remove the lower rear through bolt (B, **Figure 15**) and foot pegs. Withdraw the bolt from the left-hand side.

27. Raise the front of the engine up a little and remove the removable frame tube.

> *CAUTION*
> *The lower portions of the engine are rounded and smooth, thus it is very difficult to get a good hold on anything. Also, the engine assembly is very heavy. These final steps require a minimum of 2, preferably 3, people to safely remove the engine from the frame.*

28. Remove the upper rear through bolt nut (A, **Figure 16**).

> *NOTE*
> *The engine ground strap (B, **Figure 16**) is located between the spacer and engine.*

29. Withdraw the bolt (A, **Figure 17**) from the left-hand side. Don't lose the spacer (B, **Figure 17**) on each side between the frame brackets and the engine.

30. Pull the engine forward and slightly up. Remove it through the open portion of the frame on the right-hand side. Take it to a workbench for further disassembly.

31. Install by reversing these removal steps, noting the following.

> *NOTE*
> *Due to the weight of the complete engine assembly, it is suggested that all components removed in the preceding procedures be left off until the crankcase assembly is reinstalled into the frame. If you choose to install a completed engine assembly, it requires a minimum of 2 people. It must be installed from the right-hand side of the frame.*

32. Tighten the bolts and nuts to the following torque specifications. Refer to **Figure 18**. The letter designation on the figure relates to the text letters in the following list:

a. 8 mm flange bolt and nut: 13-18 ft.-lb. (18-25 N•m)

b. 10 mm flange bolt and nut: 22-29 ft.-lb. (30-40 N•m)

c. 12 mm flange bolt and nut: 40-47 ft.-lb. (55-65 N•m)

Tighten the drive sprocket bolt to 24-27 ft.-lb. (33-37 N•m); don't forget the O-ring seal on the bolt (**Figure 19**).

33. Be sure to install the engine ground strap (B, **Figure 16**) between the spacer and the engine.

34. Fill the crankcase with the recommended type and quantity of engine oil. Refer to Chapter Three.

35. Start the engine and check for leaks.

CYLINDER HEAD

The engine must be removed from the frame to remove the head, but it is easier to perform Steps 4-6 with the engine still in the bike's frame.

Removal/Installation

1. Place the bike on the centerstand.

2. Remove the left- and right-hand side covers and disconnect the battery negative lead (**Figure 20**).

3. Turn the fuel shutoff valve to the OFF position (**Figure 21**) and remove the fuel line to the carburetor assembly. Remove the bolt (**Figure 22**) securing the fuel tank, pull the tank to the rear and remove it.

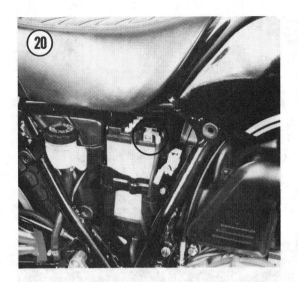

4. Remove the bolts (**Figure 23**) securing the cam cover and remove it. Remove the spark plugs.

> *NOTE*
> *Steps 5 and 6 are necessary for camshaft removal.*

5. Remove the screws (**Figure 24**) securing the ignition cover and remove the cover and gasket.

6. Use the hex spacer (**Figure 25**) on the ignition advance unit and turn the crankshaft with a 24 mm wrench (**Figure 26**). Rotate it *clockwise* until the "1.4 T" mark aligns with the fixed pointer (**Figure 27**).

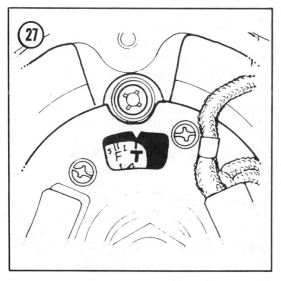

4

NOTE
Make sure the No. 1 or 4 cylinder intake and exhaust cam lobes are facing toward the spark plug. If not, rotate the crankshaft until they face the spark plug and the "1.4 T" mark aligns correctly.

7. Perform Steps 5 and 7-30 of *Engine Removal/Installation* in this chapter.

8. Remove both camshafts as described in this chapter.

9. Remove the bolts (14 mm) securing the oil line (A, **Figure 28**) and remove the oil line. Don't lose the 4 sealing washers on either side of the fittings.

10. Remove the rear cam chain tensioner locknuts (B, **Figure 28**).

11. Remove the bolts (**Figure 29**) located below the cam chain housing.

12. Remove the valve lifters and shims (A, **Figure 30**) at this time to avoid accidental mixup if they should come out while removing the head. Remove the parts for one cylinder at a time and place them into a container (like an egg carton, see **Figure 31**) marked with the specific cylinder number and "intake" or "exhaust". The No. 1 cylinder is on the left-hand side and working across from left to right are the No. 2, 3 and 4. The left-hand side refers to a rider sitting on the seat facing forward. The exhaust valves, lifters and shims are located at the front of the engine and the intake valves, lifters and shims are at the rear of the engine.

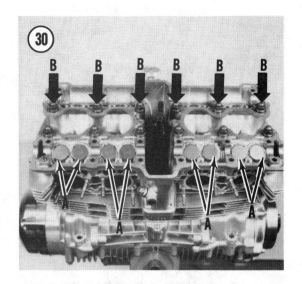

> *CAUTION*
> *The lifters must be reinstalled into their original cylinder upon assembly.*

13. To prevent warpage of the head, loosen the cylinder head cap nuts (B, **Figure 30**) 1/2 turn in the sequence shown in **Figure 32**. After all nuts (size 14 mm) have been loosened, remove them and their washers.

14. Loosen the head by tapping around the perimeter with a rubber or plastic mallet. If necessary, *gently* pry the head loose with a broad-tipped screwdriver only in the ribbed areas of the fins.

> *CAUTION*
> *Remember, the cooling fins are fragile and may be damaged if tapped or pried too hard. Never use a metal hammer.*

> *NOTE*
> *It is sometimes possible to loosen the head with engine compression. Reinstall the spark plugs and rotate the engine with the hex spacer on the ignition advance unit with a 24 mm wrench. As the pistons reach top dead center (TDC) on the compression stroke, they may pop the head loose.*

15. Untie the wire securing the cam chain and retie it to the cylinder head. Lift the cylinder head straight up and off the studs and remove it. Pull the cam chain and wire through the opening in the cylinder head and retie the cam chain up to the studs or cam chain guide.

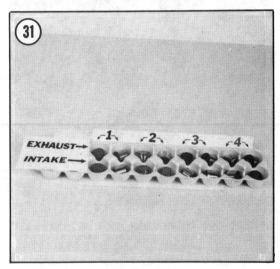

16. Remove the head gasket.

17. Place a clean shop rag into the cam chain opening in the cylinder block to prevent the entry of foreign matter.

18. Install by reversing these removal steps, noting the following.

19. Clean the cylinder head mating surfaces of any gasket material.

20. Install the rear upper and lower cam chain tensioner locknuts (B, **Figure 28**). Tighten the upper one and leave the lower one loose. Pull the rear cam chain tensioner *up* as far as it will go and tighten the lower adjusting locknut.

21. Install a new head gasket (A, **Figure 33**) and 2 locating dowels (B, **Figure 33**).

22. Install a new cam chain guide.

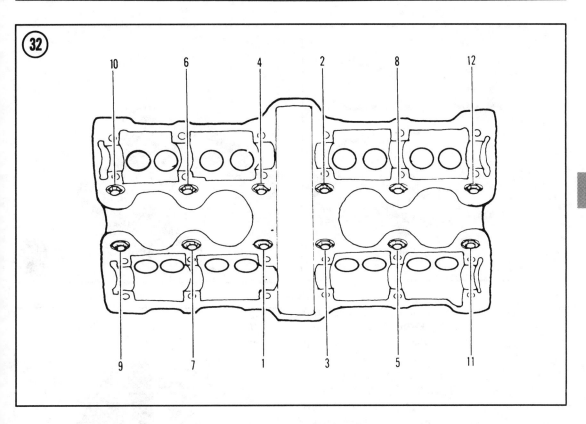

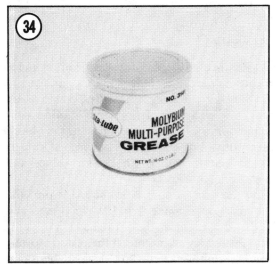

23. Install the cylinder head. Install the laminated washers, with the copper side *up*, onto each of the cylinder studs.

NOTE
*Apply molybdenum disulfide grease (**Figure 34**) to the threads of the studs prior to installing the cap nuts.*

24. Install the cap nuts and tighten to a final torque of 26-29 ft.-lb. (36-40 N•m). Use the torque sequence shown in **Figure 32**.

25. Install the lower bolts (**Figure 29**) located below the cam chain housing. Tighten them securely.

26. Install the oil line (A, **Figure 28**). Install the bolt with the larger oil hole at the top.

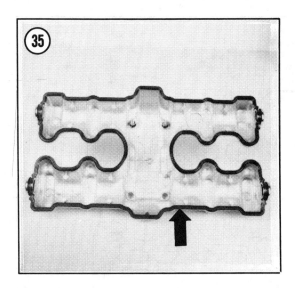

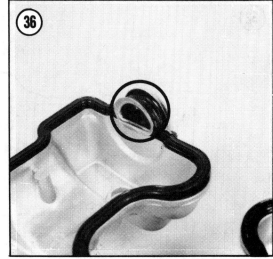

Place a sealing washer on each side of the fittings, then insert the bolts. These washers must be installed as noted to prevent an oil leak.

27. Check the condition of the sealing gasket in the cam cover (**Figure 35**); replace it if torn or deteriorated. Carefully check the end seals (**Figure 36**) as this is an oil leak problem area.

Inspection

1. Remove all traces of gasket from cylinder head and the cylinder block mating surface.
2. *Without removing the valves*, remove all carbon deposits from the combustion chambers with a wire brush. A blunt screwdriver or chisel may be used if care is taken not to damage the head, valves and spark plug threads.
3. After all carbon is removed from the combustion chambers and valve intake and exhaust ports, clean the entire head in solvent.
4. Clean away all carbon on the piston crowns. Do not remove the carbon ridge at the top of the cylinder bore.
5. Check for cracks in the combustion chamber and exhaust ports. A cracked head must be replaced.
6. After the head has been thoroughly cleaned, place a straightedge across the gasket surface (**Figure 37**) at several points. Measure warp by inserting a flat feeler gauge between the straightedge and the cylinder head at each

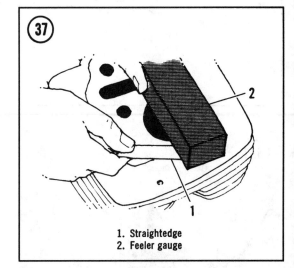

1. Straightedge
2. Feeler gauge

location. There should be no warpage; if a small amount is present, it can be resurfaced by a Honda dealer or qualified machine shop.
7. Check the cam cover mating surface using the procedure in Step 6. There should be no warpage.
8. Check the condition of the valves and valve guides as described under *Valve and Valve Components* in this chapter.

VALVE AND VALVE COMPONENTS

Removal

Refer to **Figure 38** for this procedure.

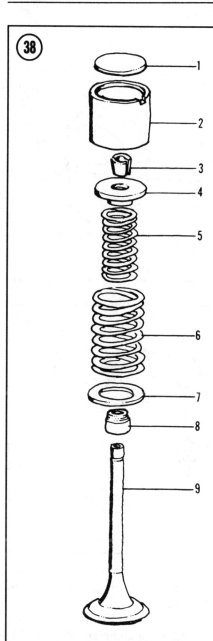

VALVE ASSEMBLY

1. Adjuster pad
2. Shim
3. Keepers
4. Spring collar
5. Inner spring
6. Outer spring
7. Seat
8. Oil seal
9. Valve—intake and exhaust

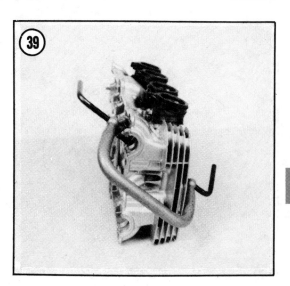

1. Remove the cylinder head as described in this chapter.

2. Remove the valve lifters and adjustment shims.

3. Compress springs with a valve spring compression tool (**Figure 39**). Remove the valve keepers and release compression.

> *CAUTION*
> *Remove any burrs from the valve stem grooves before removing the valves. Otherwise the valve guides will be damaged. You may be able to fabricate a substitute for the special tool using a 1-inch diameter piece of PVC (plumbing) pipe. Use a thick-walled section of pipe with a notch cut in one side through which the valve keepers can be removed.*

4. Remove the valve spring collars and seats, springs and valves.

> *CAUTION*
> *Remove any burrs from the valve stem grooves before removing the valves. Otherwise the valve guides will be damaged.*

5. Mark all parts as they are disassembled so that they will be installed in their same location.

Inspection

1. Clean all valves with a wire brush and solvent.

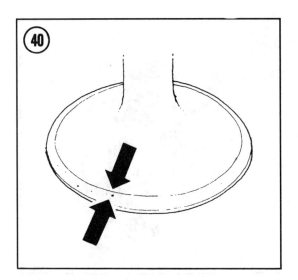

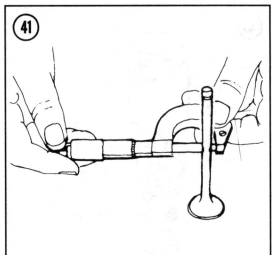

2. Inspect the contact surface of each valve for burning (**Figure 40**). Minor roughness and pitting can be removed by lapping the valve as described under *Valve Lapping* in this chapter. Excessive unevenness of the contact surface is an indication that the valve is not serviceable. The contact surface of the valve may be ground on a valve grinding machine, but it is best to replace a burned or damaged valve with a new one.

3. Measure valve stems for wear (**Figure 41**). Compare with specifications in **Table 6**.

4. Remove all carbon and varnish from the valve guides with a stiff spiral wire brush.

5. Insert each valve in its guide. Hold the valve just slightly off its seat and rock it sideways. If it rocks more than slightly, the guide is probably worn and should be replaced. As a final check, take the head to a dealer and have the valve guides measured.

6. Measure the valve spring heights with a vernier caliper (**Figure 42**). All should be of length specified in **Table 6** with no bends or other distortion. Replace defective springs in sets.

7. Check the valve spring retainer and valve keepers. If they are in good condition, they may be reused.

8. Inspect valve seats. If worn or burned, they must be reconditioned. This should be performed by your dealer or a qualified machine shop. Seats and valves in near-perfect condition can be reconditioned by lapping with a fine carborundum paste.

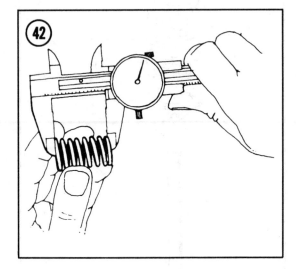

Lapping, however, is always inferior to precision grinding.

9. Measure the outside diameter of each valve lifter with a micrometer (**Figure 43**). Compare with specifications in **Table 6**. Inspect each lifter for scoring, scratches or evidence of lack of lubrication; replace any if necessary.

10. Measure the inside diameter of each valve lifter cavity in the cylinder head with a small bore gauge (**Figure 44**). Compare with specifications given in **Table 6**. Inspect each cavity for scoring, scratches or evidence of lack of lubrication. If the cavity is worn beyond the wear limit, the cylinder head will have to be replaced.

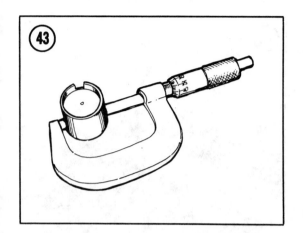

5. After all springs have been installed, gently tap the valve stems with a plastic mallet to make sure the keepers are properly seated.

Valve Guide Replacement

When guides are worn so that there is excessive stem-to-guide clearance or valve tipping, they must be replaced. Replace all, even if only one is worn. This job should only be done by a Honda dealer as special tools are required.

Valve Seat Reconditioning

This job is best left to your dealer or local machine shop. They have the special equipment and knowledge for this exacting job. You can still save considerable money by removing the cylinder head and taking just the head to the shop.

Valve Lapping

Valve lapping is a simple operation which can restore the valve seal without machining if the amount of wear or distortion is not too great.

1. Coat the valve seating area in the head with a lapping compound such as Carborundum or Clover Brand.

2. Insert the valve into the head.

3. Wet the suction cup of the lapping stick (**Figure 45**) and stick it onto the head of the

Installation

1. Coat the valve stems with molybdenum disulfide paste and insert them into the cylinder head.

2. Install the bottom spring retainers and new seals.

3. Install the valve springs with the narrow pitch end (end with coils closest together) facing the head and install the upper valve spring retainers.

> *CAUTION*
> *See CAUTION under Step 3, **Valve Removal**. This special tool or equivalent must be used.*

4. Push down on upper valve spring retainers with the valve spring compressor and install valve keepers.

> *CAUTION*
> *To avoid loss of spring tension, do not compress the springs any more than necessary to install the keepers.*

valve. Lap the valve to the seat by rotating the lapping stick in both directions. Every 5 to 10 seconds, rotate the valve 180° in the seat; continue lapping until the contact surfaces of the valve and the valve seat are a uniform grey. Stop as soon as they are, to avoid removing too much material.

4. Thoroughly clean the valves and cylinder head in solvent to remove all grinding compound. Any compound left on the valves or the cylinder head will end up in the engine and will cause damage.

After the lapping has been completed and the valve assemblies have been reinstalled into the head, the valve seal should be tested. Check the seal of each valve by pouring solvent into each of the intake and exhaust ports. There should be no leakage past the seat. If fluid leaks past any of the seats, disassemble that valve assembly and repeat the lapping procedure until there is no leakage.

CAMSHAFTS

The exhaust camshaft is driven by a chain off of the timing sprocket on the crankshaft. The intake is driven by a short chain from the exhaust cam. Both cams can be removed with the engine in the frame but it is easier with the engine removed.

> *NOTE*
> *The cylinder head cannot be removed with the engine in the frame.*

Removal

1. Perform Steps 1-6, *Cylinder Head Removal/Installation*, in this chapter.

2. Remove the bolts securing the oil pipe (A, **Figure 46**) and cam chain guide (B, **Figure 46**) and remove the oil pipe and cam chain guide.

> *NOTE*
> *Refer to **Figure 47** for letter designations of cam bearing cap for the following steps.*

3. Remove the 10 mm bolts (**Figure 48**) securing the 4 center cam bearing caps—B, C,

H and J. Remove the bearing caps and the 2 black rubber oil caps (C, **Figure 46**) fitted to the cylinder head cap nuts. Be sure to remove the 2 dowel pins fitted to each bearing cap.

4. Remove the rear cam chain guide attaching plate (**Figure 49**).

5. Loosen the front cam chain tensioner locknut and bolt (A, **Figure 50**). Press down on this lower loop of the intake cam chain with your finger. This will reduce chain tension. Tighten the locknut and bolt.

6. Loosen the lower rear cam chain tensioner adjusting locknut (**Figure 51**).

7. With a pair of pliers, pull up on the rear cam chain tensioner (B, **Figure 50**) and tighten the lower rear cam chain tensioner adjusting locknut (**Figure 51**).

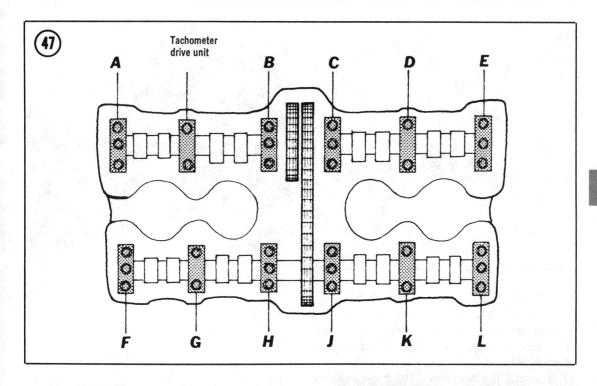

8. Check that the timing mark "1.4 T" (**Figure 52**) is still properly aligned and that the intake and exhaust cam lobes on the No. 1 and 4 cylinders are pointed toward the spark plug.

9. Remove the 10 mm bolts securing the intake cam bearing caps G and K and then F and L. Refer to **Figure 47**. Be sure to remove all dowel pins fitted to each bearing cap.

NOTE
Loosen the bolts in 2-3 stages on all 4 bearing caps to gradually release the pressure on the cam. The lobes on one cylinder will be under pressure.

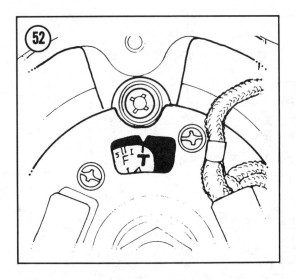

10. Lift the intake cam (**Figure 53**) up, carefully disengage the intake cam chain and remove the cam. Pull the cam chain forward and drape it over the front of the engine (**Figure 54**).

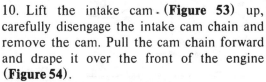

11. Loosen the exposed 10 mm exhaust sprocket bolt. Hold the intake cam chain up and taut—keep it meshed with the sprocket while performing Step 12.

> *CAUTION*
> *This is necessary to avoid letting the chain bunch up and cause damage to the cylinder head casting.*

12. Rotate the crankshaft (**Figure 55**) one full turn (360°) *counterclockwise* until the other cam sprocket bolt is exposed; remove the bolt.

13. Remove the 10 mm bolts securing the exhaust cam bearing caps A, D and E and the tachometer drive cap. Refer to **Figure 47**. Be sure to remove all dowel pins fitted to each bearing cap.

> *NOTE*
> *Loosen the bolts in 2-3 stages on all 4 bearing caps to gradually release the pressure on the cam. The lobes on one cylinder will be under pressure.*

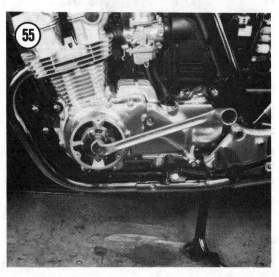

14. Lift the exhaust drive chain off the sprocket and let it rest on the cam (A, **Figure 56**).

15. Lift up on the cam and remove the intake cam drive chain (B, **Figure 56**) from the right-hand side.

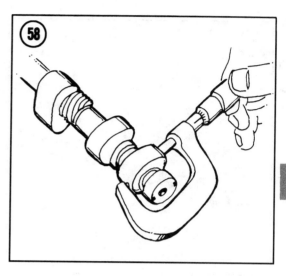

16. Lift up on the left-hand side of the cam, rotate it 180° and remove the other sprocket bolt. Slide the exhaust cam sprocket off the left-hand side of the cam.

17. Tie a piece of wire around the exhaust cam drive chain, withdraw the cam out through the chain and tie the wire to an external part of the engine (**Figure 57**).

NOTE
Be sure to tie up the exhaust cam drive chain with wire to prevent it from falling into the crankcase.

CAUTION
If the crankshaft must be rotated when the camshafts are removed, pull up on the cam drive chain and keep it taut while rotating the crankshaft. Make certain that

the chain is positioned onto the crankshaft timing sprocket. If this is not done, the chain may become kinked and may damage both the chain and the timing sprocket on the crankshaft.

Inspection

1. Check the bearing journals for wear and scoring.

2. Check the cam lobes for wear. The lobes should not be scored and the edges should be square. Slight damage may be removed with a silicon carbide oilstone. Use No. 100-200 grit initially, then polish with a No. 280-320 grit.

3. Even though the cam lobe surface appears to be satisfactory, with no visible signs of wear, the cam lobes must be measured with a micrometer as shown in **Figure 58**. Replace the shaft(s) if worn beyond the service limits (measurements less than those given in **Table 6**).

4. Check the bearing bores in the cylinder head and bearing caps. They should not be scored or excessively worn.

5. Inspect the sprockets for wear; replace if necessary.

Camshaft Bearing Clearance

This procedure requires the use of a Plastigage set. The camshafts must be installed into the heads. Prior to installation, wipe any oil from each cam bearing journal and bearing surface in the head and bearing cap.

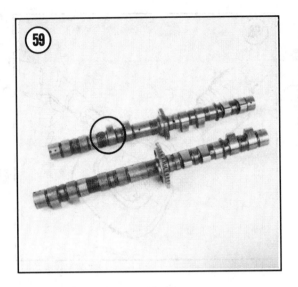

1. Make sure the No. 1 and 4 cylinders are set at TDC. Refer to Step 6, *Cylinder Head Removal*, this chapter. Readjust if necessary.

> *CAUTION*
> *Be sure to keep the camshaft drive chain taut while rotating the crankshaft.*

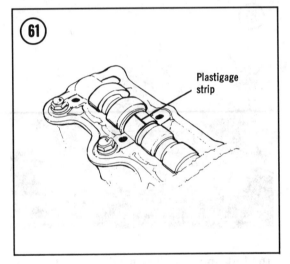

Plastigage strip

2. If the valve lifters and shims are still in place, remove them and place them in a divided container. Refer to Step 12, *Cylinder Head Removal* and to **Figure 31**.

3. Install all bearing cap locating dowels in position in the head.

4. Pull up on the camshaft drive chain and make sure it is properly engaged with the timing sprocket on the crankshaft.

5. Install the intake and exhaust cams. The exhaust cam has the tachometer drive gear on it (**Figure 59**). Install the camshafts with the notches on the left-hand side of the engine (**Figure 60**).

6. Wipe all oil from cam bearing journals prior to using Plastigage material.

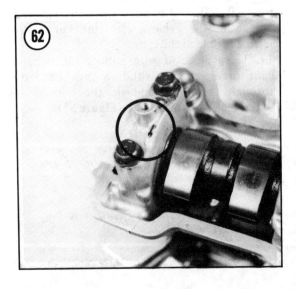

7. Place a strip of Plastigage material between the cam and each cam bearing cap, lengthwise with the cam as shown in **Figure 61**.

8. Place all bearing caps into their correct position; refer to **Figure 47** for correct placement. The letter on the bearing cap relates to the letter in the oil pocket in the cylinder head. The arrow (**Figure 62**) must point toward the front of the engine.

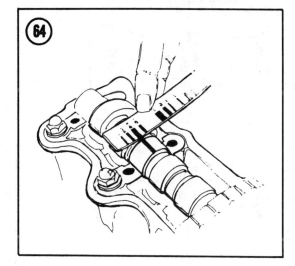

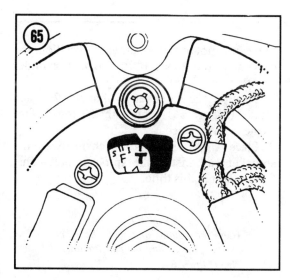

NOTE
*Bearing caps D and K have grooves in them that fit into the flange on the cam (**Figure 63**). Make sure they are installed correctly.*

9. Install all bearing cap bolts finger-tight at first; then tighten in a crisscross pattern to a final torque of 9-12 ft.-lb. (12-16 N•m).

NOTE
Do not rotate either camshaft with the Plastigage material in place.

10. Remove the bolts in the same sequence in which they were tightened. Remove the bearing caps carefully.
11. Measure the width of the flattened Plastigage according to manufacturer's instructions (**Figure 64**).
12. If the clearance exceeds the wear limit in **Table 6**, measure the cam bearing journals with a micrometer and compare to the wear limits in **Table 6**. If the cam bearing is less than the dimension specified, replace the cam. If the cam is within specifications, the cylinder head must be replaced.

Installation

1. Make sure that the No 1. and 4 cylinders are at TDC (**Figure 65**). Refer to Step 6, *Cylinder Head Removal* in this chapter. Adjust if necessary.

CAUTION
Be sure to keep the camshaft drive chain taut while rotating the crankshaft.

2. Install all valve lifters and shims.

CAUTION
The lifters and shims must be reinstalled into their original cylinder upon assembly.

3. Coat all camshaft lobes and bearing journals with assembly oil. Also coat the bearing surfaces in the cylinder head and bearing caps.
4. Loosen the rear lower cam chain tensioner adjusting locknut (**Figure 51**).
5. With a pair of pliers, pull up on the rear cam chain tensioner and tighten the locknut. This will provide maximum chain slack.

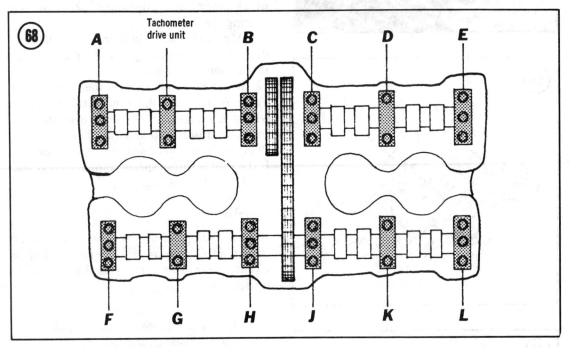

Tachometer drive unit

A B C D E

F G H J K L

6. The exhaust cam (with tachometer drive gear) is installed first. Install it with the notches in the end on the left-hand side of the engine. Install the intake cam drive chain and sprocket onto the exhaust cam. Pull up on the long exhaust cam drive chain and insert the exhaust cam through it from the right-hand side.

> NOTE
> *Install the sprocket with the larger sprocket (exhaust drive chain) to the left-hand side.*

7. Drape the intake cam chain over the front of the engine and leave the exhaust chain on the cam—not on the sprocket. Position the cam with the lobes of the No. 1 cylinder pointing toward the spark plug.

8. Position the sprocket so that the 2 punch marks (**Figure 66**) align with the top surface of the cylinder head.

9. Place the exhaust cam chain over the sprocket and install the sprocket bolt—only finger-tight at this time.

> NOTE
> *After the chain and bolt have been installed, make sure the punch marks still align (**Figure 67**).*

CAUTION
Very expensive damage could result from improper camshaft and chain alignment. Recheck your work several times to be sure alignment is correct.

10. Install both end bearing caps (A and E); refer to **Figure 68**. Be sure to install both dowel pins (**Figure 69**) on each bearing cap. Install the bearing caps with the arrow (**Figure 70**) facing toward the front of the engine.

11. Install the D bearing cap, making sure the groove in it fits into the flange on the cam (**Figure 71**). Install the tachometer drive/bearing cap; rotate the driven gear (**Figure 72**) while installing it so the gears will mesh properly. Install the 2 bolts, only finger-tight at this time.

12. Hold up on the intake cam drive chain and rotate the crankshaft *counterclockwise* 360° (the cam will rotate 180°), using a 24 mm wrench on the ignition advancer hex spacer (**Figure 73**). Install the other sprocket bolt and tighten to 13-15 ft.-lb. (18-20 N•m).

CAUTION
Keep the drive chain meshed with the sprocket while rotating the crankshaft. This is necessary to avoid letting the chain bunch up and cause damage to the cylinder head casting.

13. Repeat Step 12, rotating the crankshaft 360° *counterclockwise*, and tighten the previously installed sprocket bolt to 13-15 ft.-lb. (18-20 N•m).

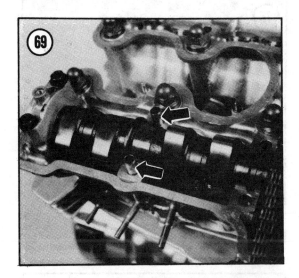

14. Tighten the bolts on the 4 bearing caps in a crisscross pattern in 2 or 3 stages to a final torque of 9-12 ft.-lb. (12-16 N•m).

> *NOTE*
> *Do not install the 2 center bearing caps (B and C) at this time.*

15. Make sure the "1.4 T" timing marks still align (**Figure 65**) and that the exhaust cam lobes on the No. 1 cylinder face toward the spark plug. Readjust as necessary. Check also that the 2 punch marks on the sprocket align with the top surface of the cylinder head (**Figure 66**).

> *CAUTION*
> *Very expensive damage could result from improper camshaft and chain alignment.*

16. Install the intake cam, through the intake cam sprocket, with the notches on the end of the cam on the left-hand side of the engine. Position the cam and sprocket so the 2 punch marks (**Figure 74**) on the sprocket align with the top surface of the cylinder head. Also the lobes on the No. 1 cylinder must point to the spark plug (**Figure 75**).

17. Install both end bearing caps (F and L); refer to **Figure 68**. Be sure to install both dowel pins (**Figure 69**) on each bearing cap. Install the bearing cap with the arrow (**Figure 70**) facing toward the front of the engine. Tighten the bolts only finger-tight at this time.

18. Install the G and K bearing caps; refer to **Figure 68**. Make sure the groove in bearing cap K (**Figure 76**) fits into the flange on the cam. Install the bolts only finger-tight at this time.

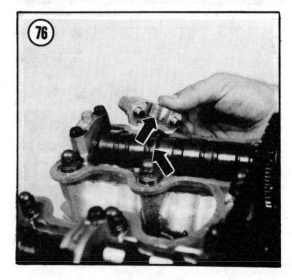

19. Tighten the bolts on the 4 bearing caps in a crisscross pattern in 2-3 stages to a final torque of 9-12 ft.-lb. (12-16 N•m).

> *NOTE*
> *Do not install the 2 center bearing caps (H and J) at this time.*

20. Make one last check of the alignment of the "1.4 T" timing mark, and that the punch marks on *both sprockets align* with the top surface of the cylinder head.

21. Install the exhaust cam chain guide attachment plate (**Figure 77**).

22. Install the 4 center bearing caps (exhaust B and C and intake H and J); refer to **Figure 68**. Install the cam chain guide and oil pipe (**Figure 78**) at the same time.

> *NOTE*
> *Be sure to install the angled clips (**Figure 79**) under the front bolts on the B and C bearing caps.*

23. Tighten the bearing cap bolts in a crisscross pattern, in 2 or 3 stages, to a final torque of 9-12 ft.-lb. (12-16 N•m).

24. Install the 2 black rubber oil caps onto the 2 center rear cylinder head cap nuts (**Figure 80**).

25. Fill the oil pockets (**Figure 81**) with fresh engine oil so the cam lobes will be covered for the initial engine start up.

26. Adjust the cam chain tensioners as described under *Camshaft Chain Tensioner Adjustment* in Chapter Three.

27. Check and adjust (if necessary) the valve clearance as described under *Valve Clearance Measurement* in Chapter Three.

CAMSHAFT CHAIN

Inspection/Replacement

The intake cam drive chain can be removed with the engine in the frame but it is easier with the engine removed.

> *NOTE*
> *To inspect and replace the exhaust cam drive chain it is necessary to disassemble the engine and remove the crankshaft.*

Intake cam

1. Perform Steps 1-15 of *Camshaft Removal* in this chapter.
2. Place the intake cam drive chain over the 2 intake sprockets.
3. Attach one sprocket so it is stationary and pull on the other sprocket with a scale (a portable fish scale will do). Apply 29 lb. (13 kg) tension on the components and measure the distance between the 2 sprockets as shown in **Figure 82**.
4. Compare the sprocket dimension with the specifications in **Table 6**. Replace the chain if the dimension exceeds the wear limit.

Exhaust cam

1. Perform Steps 1-2 of *Crankshaft Removal/Installation* in this chapter.

2. Place the exhaust cam drive chain over the 2 *intake sprockets.*

3. Attach one sprocket so it is stationary and pull on the other sprocket with a scale (a portable fish scale will do). Apply 29 lb. (13 kg) tension on the components and measure the distance between the 2 sprockets as shown in **Figure 82**.

4. Compare the sprocket dimension with the specifications in **Table 6**. Replace the chain if the dimension exceeds the wear limit.

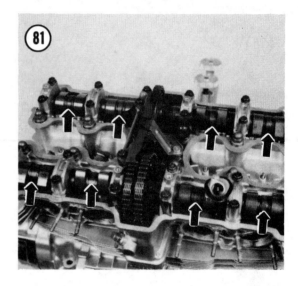

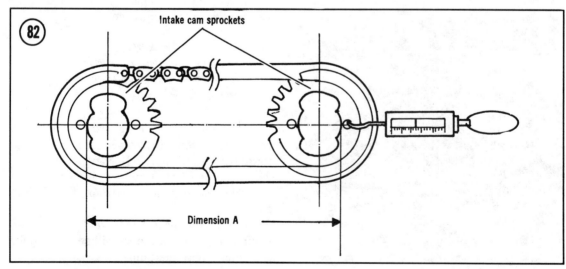

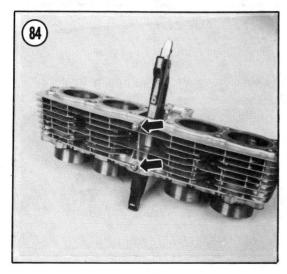

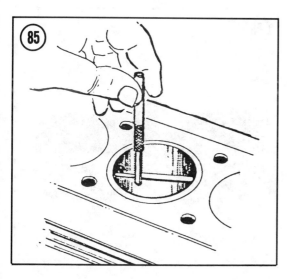

Camshaft Chain Tensioner Adjustment

After the camshaft chain has been replaced, adjust the chain as described under *Camshaft Chain Tensioner Adjustment* in Chapter Three.

Camshaft Chain Sprockets

Inspect the condition of all sprockets. Replace them if they show signs of wear or have any teeth missing.

CYLINDER BLOCK

Removal

1. Remove the cylinder head as described in this chapter.
2. Remove the bolt (A, **Figure 83**) at the lower front of the cylinder block.
3. Remove the front cam chain guide (B, **Figure 83**).
4. Loosen the cylinder block by tapping around the perimeter with a rubber or plastic mallet. If necessary, *gently* pry the cylinder block loose with a broad-tipped screwdriver only in the ribbed areas of the fins.

> *CAUTION*
> *Remember, the cooling fins are fragile and may be damaged if tapped or pried too hard. Do not use a metal hammer.*

5. Pull the cylinder block straight up and off the pistons and crankcase studs.

> *NOTE*
> *Be sure to keep the cam chain wired up to prevent it from falling into the crankcase.*

6. Remove the cylinder block base gasket and 2 locating dowels.
7. Remove the locknuts (**Figure 84**) securing the cam chain tensioner and remove the tensioner.

Inspection

1. Measure the cylinder bores with a cylinder gauge (**Figure 85**) or inside micrometer at the points shown in **Figure 86**.
2. Measure in 2 axes—in line with the piston pin and at 90° to the pin. If the taper or out-of-round is greater than 0.002 in. (0.05 mm), the cylinders must be rebored to the next oversize and new pistons and rings

installed. Rebore all cylinders even though only one may be faulty.

> *NOTE*
> *The new pistons should be obtained first before the cylinders are bored so that the pistons can be measured; slight manufacturing tolerances must be taken into account to determine the actual size and the working clearance. Piston-to-cylinder wear limit clearance is 0.004 in. (0.10 mm).*

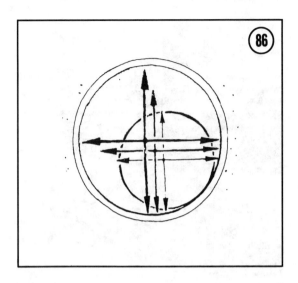

3. Check the cylinder walls for scratches; if evident, the cylinders should be rebored.

> *NOTE*
> *The maximum wear limit on a cylinder is 2.445 in. (62.10 mm). If any cylinder is worn to this limit, the cylinder block must be replaced. Never rebore a cylinder if the finished rebore diameter will be this dimension or larger.*

4. Inspect the slipper portion of the cam chain tensioner (A, **Figure 87**) for damage or excessive wear. Check the spring tension (B, **Figure 87**) for weakness. Also inspect the front cam chain guide (C, **Figure 87**) for excessive wear. Replace as necessary.

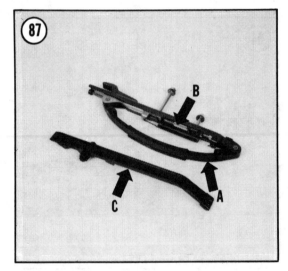

Installation

1. Check that the top surface of the crankcase and the bottom of the cylinder block are clean prior to installing new gaskets.
2. Install a new cylinder block base gasket (**Figure 88**).
3. Install the rear cam chain tensioner and locknuts (**Figure 84**).
4. Install the 2 locating dowels (A, **Figure 89**) and rubber O-rings (B, **Figure 89**) on models so equipped.
5. Install a piston holding fixture (**Figure 90**) under the 2 pistons protruding out of the crankcase.

> *NOTE*
> *These fixtures may be purchased or may be homemade units of wood. See **Figure 91** for dimensions.*

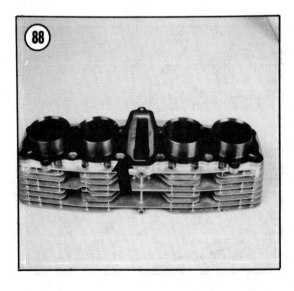

6. Apply assembly oil to the piston rings and cylinder.

4

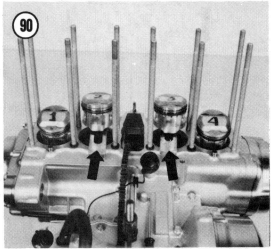

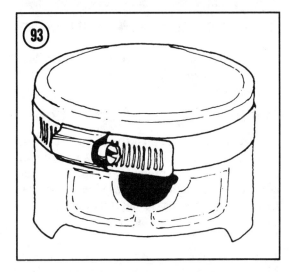

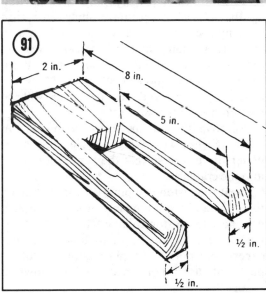

7. Carefully install the cylinder block onto the crankcase studs (**Figure 92**) and slide it down over the 2 top pistons. Feed the cam drive chain up through its opening and tie it to the chain tensioner.

8. Compress each piston ring as it enters the cylinder either with your fingers or by using aircraft type hose clamps (**Figure 93**) of appropriate size.

9. Remove the piston holding fixtures and push the cylinder block all the way down.

NOTE
Make sure the lower end of the cam chain tensioner seats correctly into the upper crankcase.

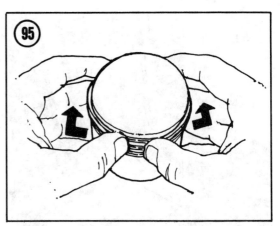

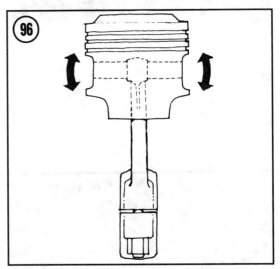

10. Install the front lower bolt (**Figure 83**) and tighten it securely.

11. Install the cylinder head as described under *Cylinder Head Installation* in this chapter.

PISTONS AND CONNECTING RODS

To remove the pistons, the engine must be removed and the cylinder head and cylinder block must be removed. To remove the connecting rods, the crankcase has to be split in order to gain access to the rod bearing caps.

Piston Removal

1. Remove the cylinder head and cylinder block as described under *Cylinder Block Removal/Installation* in this chapter.

2. Lightly mark the top of each piston with the correct cylinder number, "1", "2", "3" and "4" (**Figure 94**), so that it will be installed into the correct cylinder. Remember, the No. 1 cylinder is on the left-hand side of the bike; No. 2, 3 and 4 continue from left to right across the engine.

> *WARNING*
> *The edges of all piston rings are very sharp. Be careful when handling them to avoid cut fingers.*

3. Remove the top ring first by spreading the ends with your thumbs just enough to slide it up over the piston (**Figure 95**). Repeat for the remaining rings.

4. Before removing the piston, hold the rod tightly and rock the piston as shown in **Figure 96**. Any rocking motion (do not confuse with the normal sliding motion) indicates wear on the piston pin, rod bushing, pin bore or more likely, a combination of all three. Mark the piston, pin and rod so that they will be reassembled in the same set.

5. Remove the circlips from the piston pin bores (**Figure 97**). Wrap a clean shop cloth under the piston so that the clips will not fall into the crankcase.

6. Heat the piston and pin with a small butane torch. The pin will probably drop right out. If not, heat the piston to about 140° F (60° C), i.e., until it is too warm to touch, but not excessively hot. If the pin is still difficult to push out, use a homemade tool as shown in **Figure 98**.

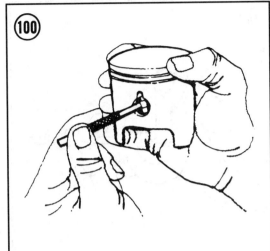

4

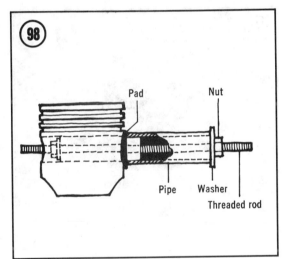

Pad   Nut

Pipe   Washer

Threaded rod

Piston Inspection

1. Carefully clean the carbon from the piston crown with a chemical remover or with a soft scraper (**Figure 99**). Do not remove or damage the carbon ridge around the circumference of the piston above the top ring. If the pistons, rings and cylinders are found to be dimensionally correct and can be reused, removal of the carbon ring from the tops of pistons or carbon ridges from the tops of cylinders will promote excessive oil consumption.

> *WARNING*
> *The rail portions of the oil scraper can be very sharp. Be careful when handling them to avoid cut fingers.*

> *CAUTION*
> *Do not wire brush piston skirts.*

2. Examine each ring groove for burrs, dented edges and wide wear. Pay particular attention to the top compression ring groove, as it usually wears more than the others.

3. Measure piston-to-cylinder clearance as described under *Piston Clearance* in this chapter.

4. If damage or wear indicates piston replacement, select a new piston as described under *Piston Clearance* in this chapter.

5. Measure the piston pin bore with a snap gauge (**Figure 100**) and measure the outside diameter of the piston pin with a micrometer

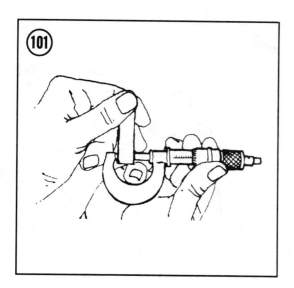

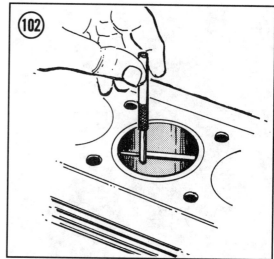

(**Figure 101**). Compare against dimensions given in **Table 6**. Any machinist can do this for you if you do not have the measuring tools. Replace the piston and piston pin set as a unit if either or both are worn.

Piston Clearance

1. Make sure the piston and cylinder walls are clean and dry.
2. Measure the inside diameter of the cylinder bore at a point 1/2 in. (13 mm) from the upper edge with a bore gauge (**Figure 102**).
3. Measure the outside diameter of the piston (**Figure 103**) at a point 1/16 in. (5 mm) from the lower edge of the piston, 90° to the piston pin axis (**Figure 104**). Check against measurement given in **Table 6**.

Piston Installation

1. Apply molybdenum disulfide grease to the inside surface of the connecting rod small end. Apply fresh engine oil to the piston pin and piston pin bore.
2. Place the piston over the connecting rod, with the "IN" mark (**Figure 105**) facing toward the rear. Be sure to install the correct piston (No. 1, 2, 3 or 4) onto the same rod from which it was removed.
3. Insert the piston pin and tap it with a plastic mallet until it slides into the connecting rod bushing. If it does not slide in easily, heat the piston until it is too warm to touch but not excessively hot (140° F or 60° C).

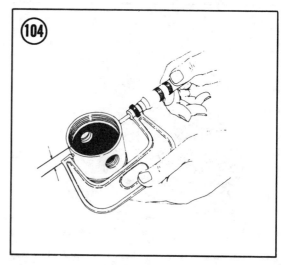

Continue to drive the piston pin while holding the piston so that the rod does not have to take any shock. Drive the piston pin in until it is centered in the rod. If the pin is still difficult to install, use the homemade tool (**Figure 98**) but eliminate the piece of pipe.

4. Install the circlip (**Figure 97**).

5. Repeat Steps 1-4 for all remaining pistons.

6. Install the rings as described under *Piston Ring Replacement* in this chapter.

Connecting Rod Inspection

1. Check each rod for obvious damage such as cracks and burns.

2. Check the piston pin bushing for wear or scoring.

3. Take the rods to a machine shop and check the alignment for twisting and bending.

4. Examine the bearing inserts for wear, scoring or burning. They are reusable if in good condition. Make a note of the bearing size (if any) stamped on the back of the insert if the bearing is to be discarded; a previous owner may have used undersize bearings.

5. Check bearing clearance and connecting rod side play as described under *Connecting Rod Bearing and Crankpin Inspection*.

Connecting Rod Bearing and Crankpin Inspection

1. Split the crankcase as described under *Crankcase Disassembly/Assembly* in this chapter.

NOTE
Prior to disassembly, mark the rods and caps. Number them "1", "2", "3" and "4" starting from the left-hand side. The left-hand side refers to the engine as it sits in the bike's frame—not as it sits on your workbench.

2. Remove the rods from the crankshaft if not already removed. Mark the back of each bearing insert with the cylinder number and "U" (upper) or "L" (lower). Install bearing inserts into the rods and caps.

CAUTION
If the old bearings are reused, be sure that they are installed in their exact original locations.

3. Wipe bearing inserts and crankpins clean. Check again that inserts and crankpins are in good condition.

4. Place a piece of Plastigage on one crankpin parallel to the crankshaft.

5. Install rod cap and tighten nuts to 22-25 ft.-lb. (30-34 N•m).

CAUTION
Do not rotate crankshaft while Plastigage is in place.

6. Remove the rod cap.

7. Measure width of flattened Plastigage according to the manufacturer's instructions. Measure at both ends of the strip. A difference of 0.001 in. (0.025 mm) or more indicates a tapered crankpin, indicating the crankshaft must be reground or replaced.

8. If the crankpin taper is within tolerance, measure the bearing clearance with the same strip of Plastigage. Used bearing clearance must not exceed 0.003 in. (0.08 mm). New bearing clearance should be 0.0008-0.0024 in. (0.020-0.060 mm). Remove the Plastigage strips.

9. If the bearing clearance is greater than specified, use the following steps for new bearing selection.

10. The connecting rods and caps are marked with code numbers 1, 2 or 3 (**Figure 106**). The crankshaft is also marked with code numbers 1, 2 or 3 (**Figure 107**) on the counterbalance weights.

4

11. Select new bearings by cross-referencing the crankpin journal code number (**Figure 107** and horizontal column, **Table 1**) to the rod bearing code number (**Figure 106** and vertical column, **Table 1**). Where the 2 columns intersect, the new replacement color is indicated. **Table 2** gives the bearing color and size.

12. After new bearings have been installed, recheck clearance (specifications given in Step 8).

13. Repeat Steps 3-12 for the other 3 cylinders.

14. Measure the inside diameter of the small ends of the connecting rods with an inside dial gauge (**Figure 108**). Check against measurements given in **Table 6**. Replace if worn.

15. Insert the bearing shells into each connecting rod and cap. Make sure they are locked in place correctly.

> *CAUTION*
> *If the old bearings are reused, be sure they are installed in their exact original positions.*

16. Lubricate the bearings and crankpins with assembly oil and install the rods. Apply molybdenum disulfide grease to the threads of the connecting rods. Install the caps and tighten the cap nuts evenly, in 2-3 stages, to 22-25 ft.-lb. (30-34 N•m).

17. Rotate the crankshaft a couple of times to make sure the bearings are not too tight.

PISTON RINGS

Replacement

> *WARNING*
> *The edges of all piston rings are very sharp. Be careful when handling them to avoid cut fingers.*

1. Remove old rings with a ring expander tool or by spreading the ring ends with your thumbs and lifting the rings up evenly (**Figure 109**).

2. Carefully remove all carbon from the ring grooves. Inspect grooves carefully for burrs, nicks or broken and cracked lands. Recondition or replace the piston if necessary.

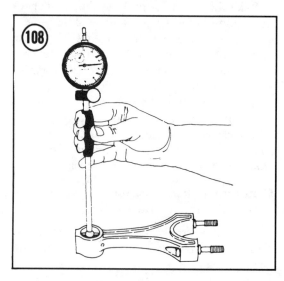

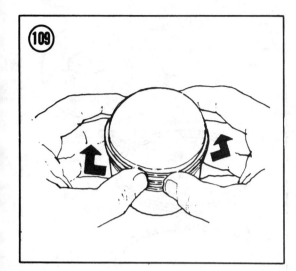

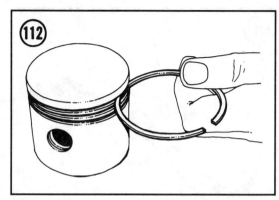

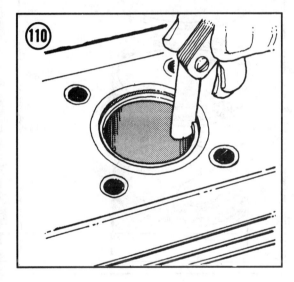

3. Check end gap of each ring. To check gap, insert the ring into the bottom of the cylinder bore and square it with the wall by tapping with the piston. The ring should be in about 5/8 in. (15 mm). Insert a feeler gauge as shown in **Figure 110**. Compare gap with **Table 6**. If the gap is smaller than specified, hold a small file in a vise, grip the ends of the ring with your fingers, and enlarge the gap. See **Figure 111**.

4. Roll each ring around its piston groove as shown in **Figure 112** to check for binding. Minor binding may be cleaned up with a fine cut file.

NOTE
Install all rings with their markings facing up.

5. Install oil ring in oil ring groove with a ring expander tool or spread the ends with your thumbs.

6. Install 2 compression rings carefully with a ring expander tool or spread the ends with your thumbs.

7. Check side clearance of each ring as shown in **Figure 113**. Compare with specifications in **Table 6**.

8. Distribute ring gaps around piston as shown in **Figure 114**. The important thing is that the ring gaps are not aligned with each other when installed.

IGNITION ADVANCE MECHANISM

The ignition advance mechanism can be removed with the engine in the frame. This procedure is shown with the engine removed for clarity.

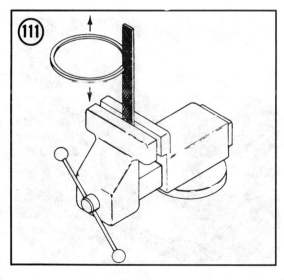

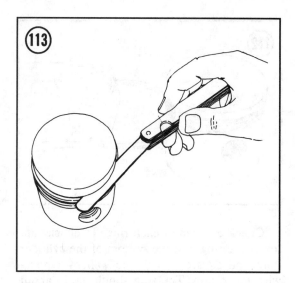

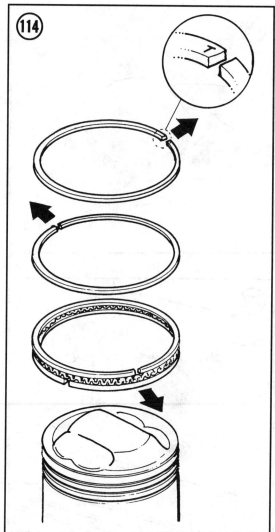

Removal/Installation

1. Place the bike on the centerstand.
2. Remove the right-hand side cover and disconnect the battery negative lead (**Figure 115**).
3. Remove the screws (**Figure 116**) securing the ignition cover and remove the cover and the gasket.
4. Remove the bolts (**Figure 117**) securing the left-hand case cover and remove it.

> *NOTE*
> *Don't lose the 2 locating dowels.*

5. To remove the advancer unit, hold the hex spacer with a 24 mm wrench and remove the inner bolt with a 12 mm wrench (**Figure 118**). Remove the advancer unit.

> *CAUTION*
> *To avoid internal damage to the advancer unit, be sure to securely hold the 24 mm hex spacer while removing the inner bolt.*

6. Inspect the advancer unit as described under *Ignition Advancer Mechanism* in Chapter Seven.
7. Install by reversing these removal steps, noting the following.
8. When installing the advancer unit, index the pin on the backside of the advancer unit into the slot in the end of the crankshaft (**Figure 119**).
9. Hold the advancer unit in place and install the hex spacer. Align the 2 notches with the 2

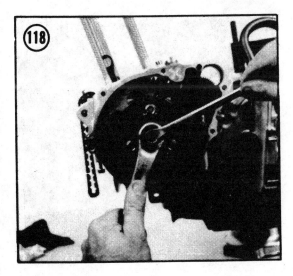

tangs (**Figure 120**) on the advancer unit. Install the 12 mm bolt and tighten to 15-18 ft.-lb. (21-25 N•m) while holding the hex space securely.

> *CAUTION*
> *To avoid internal damage to the advancer unit, securely hold the 24 mm spacer while tightening the inner bolt.*

10. Install a new gasket (A, **Figure 121**) and 2 locating dowels (B, **Figure 121**).

ALTERNATOR

Removal/Installation

Refer to *Alternator Removal/Installation* in Chapter Seven.

OIL PUMP

The oil pump is mounted on the left-hand side of the engine and can be removed with the engine in the frame. Steps 7-10 are shown with the engine removed and partially disassembled for clarity. Do not remove any components other than specified.

Removal/Installation

1. Place the bike on the centerstand. Remove the side covers, seat and fuel tank.
2. Remove the exhaust system on the left-hand side only. Refer to Chapter Six.
3. Remove the gearshift pedal.
4. Remove the bolts (**Figure 122**) securing the left-hand crankcase cover and remove the cover.
5. Loosen the bolt (**Figure 123**) securing the neutral indicator electrical wire strap. Carefully push the wire down away from the oil pump assembly.
6. Disconnect the crankcase breather hose on the oil pump cover where it attaches to the air box (**Figure 124**). Pull the hose down between the No. 1 and 2 carburetors.
7. Place a drip pan under the oil pump as a small amount of oil will drain out. Remove the bolts (**Figure 125**) securing the oil pump cover. Remove the cover and breather hose.
8. Remove the bolts (**Figure 126**) securing the oil pump assembly and remove the assembly. Don't lose the locating dowel.

4

9. Install by reversing these removal steps plus the following. Prime the oil pump prior to installation.

10. Install a new gasket (A, **Figure 127**) and install the locating dowel (B, **Figure 127**).

CAUTION
Do not tighten any of the bolts until the oil pump gears mesh properly and the assembly is up against the gasket and crankcase.

11. Install the oil pump assembly; the long bolt goes into the hole with the locating dowel. Tighten the bolts securely.

NOTE
If the drive gear will not mesh properly, shift the transmission into gear and slowly rotate the rear wheel while pushing in on the assembly. This will enable the gears to mesh properly.

12. Start the engine and check for leaks. Add oil to maintain the correct oil level. Refer to Chapter Three.

Disassembly/Inspection/Assembly

Refer to **Figure 128** for this procedure.
1. Inspect the outer cover and body for cracks.
2. Remove the 2 Phillips screws and dowel pin (**Figure 129**) securing the pump cover to the body.
3. Remove the inner and outer rotor (**Figure 130**). Check both parts for scratches and

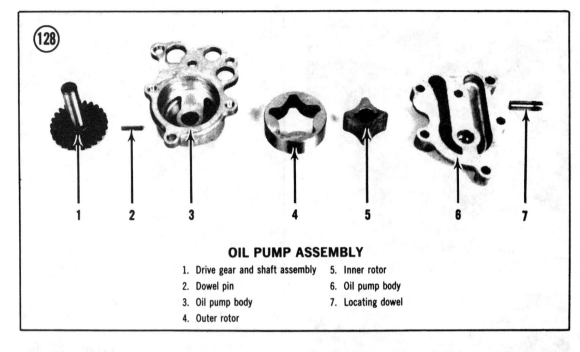

OIL PUMP ASSEMBLY

1. Drive gear and shaft assembly
2. Dowel pin
3. Oil pump body
4. Outer rotor
5. Inner rotor
6. Oil pump body
7. Locating dowel

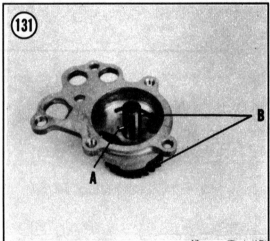

abrasions. Replace both parts if evidence of this is found.

4. Remove the dowel pin (A, **Figure 131**) and push out the drive gear and shaft assembly (B, **Figure 131**).

5. Clean all parts in solvent and thoroughly dry. Coat all parts with fresh oil prior to installation.

6. Install the drive gear and shaft assembly (B, **Figure 131**). Install the dowel pin (A, **Figure 131**) and center it on the shaft.

7. Install the outer rotor (**Figure 132**) and inner rotor (**Figure 133**) into the pump body.

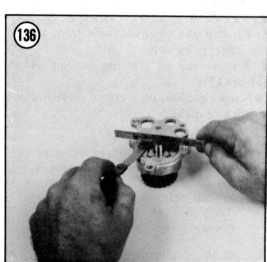

4

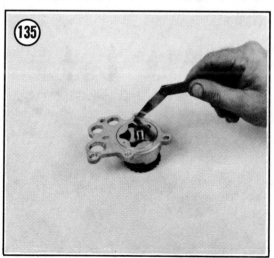

Install both parts with the punch marks facing *up*. It is not necessary to align the 2 marks upon installation. Make sure the slots in the inner rotor index correctly with the dowel pin.

8. Check the clearance between the inner and outer rotor (**Figure 134**) with a flat feeler gauge. If the clearance is 0.006 in. (0.15 mm) or greater, replace the worn part.

9. Inspect the clearance between the outer rotor and the body (**Figure 135**) with a flat feeler gauge. If the clearance is 0.014 in. (0.35 mm) or greater, replace the worn part.

10. Inspect the rotor side clearance with a straightedge and flat feeler gauge (**Figure 136**). If the clearance is 0.004 in. (0.1 mm) or greater, replace the rotors or the entire assembly.

11. Install the body cover, 2 screws and dowel pin (**Figure 129**).

12. After assembly, rotate the shaft assembly and rotor to make sure it rotates freely.

13. Install the oil pump assembly.

NOTE
If the condition of the oil pump is doubtful, run the following test to make sure the pump is functioning properly.

Oil Pump Pressure Test

If the oil pump output is doubtful, the following test can be performed.

1. Warm the engine up to normal operating temperature (176° F/80° C). Shut off the engine.

2. Place the bike on the centerstand.

3. Remove the electrical wire from the oil pressure sending switch.

4. Remove the oil pressure sending switch (**Figure 137**).

5. Screw a portable oil pressure gauge into the switch hole in the crankcase.

> *NOTE*
> *These can be purchased in an automotive or motorcycle supply store or from a Honda dealer. The Honda part numbers are No. 07506-3000000 (Oil Pressure Gauge) and No. 07510-4220100 (Oil Pressure Gauge Attachment).*

6. Start the engine and run it at fast idle (7,000 rpm). The standard pressure is 71 psi (50 kg/cm^2) at 7,000 rpm and at 176° F (80° C). If the pressure is less than specified the oil pump must be rebuilt or replaced.

7. Remove the portable oil pressure gauge.

8. Apply Loctite Lock N' Seal to the switch threads prior to installation. Tighten the switch to 11-14 ft.-lb. (15-19 N•m) and install the electrical wire to the top of the switch. This connection must be free of oil to make good electrical contact.

OIL STRAINER, OIL PATH BODY AND PRESSURE RELIEF VALVE

These components can be removed with the engine in the frame. This procedure is shown with the engine removed for clarity.

Removal/Installation

1. Drain the engine oil as described in Chapter Three.

2. Remove the bolts securing the oil pan and remove it and the gasket.

> *NOTE*
> *Don't lose the 3 copper washers and the 2 electrical wire clips.*

3. Pull off the oil strainer (**Figure 138**).

4. Remove the bolts (A, **Figure 139**) securing the oil path body and remove it.

5. Install by reversing these removal steps, noting the following.

6. Make sure the rubber grommet (B, **Figure 139**) is in good condition and is in place.

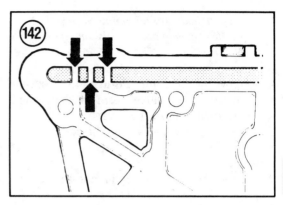

4

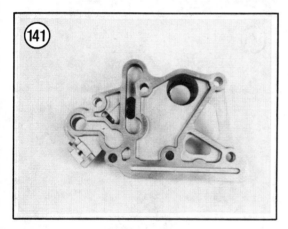

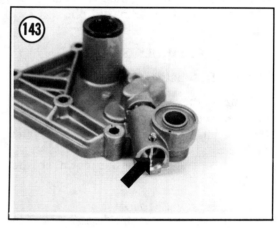

Replace it if it's deteriorating or will not hold the strainer in place securely.

7. Install a new pan gasket and install all bolts. Install the 3 copper washers under the 3 bolts as marked by a raised circle or arrow (A, **Figure 140**) on the oil pan. Tighten the bolts to 7-10 ft.-lb. (10-14 N•m).

NOTE
*Be sure to install the 2 alternator electrical wire clips as shown (B, **Figure 140**).*

8. Refill the engine with the correct amount and type engine oil. Refer to Chapter Three.
9. Start the engine and check for leaks.

Inspection

1. Wash all parts which were removed in cleaning solvent and thoroughly dry with

compressed air. Carefully scrub the strainer screen with a soft toothbrush; do not damage the screen.
2. Inspect the strainer screen for broken areas. If broken in any area, replace the strainer.
3. Inspect the oil path body (**Figure 141**) for cracks or damage; replace if necessary.

CAUTION
*The Honda factory determined there was a problem with the oil path body on the 1979 CB750K (frame serial No. 2000001-205514) and 1979 CB750K LTD (frame serial No. 3000001-201200) only. No other CB750 models were affected by this recall. A Recall Notice was sent to all registered owners of these models instructing them to have the new oil path body installed by their Honda dealer. The new part has 3 oil flow restriction dams as shown in **Figure 142**. If you are working on one of these designated models and the new*

oil path body was not replaced, install the new oil path body at this time (part No. 15311-425-305).

4. Remove the cotter pin **(Figure 143)** securing the pressure relief valve. Remove the dished washer, spring and relief valve.

5. Inspect the check valve and the cylinder that it rides for scratches or wear. Replace if defective.

6. Make sure the spring is not broken or distorted; replace if necessary.

7. Assemble by reversing Step 4. Install a new cotter pin—never reuse an old pin.

PRIMARY SHAFT

Removal/Installation

1. Remove the engine as described under *Engine Removal/Installation* in this chapter. Remove all exterior assemblies from the crankcase.

2. Turn the crankcase upside down on the workbench.

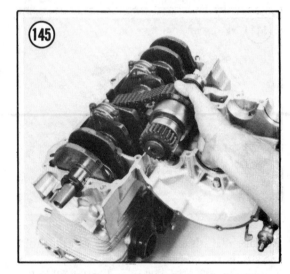

> *CAUTION*
> *If the cylinder head and cylinder have been removed, set the engine on wood blocks to protect the cylinder studs.*

3. Separate the crankcase as described under *Crankcase Disassembly* in this chapter.

4. Remove the transmission main shaft and countershaft **(Figure 144)**.

5. Lift up on the primary shaft and drive chain **(Figure 145)**; disengage the shaft from the chain and remove the shaft assembly.

6. Install by reversing these removal steps. Make sure the 1/2 circlip **(Figure 146)** is in position in the upper crankcase prior to installing the shaft assembly.

Disassembly/Inspection/Assembly

Refer to **Figure 147** for this procedure.

1. Inspect the condition of the teeth on the split primary drive gear (A, **Figure 148**), the damper housing gear (B, **Figure 148**) and the oil pump drive gear (C, **Figure 148**). Light damage can be removed with an oilstone, but if damage is severe, the gear(s) must be replaced.

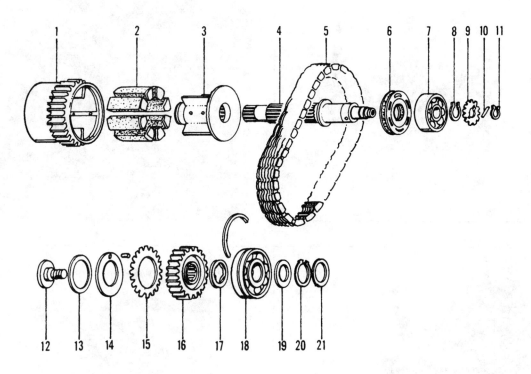

PRIMARY SHAFT ASSEMBLY

1. Outer damper housing
2. Rubber dampers (8)
3. Inner damper
4. Primary shaft
5. Primary shaft Hy-Vo chain
6. Oil seal
7. Bearing
8. Circlip
9. Oil pump drive gear
10. Pin
11. Circlip
12. Lock bolt
13. Lockwasher
14. Collar
15. Split primary drive gear (thin)
16. Split primary drive gear (large)
17. Splined washer
18. Bearing
19. Thrust washer
20. Circlip
21. Washer

NOTE
If the damper housing gear is damaged,
inspect the condition of the Hy-Vo chain
as it may be damaged also.

2. To remove the oil pump drive gear, remove the circlip and slide off the drive gear (A, **Figure 149**).

3. The bearing (B, **Figure 149**) may be removed by applying light pressure on the backside of the oil seal and sliding off both parts.

NOTE
The oil seal should be replaced if removed.

4. If the split primary gear is to be removed it is easier to reinstall the shaft assembly into the crankcase so it can be used as a holding fixture. Temporarily install the shaft assembly and install a couple of bolts to hold the cases together. Insert a soft aluminum wedge or broad-tipped screwdriver between the split gear and the crankcase in area marked A, **Figure 150**. Loosen the lock bolt and remove the shaft assembly from the crankcase.

CAUTION
Do not position the soft wedge or
*screwdriver in area marked B, **Figure 150***
as the crankcase casting will break from
the pressure exerted on it—the bolt is
tightened to 60-72 ft.-lb. (80-100 N•m).

5. Remove the lock bolt, lockwasher, collar and pin (**Figure 151**).

6. Slide off the split primary drive gear and splined washer (A, **Figure 152**).

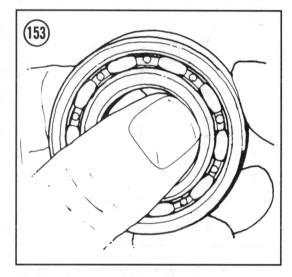

7. Remove the bearing, thrust washer and circlip (B, **Figure 152**).

8. Remove thrust washer and slide off the damper assembly (C, **Figure 152**).

9. Separate the damper assembly and inspect the condition of the damper rubbers. Replace as a set if any are worn or starting to deteriorate.

10. Inspect the condition of the splines on the primary shaft; replace if necessary.

11. Inspect the condition of the 2 bearings. Turn each bearing by hand (**Figure 153**). Make sure the bearings turn smoothly. Check the balls for evidence of wear, pitting or excessive heat (bluish tint). Replace the bearing(s) if necessary.

12. Assemble by reversing these disassembly steps, noting the following.

13. Install the split primary drive gear with the pin facing out. Install the collar, making sure the hole in the collar fits onto the pin on the gear. Install the lockwasher and lock bolt (**Figure 151**). Install the shaft assembly into the crankcase as described in Step 4. This time position the soft wedge or broad-tipped screwdriver in the area as marked C, **Figure 150**. Tighten the lock bolt to 60-72 ft.-lb. (80-100 N•m).

PRIMARY SHAFT TENSIONER

Removal

1. Perform Steps 1-9, *Crankcase Disassembly* in this chapter.

2. Remove the clip on the pivot pin (**Figure 154**).

3. Lift up on the tensioner slipper and remove the plunger and spring (**Figure 155**).

4. Turn the lower crankcase over and unscrew the tensioner fluid valve (A, **Figure 156**).

5. Remove the nut (B, **Figure 156**) on the oil line.

6. Remove the upper washer, oil line assembly and lower washer.

7. Turn the crankcase over and remove the 3 bolts (**Figure 157**) securing the slipper base assembly and remove it.

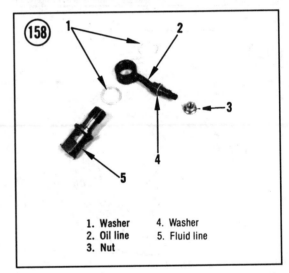

1. Washer
2. Oil line
3. Nut
4. Washer
5. Fluid line

Inspection

Refer to **Figure 158** for this procedure.

1. Inspect the condition of the rubber slipper (A, **Figure 159**); replace if worn or showing signs of deterioration.

2. Make sure the plunger (B, **Figure 159**) slides easily within the cylinder (C, **Figure 159**) with no binding; replace if necessary.

3. Make sure the spring is not distorted and does not show signs of sagging. It must maintain pressure on the slipper at all times for the tensioner to work properly.

4. Remove the cotter pin in the end of the tensioner fluid valve. Remove the dished washer, spring and check ball.

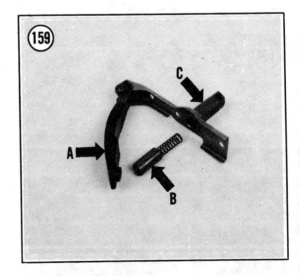

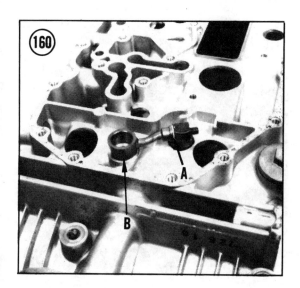

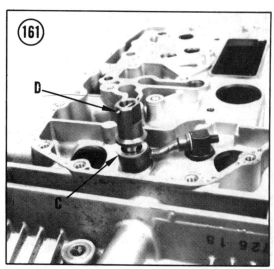

5. Clean all parts in cleaning solvent and thoroughly dry with compressed air.

6. Make sure all oil holes are clean and open in the oil pipe assembly, fluid valve and plunger. If necessary, clean out with fine wire.

7. Assemble the tensioner fluid valve. Install the check ball, spring, dished washer and new cotter pin—never reuse a cotter pin.

Installation

1. Install the slipper base assembly (**Figure 157**) and tighten the bolts to 6-9 ft.-lb. (8-12 N•m).

2. Install the spring and plunger (**Figure 155**) and the clip (**Figure 154**).

> *NOTE*
> *In order to hold the slipper in position and keep the plunger and spring from falling out, use a screwdriver and bend down the long portion of the pin firmly against the slipper base.*

3. Turn the crankcase over. Install one washer onto the oil line (A, **Figure 160**) and install the oil line into the tensioner base cylinder. Place one washer (B, **Figure 160**) onto the crankcase threads under the oil line cylinder.

4. Place another washer on top of the oil line cylinder (C, **Figure 161**) and screw in the tensioner fluid valve (D, **Figure 161**). Install the nut on the oil line (B, **Figure 156**). Tighten the valve securely.

5. Perforn Steps 7-20, *Crankcase Assembly* in this chapter.

CRANKCASE

Service to the lower end requires that the crankcase be removed from the bike's frame.

Disassembly

1. Remove the engine from the frame as described in this chapter. Remove all exterior assemblies (cylinder head, cylinder, alternator, clutch, etc.) from the crankcase.

2. Loosen the upper crankcase bolts in 2 or 3 stages in a crisscross pattern to avoid warpage. Remove all bolts.

3. Turn the engine upside down on the workbench.

> *CAUTION*
> *Set the engine on wood blocks to protect the cylinder studs.*

4. Remove the oil pan, oil strainer and oil path body as described in this chapter.

5. Loosen the lower crankcase bolts in 2 or 3 stages in a crisscross pattern to avoid warpage. Leaving the 10 crankshaft bearing bolts for last, remove all bolts.

> *NOTE*
> *Don't lose the washers under the crankshaft bearing bolts.*

6. Tap around the perimeter of the crankcase halves with a plastic mallet—do not use a

metal hammer as it will cause damage. Separate the case halves. Don't lose the 2 locating dowels.

> *CAUTION*
> *Honda's thin-walled crankcase castings are just that—thin. To avoid damage to the cases do not hammer on the projected walls that surround the clutch or alternator (**Figure 162**). These areas are easily damaged if stressed beyond what they are designed for.*

> *CAUTION*
> *If it is necessary to pry the crankcase apart, do it very carefully so that you do not mar the gasket surfaces. If you do, the cases will leak and must be replaced. They cannot be repaired.*

7. Remove the transmission assemblies and the primary shaft (**Figure 163**).

8. Remove the chain oil feed nozzle and O-ring (A, **Figure 164**). Also remove the O-ring located under it (**Figure 165**).

9. Lift out the crankshaft, exhaust cam chain and primary drive chain.

10. Remove the gearshift drum and forks as described under *Gearshift Drum and Forks Removal* in Chapter Five.

11. Remove the primary shaft tensioner assembly as described in this chapter.

12. Remove the crankcase main bearing inserts from the upper and lower crankcase halves.

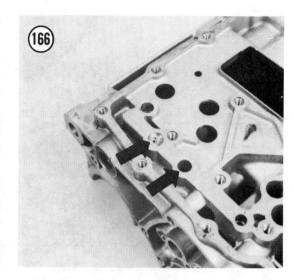

halves. Mark the backsides of the inserts with No. "1", "2", "3" and "4" and "U" (upper) or "L" (lower) starting from the left-hand side, so they will be installed into the same position.

NOTE
The left-hand side refers to the engine as it sits in the bike's frame—not necessarily as it sits on your workbench.

Inspection

1. Thoroughly clean the inside and outside of both crankcase halves with cleaning solvent. Dry with compressed air. Make sure there is no solvent residue left in the cases as it will contaminate the engine oil.
2. Make sure all oil passages are clean, especially the 2 oil control orifices in the lower crankcase (**Figure 166**) and the one in the upper crankcase (**Figure 167**). After cleaning, blow dry both case halves with compressed air.
3. Check the crankcases for possible damage such as cracks or other damage. Inspect the mating surfaces of both halves. They must be free of gouges, burrs or any damage that could cause an oil leak.
4. Make sure the cylinder studs are not bent and the threads are in good condition. Make sure they are screwed into the crankcase tightly.

Assembly

Prior to installation of all parts, coat surfaces with assembly oil or engine oil. Assemble with the engine upside-down.

1. Install the main bearing inserts in both the upper and lower crankcase halves (**Figure 168**). If reusing old bearings, make sure that they are installed in the same location. Refer to marks made in *Disassembly*, Step 12. Make sure they are locked in place (**Figure 169**).
2. Install the primary shaft tensioner as described in this chapter.
3. Install the gearshift drum and forks as described under *Gearshift Drum and Forks Installation* in Chapter Five.
4. Apply assembly oil to the main bearing inserts and install the crankshaft, exhaust cam drive chain and primary shaft drive chain.

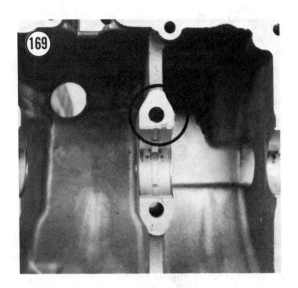

NOTE
*Make sure the oil seal (**Figure 170**) is positioned in the groove properly.*

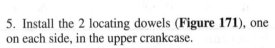

5. Install the 2 locating dowels (**Figure 171**), one on each side, in the upper crankcase.

6. Install the lower O-ring seal (**Figure 165**) and chain oil feed nozzle and O-ring (A, **Figure 164**). Make sure the locating tab is located correctly in the groove in the crankcase (B, **Figure 164**).

7. Install the primary shaft and both transmission shaft assemblies (**Figure 172**). Make sure the dowel pin (A, **Figure 173**) and both 1/2 circlips (B, **Figure 173**) are in place in the upper crankcase prior to installing the transmission assemblies.

8. Make sure case half sealing surfaces are perfectly clean and dry.

9. Apply a light coat of gasket sealer to the sealing surfaces of both halves. Cover only flat surfaces, not curved bearing surfaces. Make the coating as thin as possible or the case can shift and hammer out the bearings. Do not apply sealant close to the edge of the bearing inserts (**Figure 174**) as it would restrict oil flow.

NOTE
Use Gasgacinch Gasket Sealer, or equivalent. When selecting an equivalent, avoid thick or hard setting materials.

Do not coat this area with sealant

NOTE
Make sure the lower crankcase main bearing inserts are in place and correctly positioned.

10. On the transmission countershaft, slide the 4th gear (A, **Figure 175**) into the recess in the 1st gear (B, **Figure 175**). Apply molybdenum disulfide grease to the groove in the main shaft 3rd gear (C, **Figure 175**). *Make sure all other gears are not engaged.*

11. In the upper crankcase, position the shift drum into 1st gear. The shift forks should be located in the position shown in **Figure 176**.

12. Position the lower crankcase onto the upper crankcase. Set the front portion down first and lower the rear while making sure the shift forks engage properly into the transmission assemblies. Make sure the primary chain tensioner slipper stays in the depressed position and that the plunger and spring are still in place. If they work loose and become cocked, the crankcase will not seat completely. If they work loose, remove the lower crankcase and reposition the spring and plunger. Rebend the clip against the base as described in Step 2 of *Primary Shaft Tensioner Installation* in this chapter.

13. Lower the crankcase completely, making sure the outer bearing race on the countershaft is still engaged into the dowel pin. This could also keep the crankcase from completely seating if disengaged.

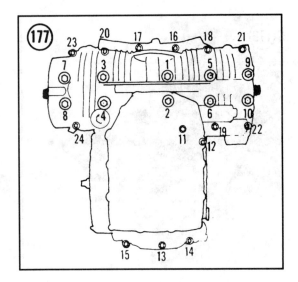

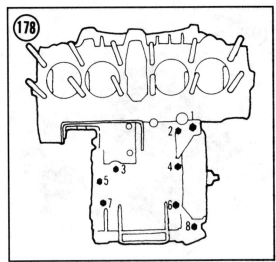

CAUTION
Do not install any crankcase bolts until the sealing surface around the entire crankcase perimeter has seated completely.

14. Prior to installing the bolts, slowly spin the transmission main shaft and shift the transmission through all 5 gears. This is to check that the shift forks are properly engaged.
15. Apply oil to the threads of all crankcase bolts. Install the lower crankcase bolts only finger-tight at this time. Be sure to place a flat washer under all 10 crankshaft bearing bolts (No. 1-10, **Figure 177**).
16. Tighten all bolts in 2 or 3 stages in the torque sequence shown in **Figure 177**. Tighten to the following specifications:
    a. 6mm bolts: 7-10 ft.-lb. (10-14 N•m)
    b. 8mm bolts: 15-18 ft.-lb. (21-25 N•m)
    c. 10mm bolts: 33-36 ft.-lb. (45-50 N•m)
17. Turn the crankcase over and install all upper crankcase bolts only finger-tight. Tighten the bolts in 2 or 3 stages in the torque sequence shown in **Figure 178**. Tighten to the preceding specifications.
18. Install all engine assemblies that were removed.
19. Install the engine as described in this chapter.
20. Fill the crankcase with the recommended type and quantity of engine oil. Refer to Chapter Three.

CRANKSHAFT

Removal/Installation

1. Split the crankcases as described under *Crankcase Disassembly* in this chapter. Remove the primary shaft assembly.
2. Remove the crankshaft assembly and remove the connecting rods.

NOTE
Prior to disassembly, mark the rods and caps. Number them "1", "2", "3" and "4" starting from the left-hand side. The left-hand side refers to the engine as it sits in the bike's frame—not as it sits on your workbench.

3. Install by reversing these removal steps, noting the following procedures.
4. If removed, insert the bearing shells into each connecting rod and cap. Make sure they are locked in place correctly.

CAUTION
If the old bearings are reused, be sure they are installed in their exact original positions.

5. Lubricate the bearings and crankpins with assembly oil and install the rods. Apply molybdenum disulfide grease to the threads of the connecting rods. Install the caps and tighten the cap nuts evenly, in 2-3 stages, to 22-25 ft.-lb. (30-34 N•m).

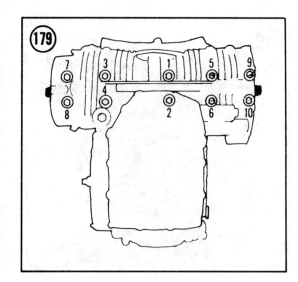

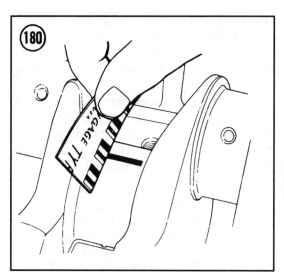

6. Rotate the crankshaft a couple of times, after the crankcases are bolted together, to make sure the bearings are not too tight.

Crankshaft Inspection

1. Clean crankshaft thoroughly with solvent. Clean oil holes with rifle cleaning brushes; flush thoroughly and dry with compressed air. Lightly oil all journal surfaces immediately after cleaning to prevent rust.
2. Carefully inspect each journal for scratches, ridges, scoring, nicks, etc. Very small nicks and scratches may be removed with emery cloth. More serious damage must be removed by grinding—a job for a machine shop.
3. If the surface on all journals is satisfactory, take the crankshaft to your dealer or local machine shop. They can check out-of-roundness, taper and wear on the journals. They can also check crankshaft alignment and inspect for cracks. Check against measurements given in **Table 6** at the end of this chapter.

Main Bearing and Journal Inspection

1. Check the inside and outside surfaces of the bearing inserts for wear, bluish tint (burned), flaking, abrasion and scoring. If the bearings are good, they may be reused. If any insert is questionable, replace the entire set.

2. Measure the main bearing oil clearance. Clean the bearing surfaces of the crankshaft and the main bearing inserts.
3. Set the upper crankcase upside down on the workbench on wood blocks to prevent damage to the cylinder studs.
4. Install the existing inserts into the upper crankcase.
5. Install the crankshaft into the upper crankcase.
6. Place a strip of Plastigage over each main bearing journal parallel to the crankshaft.

> *NOTE*
> *Do not rotate the crankshaft while the Plastigage strips are in place.*

7. Install the existing bearing inserts into the lower crankcase.
8. Carefully turn the crankcase over and install it onto the upper crankcase.
9. Apply oil to the bolt threads and install bolts No. 1-10, **Figure 179**. Tighten them in the torque sequence shown in **Figure 179**. Tighten to 15-18 ft.-lb. (21-25 N•m).
10. Remove the bolts No. 1-10 in the reverse order of installation.
11. Measure the width of the flattened Plastigage according to manufacturer's instructions. Measure both ends of Plastigage strip (**Figure 180**). A difference of 0.001 in. (0.025 mm), or more, indicates a tapered journal. Confirm by measuring with a micrometer. New bearing clearance should be

0.0008-0.0024 in. (0.020-0.060 mm) and the service limit is 0.003 in. (0.08 mm).

12. If the bearing clearance is greater than specified, use the following steps for new bearing selection.

13. The crankshaft main journals are marked with letters "A", "B" or "C" (**Figure 181**). The exterior of the upper rear portion of the upper crankcase is also marked with a series of letters "A", "B" or "C" (**Figure 182**).

NOTE
The letter on the left-hand end relates to the bearing insert on the left-hand side and so on working across from left to right. Remember the left-hand side relates to the engine as it sits in the bike's frame, not as it sits on your workbench.

14. Select new bearings by cross-referencing the main journal letter (**Figure 181**) in the horizontal column of **Table 3** to the crankcase bearing letter (**Figure 182**) in the vertical column of **Table 3**. Where the 2 columns intersect, the new bearing insert color is indicated. **Table 4** gives the bearing color and thickness. Always replace a set of 10 at the same time.

15. After new bearings have been installed, recheck clearance comparing to the specifications given in **Table 6**.

ELECTRIC STARTER GEARS

The electric starter gears can be removed with the engine in the frame. This procedure is shown with the engine removed for clarity.

Removal/Installation

1. Place the bike on the centerstand.
2. Remove the right-hand side cover and disconnect the battery negative lead (**Figure 183**).
3. Remove the screws (**Figure 184**) securing the ignition cover and remove the cover and the gasket.
4. Remove the bolts (**Figure 185**) securing the left-hand crankcase cover and remove the cover and gasket.

NOTE
Don't lose the 2 locating dowels.

4

5. To remove the advancer unit, hold the hex spacer with a 24 mm wrench and remove the inner bolt with a 12 mm wrench (**Figure 186**). Remove the advancer unit.

6. Remove the starter clutch assembly (**Figure 187**).

7. Remove the starter driven gear and shaft (**Figure 188**).

8. Install by reversing these removal steps, noting the following.

9. When installing the advancer unit, index the pin on the backside of the advancer unit into the slot in the end of the crankshaft (**Figure 189**).

10. Hold the advancer unit in place and install the hex spacer. Align the 2 notches with the 2

tangs (**Figure 190**) on the advancer unit. Install the 12 mm bolt and tighten to 15-18 ft.-lb. (21-25 N•m) while securely holding the hexspacer.

CAUTION
To avoid internal damage to the advancer unit, securely hold the 24 mm spacer while tightening the inner bolt.

11. Install a new gasket (A, **Figure 191**) and 2 locating dowels (B, **Figure 191**).

Inspection

1. Inspect the condition of the gears on the starter clutch assembly and starter driven gear. Check for chipped or missing teeth. Look for uneven or excessive wear on the gear faces. Replace if necessary.

2. Check the rollers (**Figure 192**) in the starter clutch for uneven or excessive wear; replace as a set if any are bad.

3. To replace the rollers, remove the bolts (**Figure 193**) securing the starter clutch together. Apply Loctite Lock N' Seal to the threads prior to installing them and tighten to 19-22 ft.-lb. (26-30 N•m).

4. Check the condition of the bushing (A, **Figure 194**); if damaged, the starter gear must be replaced.

5. Measure the OD of the starter gear (B, **Figure 194**). The standard dimension is 1.664-1.665 in. (42.275-42.300 mm); replace if its dimension is 1.6636 in. (42.255 mm) or less.

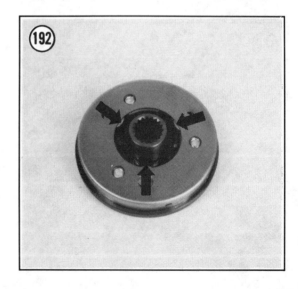

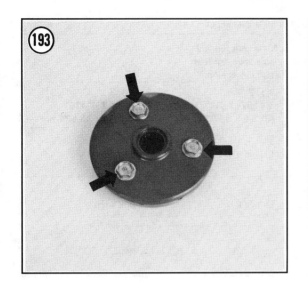

BREAK-IN

Following cylinder servicing (boring, honing, new rings, etc.) or major lower end work, the engine should be broken in just as though it were new. The performance and service life of the engine depend greatly on a careful and sensible break-in. For the first 500 miles (805 km), no more than one-third throttle should be used and speed should be varied as much as possible within the one-third throttle limit. Prolonged, steady running at one speed, no matter how moderate, is to be avoided, as is hard acceleration.

Following the first 500 miles (805 km), increasingly more throttle can be used, but full throttle should not be used until the motorcycle has covered at least 1,000 miles (1,600 km) and then it should be limited to short bursts until 1,500 miles (2,400 km) have been logged.

The mono-grade oils recommended for break-in and normal use provide a better bedding pattern for rings and cylinders than do multi-grade oils. As a result, piston ring and cylinder bore life are greatly increased. During this period, oil consumption will be higher than normal. It is therefore important to frequently check and correct the oil level. At no time, during break-in or later, should the oil level be allowed to drop below the bottom line on the dipstick; if the oil level is low, the oil will become overheated resulting in insufficient lubrication and increased wear.

500 Mile (805 km) Service

It is essential that oil and filter be changed after the first 500 miles (805 km). In addition, it is a good idea to change the oil and filter at the completion of break-in (about 1,500 miles/2,400 km) to ensure that all of the particles produced during break-in are removed from the lubrication system. The small added expense may be considered a smart investment that will pay off in increased engine life.

Tables are on the following pages.

TABLE 1 CONNECTING ROD BEARING SELECTION

| Connecting rod ID number and dimension | Crankpin journal size code number and dimension | | |
	No. 1 1.4170–1.4173 in. (35.992–35.600mm)	No. 2 1.4167–1.4170 in. (35.984–35.992mm)	No. 3 1.4163–1.4167 in. (35.975–35.984mm)
No. 1 1.5354–1.5357 in. (39.000–39.008mm)	Yellow (E)	Green (D)	Brown (C)
No. 2 1.5357–1.5360 in. (39.008–39.016mm)	Green (D)	Brown (C)	Black (B)
No. 3 1.5360–1.5364 in. (39.016–39.024mm)	Brown (C)	Black (B)	Blue (A)

TABLE 2 CONNECTING ROD BEARING THICKNESS

Color	Inches	Millimeters
Blue (A)	0.0591–0.0593	1.502–1.506
Black (B)	0.0590–0.0591	1.498–1.502
Brown (C)	0.0588–0.0590	1.494–1.498
Green (D)	0.0587–0.0588	1.490–1.494
Yellow (E)	0.0585–0.0587	1.486–1.490

TABLE 3 MAIN JOURNAL BEARING SELECTION

Main journal size code letter and dimension	Letter A 1.4170–1.4173 in. (35.992–36.000mm)	Letter B 1.4167–1.4170 in. (35.985–35.992mm)	Letter C 1.4163–1.4167 in. (35.975–35.984mm)
Crankcase ID code letter and dimension	Color Identification		
Letter A 1.5354–1.5357 in. (39.000–39.008mm)	Yellow (E)	Green (D)	Brown (C)
Letter B 1.5357–1.5360 in. (39.008–39.016mm)	Green (D)	Brown (C)	Black (B)
Letter C 1.5360–1.5364 in. (39.016–39.024mm)	Brown (C)	Black (B)	Blue (A)

TABLE 4 MAIN JOURNAL BEARING THICKNESS

Color	Inches	Millimeters
Black (A)	0.0590–0.0591	1.498–1.502
Brown (B)	0.0588–0.0590	1.494–1.498
Green (C)	0.0587–0.0588	1.490–1.494
Yellow (D)	0.0585–0.0587	1.486–1.490
Blue (E)	0.0591–0.0593	1.502–1.506

TABLE 5 ENGINE TORQUE SPECIFICATIONS

Item	Foot-pounds (ft.-lb.)	Newton meters (N·m)
Engine mounting bolts		
8mm	13–18	18–25
10mm	22–29	30–40
12mm	40–47	55–65
Drive sprocket	24–27	33–37
Cylinder head cap nuts	26–29	36–40
Camshaft bearing cap bolts	9–12	12–16
Camshaft sprocket bolts	13–15	18–20
Rod bearing cap nuts	22–25	30–34
Ignition advance 12mm bolts	15–18	21–25
Oil pressure sending unit	11–14	15–19
Oil pan bolts	7–10	10–14
Primary shaft lockbolt	60–72	80–100
Primary chain tensioner base bolts	6–9	8–12
Crankcase bolts		
6mm	7–10	10–14
8mm	15–18	21–25
10mm	33–36	45–50
Starter clutch assembly bolts	19–22	26–30

TABLE 6 ENGINE SPECIFICATIONS

Item	Specifications	Wear Limit
General		
Number of cylinders	4	
Bore and stroke	2.44 × 2.44 in. (62.0 × 62.0mm)	
Displacement	45.7 cu.in. (749cc)	
Compression ratio	9.0 to 1	
Compression pressure	170 ± 14 psi (12 ± 1.0 kg/cm²)	
Engine weight	195 lb. (88.5 kg)	
Cylinders		
Bore	2.4409–2.4413 in. (62.000–62.010mm)	2.445 in. (62.10mm)
Out-of-round	— — — —	0.004 in. (0.10mm)
Cylinder/piston clearance	— — — —	0.004 in. (0.10mm)
Pistons		
Diameter	2.439–2.440 in. (61.95–61.98mm)	2.437 in. (61.90mm)
Clearance in bore	— — — —	0.004 in. (0.10mm)
Wrist pin bore	0.5906–0.5909 in. (15.002–15.008mm)	0.593 in. (15.05mm)
Wrist pin outer diameter	0.5903–0.5906 in. (14.994–15.000mm)	0.590 in. (14.98mm)
Piston Rings		
Number per cylinder		
Compression	2	
Oil control	1	

(continued)

Table 6   ENGINE SPECIFICATIONS (continued)

Item	Specifications	Wear Limit
Ring end gap		
Top and second	0.004–0.012 in. (0.10–0.30mm)	0.020 in. (0.5mm)
Oil (side rail)	0.012–0.035 in. (0.3–0.9mm)	0.043 in. (1.1mm)
Ring side clearance		
Top	0.0012–0.0026 in. (0.030–0.065mm)	0.004 in. (0.09mm)
Second	0.0010–0.0022 in. (0.025–0.055mm)	0.004 in. (0.09mm)
Connecting Rod		
Small end inner diameter	0.5912–0.5919 in. (15.016–15.034mm)	0.593 in. (15.07mm)
Crankshaft		
Main bearing oil clearance	0.0008–0.0024 in. (0.020–0.060mm)	0.003 in. (0.08mm)
Connecting rod oil clearance	0.0008–0.0024 in. (0.020–0.060mm)	0.003 in. (0.08mm)
Connecting rod big end side clearance	0.0020–0.008 in. (0.05–0.20mm)	0.01 in. (0.3mm)
Camshaft		
Valve timing		
Intake	Opens 5° BTDC @ 1mm lift, closes 35° ABDC	
Exhaust	Opens 35° BBDC @ 1mm lift, closes 5° ATDC	
Cam lobe height		
Intake	1.4567–1.4630 in. (37.000–37.160mm)	1.45 in. (36.9mm)
Exhaust	1.4763–1.4827 in. (37.500–37.660mm)	1.47 in. (37.4mm)
Runout limit	— — —	0.002 in. (0.05mm)
Camshaft to bearing cap oil clearance		
Cap letter:		
A,E,F,L	0.0016–0.0032 in. (0.040–0.082mm)	0.0051 in. (0.13mm)
Tachometer gear,D,G,K	0.0024–0.0043 in. (0.062–0.109mm)	0.0063 in. (0.16mm)
B,C,H,J	0.0033–0.0055 in. (0.085–0.139mm)	0.0075 in. (0.19mm)
Camshaft Chain Length		
Intake	6.917–6.926 in. (175.70–175.92mm)	6.97 in. (177mm)
Exhaust	12.167–12.179 in. (309.05–309.35mm)	12.28 in. (311.8mm)
Valves		
Valve stem outer diameter		
Intake	0.2156–0.2161 in. (5.475–5.490mm)	0.215 in. (5.47mm)
Exhaust	0.2148–0.2154 in. (5.455–5.470mm)	0.214 in. (5.44mm)

(continued)

Table 6   ENGINE SPECIFICATIONS (continued)

Item	Specifications	Wear Limit
Valve guide inner diameter		
Intake and exhaust	0.2165–0.2171 in. (5.500–5.515mm)	0.218 in. (5.54mm)
Stem to guide clearance		
Intake	— — — —	0.003 in. (0.07mm)
Exhaust	— — — —	0.004 in. (0.09mm)
Valve seat width	0.039–0.050 in. (0.99–1.27mm)	0.06 in. (1.5mm)
Valve springs		
Free length		
Outer—intake and exhaust	1.73 in. (43.9mm)	1.67 in. (42.5mm)
Inner—intake and exhaust	1.60 in. (40.7mm)	1.57 in. (39.8mm)
Length under load		
Outer—intake and exhaust	1.48 in. @ 28–32 lbs. (37.5mm @ 13–14 kg)	1.48 in. @ 26.5 lbs. (37.5mm @ 12.0 kg)
Inner—intake and exhaust	1.36 in. @ 14–17 lbs. (34.5mm @ 6.8 kg)	1.36 in. @ 13 lbs. (34.5mm @ 6.0 kg)
Valve lifters		
Valve lifter outer diameter	1.1013–1.1021 in. (27.972–27.993mm)	1.101 in. (27.96mm)
Valve lifter bore in cylinder head	1.1024–1.1030 in. (28.000–28.016mm)	1.104 in. (28.04mm)

4

CLUTCH AND TRANSMISSION

CLUTCH

The clutch in the Honda CB750 is a wet multiplate type which operates immersed in the engine oil. It is mounted on the right-hand end of the transmission main shaft. The inner clutch hub is splined to the main shaft and the outer hub can rotate freely on the main shaft. The outer hub is geared to the primary shaft.

The clutch release mechanism is mounted inside the clutch cover. The mechanism consists of a lifter shaft, operated by the clutch cable and adjusting arm. Pulling the clutch lever and cable pivots the lifter shaft which in turn raises the adjusting arm. The arm pushes in on the lifter guide and the lifter plate disengages the clutch mechanism.

Refer to **Table 1** for all clutch torque specifications. **Tables 1-4** are located at the end of this chapter.

Refer to **Figure 1** for the clutch assembly and **Figure 2** for the clutch lifter mechanism.

Removal/Disassembly

1. Place the bike on the centerstand.
2. Drain the engine oil as described under *Changing Engine Oil and Filter* in Chapter Three.
3. Slacken the clutch cable at the hand lever (**Figure 3**) and remove the cable.

4. Loosen the locknut, (A, **Figure 4**) at the lower adjuster and remove the cable from the lever.
5. Remove the rear brake lever (B, **Figure 4**).
6. Remove the bolts (**Figure 5**) securing the clutch cover and remove the cover and gasket. Don't lose the 2 locating dowels.

NOTE
Figures 5-30 are shown with the engine removed and partially disassembled. It is not necessary to do so for clutch removal.

7. Remove the clutch bolts (**Figure 6**) securing the lifter plate in a crisscross pattern.
8. Remove the lifter plate and the clutch springs (**Figure 7**).
9. Straighten out the locking tab (**Figure 8**) on the clutch nut washer.
10. Remove the clutch nut, lockwasher and washer. To keep the clutch housing from turning, hold it with a strap wrench (**Figure 9**).

NOTE
Nut removal requires a special tool available from a Honda dealer (Locknut Wrench part No. 07716-0020100); refer to Figure 10.

11. Remove the clutch center, plates, discs and pressure plate (**Figure 11**).

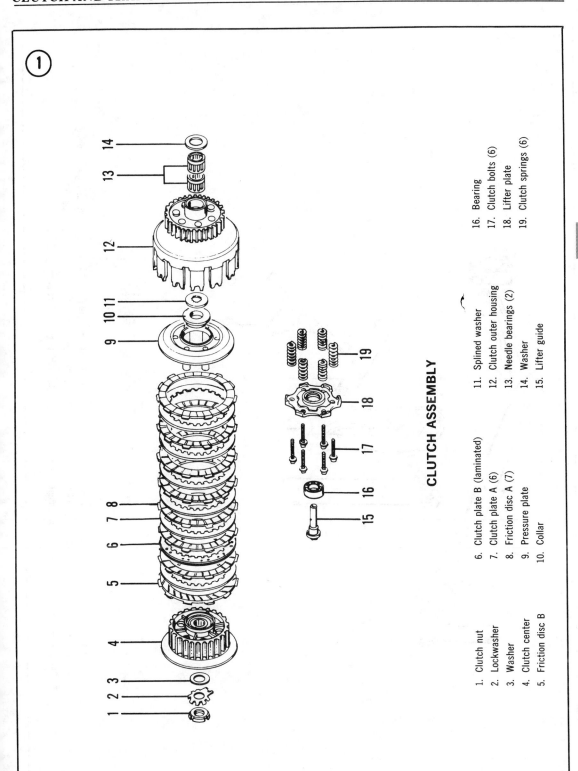

CLUTCH ASSEMBLY

1. Clutch nut
2. Lockwasher
3. Washer
4. Clutch center
5. Friction disc B
6. Clutch plate B (laminated)
7. Clutch plate A (6)
8. Friction disc A (7)
9. Pressure plate
10. Collar
11. Splined washer
12. Clutch outer housing
13. Needle bearings (2)
14. Washer
15. Lifter guide
16. Bearing
17. Clutch bolts (6)
18. Lifter plate
19. Clutch springs (6)

5

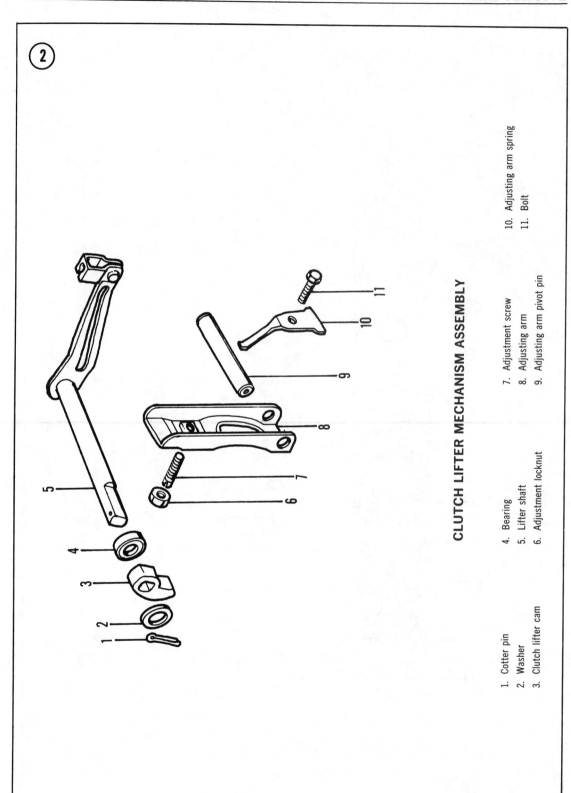

CLUTCH LIFTER MECHANISM ASSEMBLY

1. Cotter pin
2. Washer
3. Clutch lifter cam
4. Bearing
5. Lifter shaft
6. Adjustment locknut
7. Adjustment screw
8. Adjusting arm
9. Adjusting arm pivot pin
10. Adjusting arm spring
11. Bolt

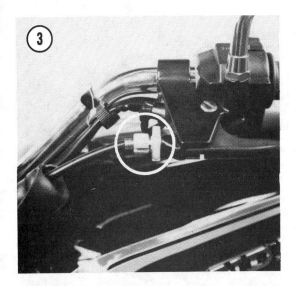

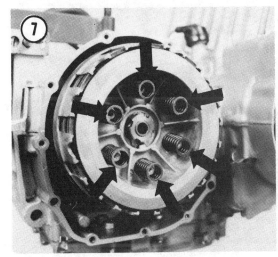

5

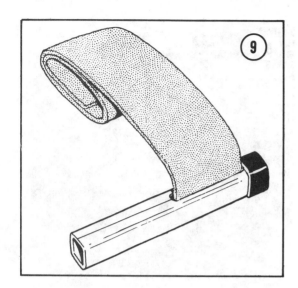

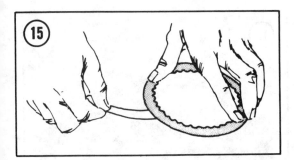

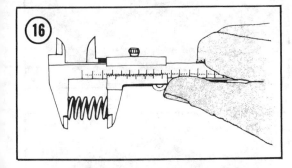

NOTE
The clutch outer housing will not come off with these parts as a splined washer is holding it in place on the transmission shaft.

12. Remove the collar (**Figure 12**), splined washer (**Figure 13**), clutch outer housing and washer from the transmission main shaft.

Inspection

Refer to **Table 2** for clutch specifications.

1. Clean all clutch parts in petroleum-based solvent such as kerosene and thoroughly dry with compressed air.

2. Measure the thickness of each friction disc at several places around the disc as shown in **Figure 14**. A new friction disc measures 0.146-0.153 in. (3.7-3.88 mm). Replace any that measure 0.13 in. (3.4 mm) or less.

NOTE
These dimensions relate both to the 7 friction discs "A" and the one friction disc "B".

3. Check the clutch plates for warpage as shown in **Figure 15**. Replace any that are warped more than 0.012 in. (0.3 mm).

4. Measure the free length of each clutch spring as shown in **Figure 16**. Replace all springs if any are 1.29 in. (32.8 mm) or less.

5. Inspect the teeth of the outer housing (**Figure 17**) for damage. Remove any small nicks on the gear teeth with an oilstone. If damage is severe, the housing must be replaced. Also check the teeth on the driven gear (**Figure 18**); it may also need replacing.

6. Inspect the condition of the 2 needle bearings (**Figure 19**) within the clutch outer housing. Make sure they rotate smoothly with no signs of wear; replace if necessary.

7. Inspect the condition of the slots in the clutch outer housing (**Figure 20**) for cracks, nicks or galling where they come in contact

with the friction disc tabs. If any severe damage is evident, the housing must be replaced.

8. Inspect the condition of the inner splines (A, **Figure 21**) and outer grooves (B, **Figure 21**) of the clutch center. Replace if necessary.

9. Check the rotation of the ball bearing in the lifter plate (**Figure 22**). Make sure it rotates smoothly; replace if necessary.

10. Check the movement of the clutch adjuster arm and lifter shaft in the clutch cover (**Figure 23**). It must operate smoothly or be replaced.

Assembly/Installation

1. Install the clutch friction disc "B" (**Figure 24**) onto the clutch center.

> *CAUTION*
> *It must be installed as shown in **Figure 24** and **Figure 25** to prevent clutch damage and improper clutch operation.*

2. Install a clutch plate "A," friction disc "A" and laminated plate "B" (**Figure 26**). Continue to install a friction disc "A," then clutch plate, and alternate them until all are installed.

> *CAUTION*
> *If either or both friction discs and clutch plates have been replaced with new ones, apply new engine oil to all surfaces to avoid having the clutch lock up when used for the first time.*

3. Align the teeth of the split drive gear with the crankcase split line (**Figure 27**). This is necessary for the installation of the clutch outer housing in Step 5.

> *NOTE*
> *The drive gear is split; the outer thin gear is spring-loaded and has one more tooth than the main gear. This helps to reduce noise and backlash.*

4. Install the washer (**Figure 28**) onto the transmission main shaft.

5. Install the clutch outer housing onto the shaft. The teeth must mesh properly with the split drive gear for the housing to be installed onto the shaft completely. Push it on until it stops.

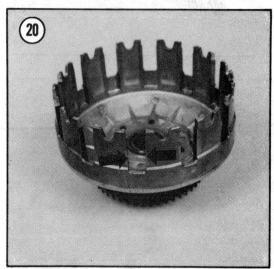

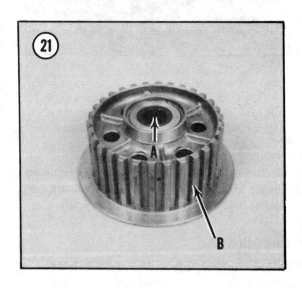

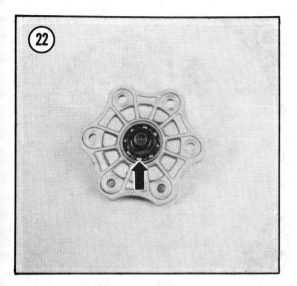

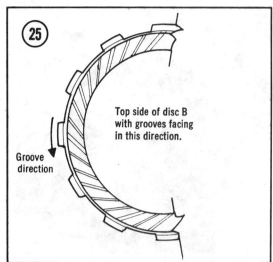

Top side of disc B with grooves facing in this direction.

Groove direction

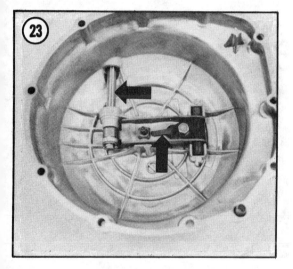

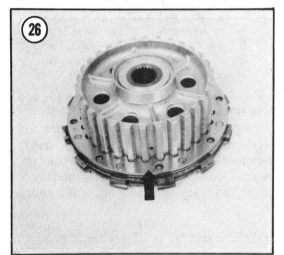

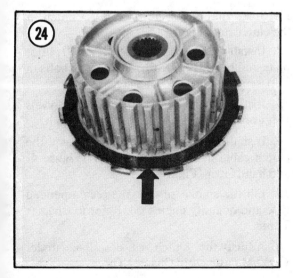

5

CAUTION
Do not force it on if it will not go on easily. Pull the housing back off and repeat Step 3. If you still have trouble, try moving the housing in a slight back and forth rotating motion while pushing on it.

6. Install the splined washer (**Figure 13**) and collar (**Figure 12**).

7. Install the clutch center, clutch plates and friction discs assembly (components assembled in Steps 1 and 2). Push the assembly on slowly while aligning the tabs of the friction discs into the slots in the clutch outer housing.

NOTE
Friction disc "B," installed in Step 1, has wider tabs and will only fit into the outermost section of the clutch outer housing. This is a cross-check for correct location of disc "B" onto the clutch center.

8. Install the washer (**Figure 29**) with the dished side facing toward the outside. Some models may have the word "OUTSIDE" stamped on it; this side must face toward the outside.

9. Install the lockwasher; make sure it is positioned into the locating bar (**Figure 30**). If it does not sit back far enough to properly engage, tap it lightly with a screwdriver blade and hammer. It must lock against the bar to lock properly.

10. Install the clutch nut and tighten it to 33-40 ft.-lb. (45-55 N•m). Use the same tool used for removal (**Figure 10**).

11. Stake the lockwasher tab into a notch in the clutch nut (**Figure 8**).

12. Install the clutch springs (**Figure 7**), lifter plate and bolts (**Figure 6**). Tighten the bolts in a crisscross pattern in 2 or 3 stages.

13. Install a new gasket and 2 locating dowels (**Figure 31**) to the clutch cover and install it.

14. Install the rear brake lever and install the clutch cable in the lower adjuster (**Figure 4**) and hand lever (**Figure 3**).

15. Fill the crankcase with the recommended type and quantity engine oil. Refer to Chapter Three.

16. Adjust the clutch as described under *Clutch Adjustment* in Chapter Three.

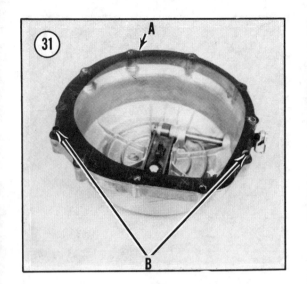

CLUTCH CABLE

Removal/Installation

In time, the cable will stretch to the point where it is no longer useful and will have to be replaced.

1. Pull back on the rubber protective boot (**Figure 32**) covering the cable adjusters.

2. Loosen the locknut and adjuster nut at the hand lever (**Figure 33**) and remove the cable from the lever.

3. Remove the right- and left-hand side covers and fuel tank (**Figure 34**).

4. At the lower adjuster, loosen the locknut (**Figure 35**) and remove the cable from the lever.

> *NOTE*
> *Prior to removing the cable, make a drawing (or take a Polaroid picture) of the cable routing through the frame. It is very easy to forget how it was, once it has been removed. Replace it exactly as it was, avoiding any sharp turns.*

5. Remove the cable from the frame and replace it with a new one.

6. Route the new cable through the loop (**Figure 36**) on the front fork and through the frame as shown in **Figure 37**.

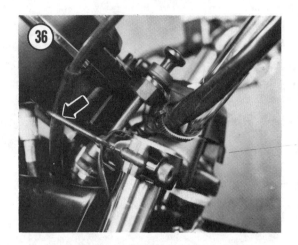

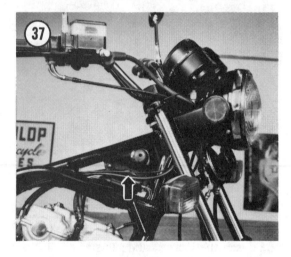

7. Attach the cable at both ends and adjust as described under *Clutch Adjustment* in Chapter Three.

DRIVE SPROCKET

Removal/Installation

1. Place the bike on the centerstand.
2. Remove the left-hand side cover.
3. Remove the shift lever and left-hand rear crankcase cover (**Figure 38**).
4. Remove the rear axle nut cotter pin and loosen the axle nut (A, **Figure 39**).
5. Loosen the locknuts and the drive chain adjusters (B, **Figure 39**) to allow slack in the drive chain.
6. Have an assistant apply the rear brake to keep the drive chain taut and keep the drive sprocket from turning. Remove the bolt, washer and O-ring (**Figure 40**).

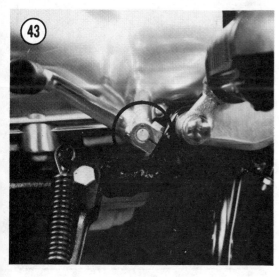

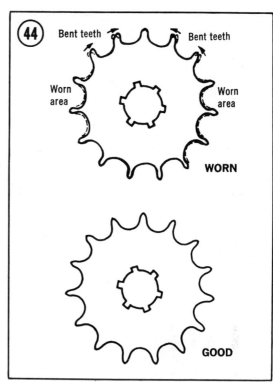

7. Move the rear wheel slightly forward and remove the drive chain from the sprocket (**Figure 41**) and remove the drive sprocket.

> *WARNING*
> *The drive chain is manufactured as a continuous closed loop with no master link. Do not cut it with a chain cutter as it will result in future chain failure and possible loss of control under riding conditions.*

8. Installation is the reverse of these removal steps, noting the following.

9. Be sure to install the oil seal O-ring on the bolt (**Figure 42**).

10. Tighten the bolt to 24-27 ft.-lb. (33-37 N•m).

11. Align the punch marks (**Figure 43**) on the shift lever and shaft when installing it.

12. Adjust the drive chain as described under *Drive Chain Adjustment* in Chapter Three.

Inspection

Inspect the teeth of the sprocket. If the teeth are visibly worn (**Figure 44**), replace the sprocket with a new one.

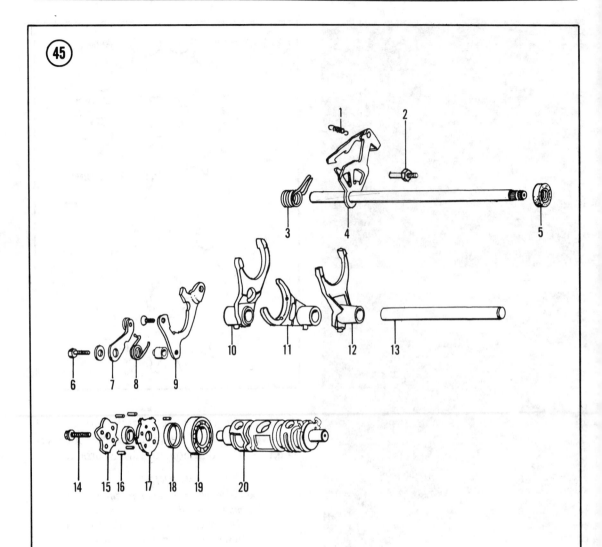

GEARSHIFT DRUM AND FORKS

1. Shift arm return spring
2. Spindle assembly stopper
3. Gearshift return spring
4. Gearshift spindle assembly
5. Oil seal
6. Shift pawl bolt
7. Shift pawl
8. Return spring
9. Shift drum bearing retainer
10. Left-hand shift fork
11. Center shift fork
12. Right-hand shift fork
13. Shift fork shaft
14. Bolt
15. Shift drum cam plate
16. Pin (5)
17. Cam plate base plate
18. Collar
19. Shift drum bearing
20. Shift drum

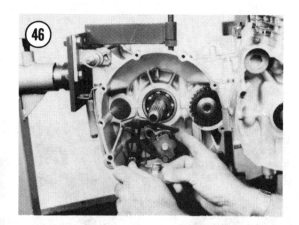

If the sprocket requires replacement, the drive chain is probably worn also. Refer to *Drive Chain Cleaning, Inspection and Lubrication* in Chapter Three.

SHIFTING MECHANISM

Refer to **Figure 45** for this procedure.

Removal

1. Remove the clutch assembly as described under *Clutch Removal/Disassembly* in this chapter.

> *NOTE*
> *This procedure is shown with the engine removed and partially disassembled for clarity. Do not remove it.*

2. Disengage the shift arm from the shift drum (**Figure 46**) and pull the gear shift spindle assembly out.
3. Remove the bolt (A, **Figure 47**) securing the shift pawl and remove it and the spring.

4. Remove the bolt (B, **Figure 47**) securing the shift drum cam plate. Remove the cam plate, pins, cam plate base plate, collar and pin.

Installation

1. Install the collar into the shift drum.
2. Align the pin on the shift drum with the hole on the cam plate base plate and install it.
3. Insert the pins into the base plate and install the cam plate. Install the bolt and tighten securely.
4. Position the shift pawl and return spring and install the bolt. Slowly tighten the bolt part way in; correctly position the shift pawl and tighten the bolt the rest of the way.
5. Install the gearshift spindle assembly.
6. Temporarily install the shift lever on the left-hand side and shift the transmission through all 5 gears to make sure it operates smoothly and properly.
7. Install the clutch assembly as described under *Clutch Assembly/Installation* in this chapter.

TRANSMISSION

The crankcase must be disassembled to gain access to the transmission components.

Specifications for all transmission components are listed in **Table 3**.

Refer to **Table 1** for transmission torque specifications.

Removal/Installation

1. Perform Steps 1-6 of *Crankcase Disassembly* in Chapter Four.
2. Remove the countershaft assembly (**Figure 48**).
3. Remove the main shaft assembly (**Figure 49**).
4. Install by reversing these removal steps, noting the following.

> *NOTE*
> *Prior to installing any components, coat all bearing surfaces with assembly oil.*

5. Install the main shaft and countershaft assemblies. Make sure the locating pin (A, **Figure 50**) is in position in the upper crankcase.

6. Make sure the bearing locating 1/2 circlips (B, **Figure 50**) are in place. Each shaft has one on the large bearing.

7. Make sure the oil seal on the countershaft is seated correctly in the upper crankcase (**Figure 51**).

Main Shaft Disassembly/Assembly

Refer to **Figure 52** for this procedure.

1. Slide off the bearing, washer, the 2nd gear and thrust washer (**Figure 53**).

2. Remove the 5th gear, the 5th gear bushing and the splined washer (**Figure 54**).

3. Remove the circlip and slide off the 3rd gear (**Figure 55**).

4. Remove the circlip, splined washer and slide off the 4th gear (**Figure 56**).

5. If necessary, remove the ballbearing (**Figure 57**) from the shaft.

6. Clean all parts in cleaning solvent and thoroughly dry.

7. Check each gear for excessive wear, burrs, pitting, or chipped or missing teeth. Make sure the lugs on the ends of gears are in good condition (**Figure 58**).

NOTE
Defective gears should be replaced, and it is a good idea to replace the mating gear on the countershaft even though it may not show as much wear or damage.

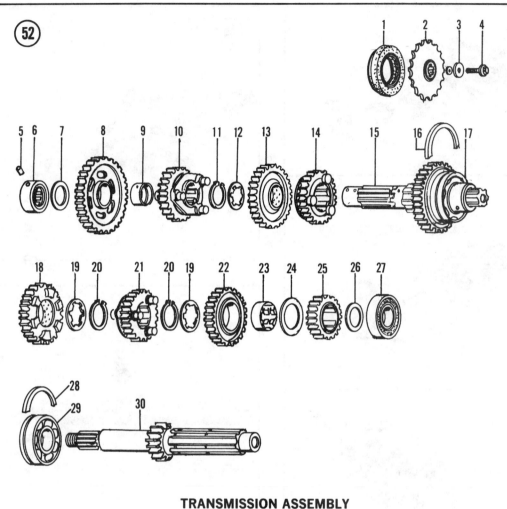

TRANSMISSION ASSEMBLY

1. Oil seal
2. Drive sprocket
3. Washer
4. Drive sprocket bolt
5. Locating dowel
6. Bearing and outer race
7. Washer
8. Countershaft first gear
9. Countershaft first gear spacer
10. Countershaft fourth gear
11. Circlip
12. Splined washer
13. Countershaft third gear
14. Countershaft fifth gear
15. Countershaft (including second gear)
16. Half circlip
17. Bearing and outer race
18. Main shaft fourth gear
19. Splined washer
20. Circlip
21. Main shaft third gear
22. Main shaft fifth gear
23. Main shaft fifth gear spacer
24. Thrust washer
25. Main shaft second gear
26. Washer
27. Bearing
28. Half circlip
29. Bearing
30. Main shaft (including first gear)

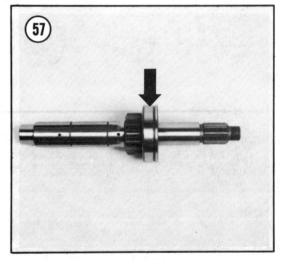

NOTE
*The 1st gear is part of the main shaft,
therefore, if the gear is defective the shaft
must be replaced.*

8. Make sure that all gears slide smoothly on
the main shaft splines.

9. Check the condition of the bearing. Make
sure it rotates smoothly (**Figure 59**) with no
signs of wear or damage. Replace if necessary.

10. Measure the inside and outside diameter
of the 5th gear bushing (A, **Figure 60**) and the
inside diameter of the 5th gear (B, **Figure 60**).
Compare with dimensions given in **Table 3**.
Replace any worn parts.

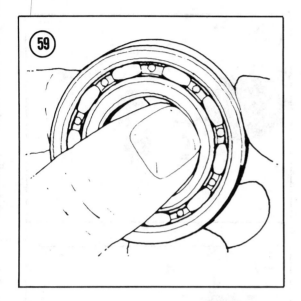

11. Measure the outside diameter of the shaft at the location of the 5th gear bushing (**Figure 61**). Compare with dimension given in **Table 3**. Replace if worn.

12. Assemble by reversing these disassembly steps. Refer to **Figure 62** for correct placement of the gears. Make sure all circlips are seated correctly in the main shaft grooves.

13. Be sure to install the bearing with the sealed side facing out (**Figure 63**). Align the oil hole in the 5th gear bushing with the hole in the main shaft.

14. Make sure each gear engages properly with the adjoining gears where applicable.

Countershaft Disassembly/Assembly

Refer to **Figure 52** for this procedure.

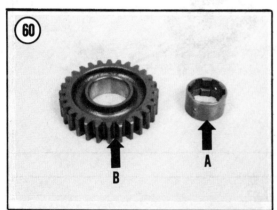

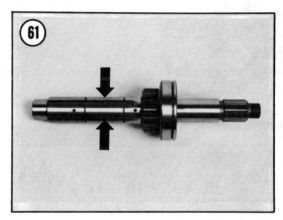

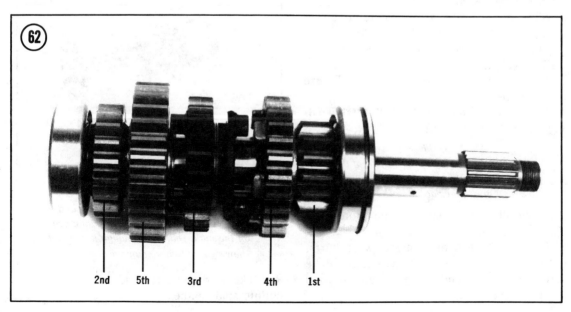

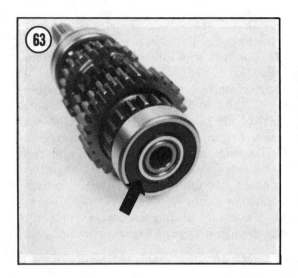

1. Slide off the outer bearing race, needle bearing and the washer (**Figure 64**).

2. Slide off the 1st gear and the 1st gear bushing (**Figure 65**).

3. Slide off the 4th gear and remove the circlip and splined washer (**Figure 66**).

4. Slide off the 3rd gear and the 3rd gear bushing (**Figure 67**).

5. Carefully remove the oil seal (A, **Figure 68**) from the shaft.

6. If necessary, remove the ball bearing (B, **Figure 68**) from the shaft.

> NOTE
> *The 2nd gear (C, **Figure 68**) is part of the shaft and cannot be removed. If damaged, the shaft must be replaced.*

7. Clean all parts in solvent and thoroughly dry.

8. Check each gear for excessive wear, burrs, pitting, or chipped or missing teeth. Make sure the lugs on ends of gears are in good condition (**Figure 69**).

> NOTE
> *Defective gears should be replaced, and it is a good idea to replace the mating gear on the main shaft even though it may not show signs of wear or damage.*

9. Make sure all gears slide smoothly on the countershaft splines.

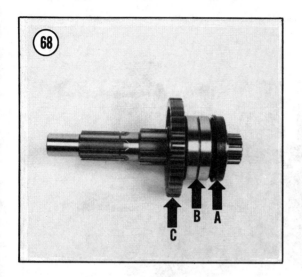

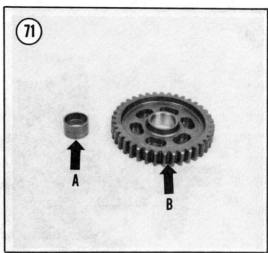

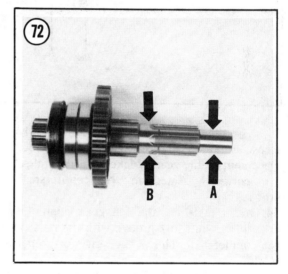

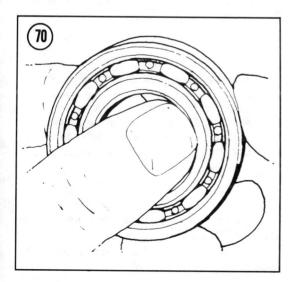

10. Check the condition of the bearing. Make sure it rotates smoothly (**Figure 70**) with no signs of wear or damage. Replace it if necessary.

11. Measure the inside and outside diameter of the 3rd gear bushing (A, **Figure 71**) and the inside diameter of the 3rd gear (B, **Figure 71**). Compare with the dimensions given in **Table 3** at the end of this chapter. Replace any worn parts.

12. Measure the outside diameter of the shaft at the location of the 1st gear bushing (A, **Figure 72**) and 3rd gear bushing (B, **Figure 72**). Compare with dimensions give in **Table 3**. Replace if worn.

73

2nd   5th   3rd   4th   1st

13. Assemble by reversing these disassembly steps. Refer to **Figure 73** for the correct placement of the gears. Make sure all circlips are correctly seated in the countershaft grooves.

14. When installing the 5th gear, align the hole in the shift fork groove with the hole in the countershaft. This is necessary for proper oil flow.

15. If the oil seal (A, **Figure 68**) is replaced, be sure to replace it with one having the embossed numbers "40 x 62 x 13.5" only. Slide it on until it seats up against the right-hand bearing.

16. Make sure each gear engages properly with the adjoining gear where applicable.

GEARSHIFT DRUM AND FORKS

Refer to **Figure 74** for this procedure.

Removal

1. Remove the engine as described under *Engine Removal/Installation* in Chapter Four.

2. Remove the shift mechanism as described in this chapter.

3. Separate the crankcases and remove the transmission components as described under *Transmission Removal/Installation* in this chapter.

4. Withdraw the shift fork shaft (**Figure 75**) and remove the shift forks (**Figure 76**).

5. Remove the bolt (A, **Figure 77**) securing the shift pawl and remove it.

6. Remove the Phillips screw (B, **Figure 77**) and the spindle assembly stopper bolt (C, **Figure 77**).

NOTE
This screw and bolt had a locking agent applied to their threads at time of manufacture and will be difficult to remove the first time. It is suggested that the Phillips screw be removed with an impact driver and suitable size bit to prevent damage to the screw head.

7. Remove the shift drum bearing stopper plate (D, **Figure 77**).

8. Remove the shift drum out through the right-hand side (**Figure 78**).

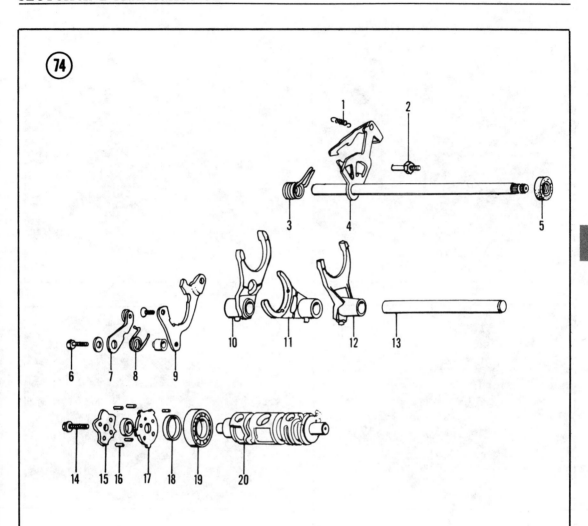

GEARSHIFT DRUM AND FORKS

1. Shift arm return spring
2. Spindle assembly stopper
3. Gearshift return spring
4. Gearshift spindle assembly
5. Oil seal
6. Shift pawl bolt
7. Shift pawl
8. Return spring
9. Shift drum bearing retainer
10. Left-hand shift fork
11. Center shift fork
12. Right-hand shift fork
13. Shift fork shaft
14. Bolt
15. Shift drum cam plate
16. Pin (5)
17. Cam plate base plate
18. Collar
19. Shift drum bearing
20. Shift drum

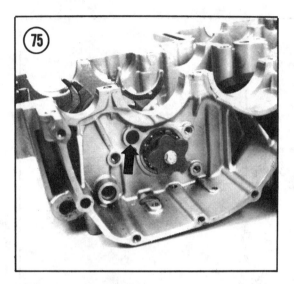

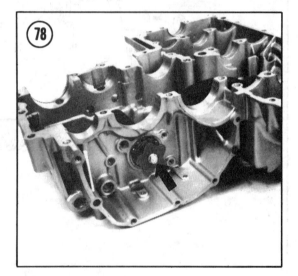

CAUTION
Do not damage the neutral indicator plate
*(**Figure 79**) on the left-hand end of the*
shift drum during removal.

Inspection

Refer to **Table 4** for the shift fork and shaft
specifications.

1. Inspect each shift fork for signs of wear or
cracking. Make sure the forks slide smoothly
on their respective shafts. Make sure the
shafts are not bent. See **Figure 80**.

NOTE
Check for any arc-shaped wear or burned
*marks on the shift forks (**Figure 81**). If*

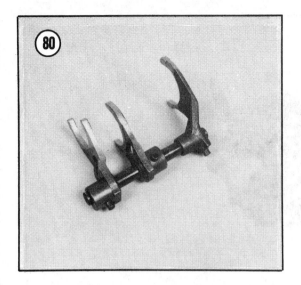

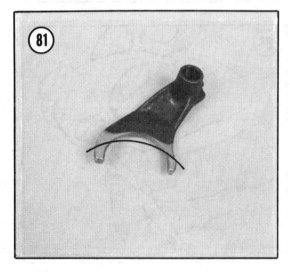

this is apparent, the shift fork has come in contact with the gear, indicating that the fingers are worn beyond use and the fork must be replaced.

2. Check grooves in the shift drum (**Figure 82**) for wear or roughness.

NOTE
The shift drum is dark in color due to a manufacturing hardening process. It is not caused by a lack of oil pressure or excessive engine heat.

3. Check the shift drum bearing (A, **Figure 83**). Make sure it operates smoothly with no signs of wear or damage.

4. Check the cam pin followers in each shift fork. They should fit snugly but not too tight. Check the end that rides in the shift drum for wear or burrs. Replace as necessary.

5. Check the stopper plate for wear (B, **Figure 83**); replace as necessary.

6. Measure the inside diameter of the shift forks with an inside micrometer (**Figure 84**). Replace the ones worn beyond the wear limits given in **Table 4**.

7. Measure the width of the gearshift fingers with a micrometer (**Figure 85**). Replace the ones worn beyond the wear limit given in **Table 4**.

8. Measure the outside diameter of the shift fork shaft with a micrometer. Replace if worn beyond the wear limits given in **Table 4**.

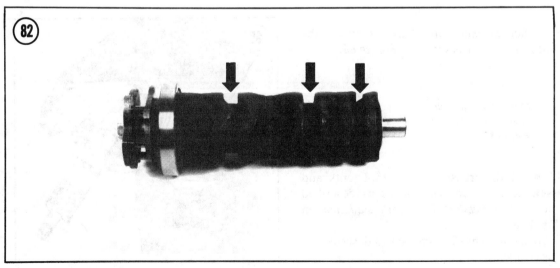

9. Inspect the condition of all bearing surfaces in the lower crankcase where the shift fork shaft and shift drum ride. Check for scoring or scratches.

Installation

1. Coat all bearing surfaces with assembly oil.
2. Install the shift drum and bearing stopper plate.

> *NOTE*
> *Apply Loctite Lock N' Seal to the threads of the screw and bolt prior to installation. Stake the side of the screw head with a punch after final tightening.*

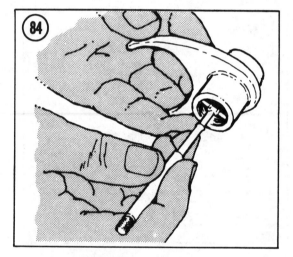

3. Install the shift fork shaft and install the shift forks onto it as shown in **Figure 86**.

> *NOTE*
> *Make sure the guide pins are properly meshed into the shift drum as shown in* ***Figure 87***.

4. Install the transmission components and assemble the crankcase halves as described under *Transmission Removal/Installation* in this chapter.
5. Install the shift mechanism as described in this chapter.

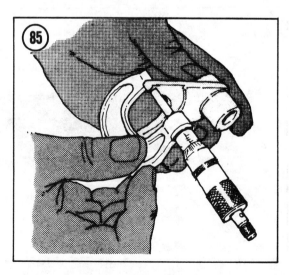

Tables are on the following pages.

TABLE 1 CLUTCH AND TRANSMISSION TORQUE SPECIFICATIONS

Item	Foot-Pounds (ft.-lb.)	Newton Meters (N·m)
Clutch locknut	33–40	45–55
Drive sprocket bolt	24–27	33–37
Shift pedal bolt	6–9	8–12

TABLE 2 CLUTCH SPECIFICATIONS

Item	Specification	Wear Limit
Lever free play (at tip)	⅜–¾ in. (10–20mm)	— — — —
Clutch spring free length	1.35 in. (34.2mm)	1.29 in. (32.8mm)
Friction disc thickness (Disc "A" and "B")	0.146–0.153 in. (3.72–3.88mm)	0.13 in. (3.4mm)
Metal plate warpage	— — — —	0.012 in. (0.3mm)

TABLE 3 TRANSMISSION SPECIFICATIONS

Item	Specification	Wear Limit
Gear backlash	0.0009–0.0029 in. (0.024–0.074mm)	0.005 in.(0.12mm)
Gear I.D./Mainshaft		
4th gear	1.1031–1.1040 in. (28.020–28.041mm)	1.105 in.(28.06mm)
5th gear	1.2215–1.2224 in. (31.025–31.050mm)	1.223 in.(31.07mm)
Gear I.D./Countershaft		
1st gear	0.9843–0.9851 in. (25.000–25.021mm)	0.987 in.(25.06mm)
3rd gear	1.1031–1.1040 in. (28.020–28.041mm)	1.105 in.(28.07mm)
Gear bushing		
Mainshaft 5th gear O.D.	1.2185–1.2195 in. (30.950–30.975mm)	1.218 in.(30.93mm)
Countershaft 1st gear O.D.	0.9826–0.9835 in. (24.959–24.980mm)	0.981 in.(24.93mm)
Countershaft 1st gear I.D.	0.8661–0.8670 in. (22.000–22.021mm)	0.869 in.(22.06mm)
Mainshaft O.D. at 4th gear	1.1007–1.1016 in. (27.959–27.980mm)	1.100 in.(27.93mm)
Countershaft O.D. At 1st gear bushing	0.8656–0.8661 in. (21.987–22.000mm)	0.863 in.(21.93mm)
Countershaft O.D. At 3rd gear	1.1007–1.1016 in. (27.959–27.980mm)	1.100 in.(27.93mm)
Gear to shaft or bushing clearance		
Mainshaft 4th gear to shaft	— — — —	0.004 in.(0.10mm)
Mainshaft 5th gear to bushing	— — — —	0.005 in.(0.12mm)
Countershaft 1st gear to bushing	— — — —	0.004 in.(0.10mm)
Countershaft 1st gear bushing to shaft	— — — —	0.004 in.(0.10mm)
Countershaft 3rd gear to shaft	— — — —	0.004 in.(0.10mm)

TABLE 4 SHIFT FORK AND SHAFT SPECIFICATIONS

Item	Specification	Wear Limit
Shift fork I.D. Center, left, and right	0.5118–0.5125 in. (13.000–13.018mm)	0.513 in.(13.04mm)
Shift fork finger thickness	0.253–0.256 in. (6.43–6.50mm)	0.24 in.(6.1mm)
Shift fork shaft	0.5104–0.5112 in. (12.966–12.984mm)	0.508 in.(12.90mm)

5

CHAPTER SIX

FUEL AND EXHAUST SYSTEMS

The fuel system consists of the fuel tank, shutoff valve, fuel filter, 4 Keihin constant velocity carburetors and an air cleaner.

The exhaust system consists of either 4 exhaust pipes and 4 mufflers or 4 exhaust pipes, 2 collectors and 2 mufflers, depending on the model.

This chapter includes service procedures for all parts of the fuel and exhaust systems. **Table 1** is at the end of the chapter.

AIR CLEANER

The air cleaner must be cleaned every 4,000 miles (6,400 km) or more frequently in dusty areas.

Service the air cleaner element as described under *Air Cleaner* in Chapter Three.

CARBURETORS

Basic Principles

An understanding of the function of each of the carburetor components and their relationship to one another is a valuable aid for pinpointing a source of carburetor trouble.

The carburetor's purpose is to supply and atomize fuel and mix it in correct proportions with air that is drawn in through the air intake. At the primary throttle opening—at idle—a small amount of fuel is siphoned through the pilot jet by the incoming air. As the throttle is opened further, the air stream begins to siphon fuel through the main jet and needle jet. The tapered needle increases the effective flow capacity of the needle jet as it is lifted with the air slide, in that it occupies decreasingly less of the area of the jet. In addition, the amount of cutaway in the leading edge of the throttle slide aids in controlling the fuel/air mixture during partial throttle openings.

At full throttle the carburetor venturi is fully open and the needle is lifted far enough to permit the main jet to flow at full capacity.

Service

The carburetor service recommended at 10,000 mile (16,100 km) intervals involves routine removal, disassembly, cleaning and inspection. Alterations in jet size, throttle slide cutaway, changes in needle position, etc., should be attempted only if you're experienced in this type of "tuning" work; a bad guess could result in costly engine damage or, at the very least, poor performance. If, after servicing the carburetors and making the adjustments described in Chapter Three, the motorcycle does not perform correctly (and assuming that other factors affecting performance are correct, such as ignition timing and condition, valve adjustment, etc.), the motorcycle should be checked by a Honda

dealer or a qualified performance tuning specialist. Refer to **Table 1** for complete carburetor specifications.

Removal/Installation

1. Place the bike on the centerstand and remove the right- and left-hand side covers (**Figure 1**).
2. Hinge up the seat and remove it.
3. Disconnect the battery negative (**Figure 2**) and positive leads and remove the battery and the tray from the frame. Disconnect the hoses from the crankcase breather collector tank (**Figure 3**) and remove the tank.
4. Remove the bolts securing the battery holder; don't remove the holder, just move it toward the rear as much as possible.
5. Turn the fuel shutoff valve to the OFF position (**Figure 4**) and remove the fuel line from the valve.
6. Remove the bolt (**Figure 5**) securing the fuel tank; pull the tank to the rear and remove it.
7. Remove the bolts (**Figure 6**) securing the air cleaner box.
8. At the hand throttle, loosen the throttle cable locknut and turn the adjusting barrel (**Figure 7**) all the way in. This provides the necessary slack for ease of cable removal at the carburetor assembly.
9. Loosen the clamping screws (**Figure 8**) on each of the carburetors.
10. Slide the clamps off the carburetors.

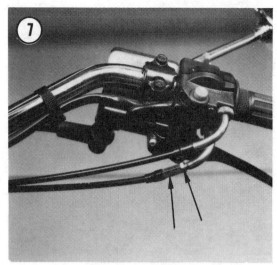

11. Push the air cleaner box rearward off of the carburetor throats. Push the box as far back as possible as you need all available room to remove the carburetor assembly.

12. Remove the drain tube (**Figure 9**) from each carburetor.

13. Pull the carburetor assembly to the rear, out of the rubber intake tubes on the cylinder head.

14. Partially pull the carburetor assembly out toward the right-hand side.

15. Disconnect the throttle cables (**Figure 10**) and choke cable (**Figure 11**). Tie the loose ends of the cables up out of the way onto the frame.

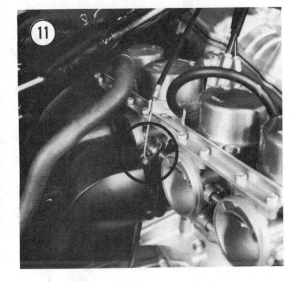

16. Continue to pull the carburetor assembly out through the right-hand side.

NOTE
This is not an easy task and it is a lot easier with two people. One or more of the rubber intake tubes on the air cleaner box may come off during removal; just push it back into place after carburetor removal.

17. Install by reversing these removal steps, noting the following.

18. Prior to installing the carburetor assembly, move each carburetor clamp on the engine intake tube all the way forward (**Figure 12**). This will allow the tube to flex the maximum amount for ease of installation.

19. Be sure the throttle cables and choke cable are in the same position in the frame and that they are not twisted or kinked and do not have any sharp bends. Tighten the locknuts (**Figure 13**) securely.

20. Route the carburetor drain tubes to the right-hand rear side of the engine.

21. Adjust the throttle cable as described under *Throttle Operation/Adjustment* in Chapter Three.

Disassembly/Assembly

Refer to **Figure 14** for this procedure.

It is recommended that only one carburetor be disassembled and cleaned at one time. This will prevent the intermix of parts.

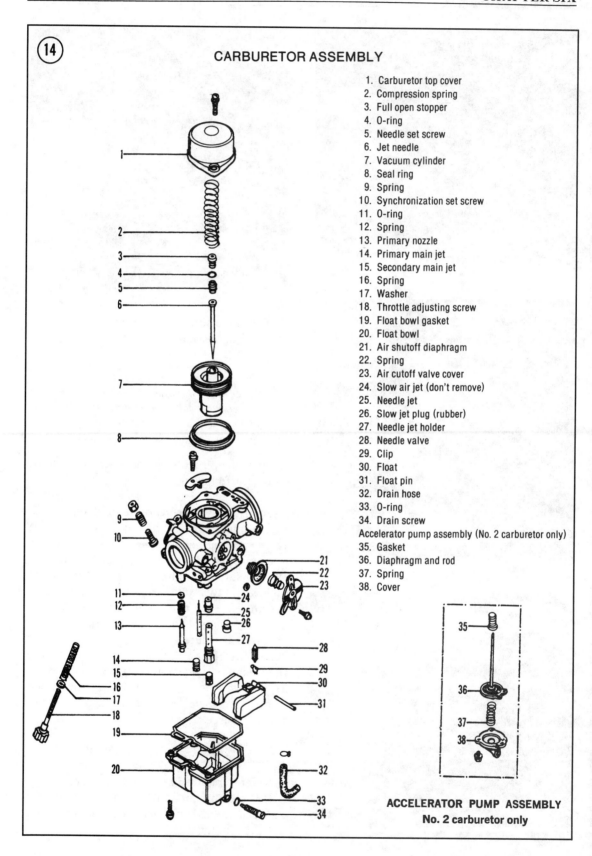

⑭

CARBURETOR ASSEMBLY

1. Carburetor top cover
2. Compression spring
3. Full open stopper
4. O-ring
5. Needle set screw
6. Jet needle
7. Vacuum cylinder
8. Seal ring
9. Spring
10. Synchronization set screw
11. O-ring
12. Spring
13. Primary nozzle
14. Primary main jet
15. Secondary main jet
16. Spring
17. Washer
18. Throttle adjusting screw
19. Float bowl gasket
20. Float bowl
21. Air shutoff diaphragm
22. Spring
23. Air cutoff valve cover
24. Slow air jet (don't remove)
25. Needle jet
26. Slow jet plug (rubber)
27. Needle jet holder
28. Needle valve
29. Clip
30. Float
31. Float pin
32. Drain hose
33. O-ring
34. Drain screw
Accelerator pump assembly (No. 2 carburetor only)
35. Gasket
36. Diaphragm and rod
37. Spring
38. Cover

ACCELERATOR PUMP ASSEMBLY
No. 2 carburetor only

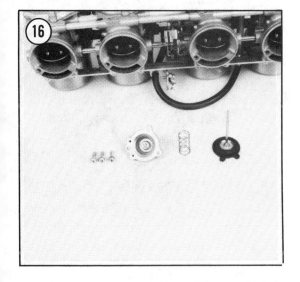

NOTE
All 4 carburetors look the same, but slight differences exist between all of them. Take note of this prior to disassembly.

All components that require cleaning can be removed from the carburetor body without removing the carburetors from the mounting plates. If separation is necessary, it is covered in a separate procedure in this chapter. The carburetors are not separated in this procedure to help simplify the presentation of this material.

1. On the No. 2 carburetor only, disassemble the accelerator pump assembly. Remove the screws (**Figure 15**) securing the accelerator pump cover and remove it. Remove the spring and diaphragm (**Figure 16**).

NOTE
The carburetors are numbered in the same sequence as the engine cylinders. The No. 1 carburetor is located on the left-hand side and No. 2, 3 and 4 continue from left to right.

2. On the No. 1 carburetor only, disassemble the air cutoff valve. Remove the screws (**Figure 17**) securing the air cutoff valve cover and remove it. Remove the spring and diaphragm (**Figure 18**). Remove the small O-ring seal (**Figure 19**).

3. Remove the screws (**Figure 20**) securing the carburetor top cover to the main body and remove the cover.

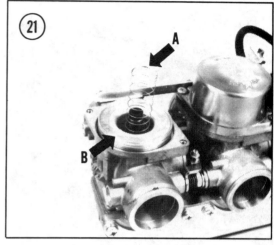

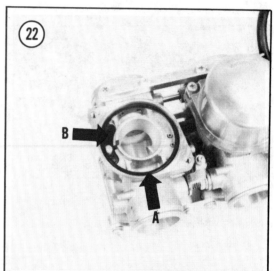

4. Remove the compression spring (A, **Figure 21**) and vacuum cylinder assembly (B, **Figure 21**).

5. Remove the O-ring seal (A, **Figure 22**) and the air jet cover (B, **Figure 22**).

6. Disassemble the vacuum cylinder assembly (**Figure 23**).

7. Remove the screws (**Figure 24**) securing the float bowl to the main body and remove it.

8. Remove the gasket from the float bowl (**Figure 25**).

9. Remove the primary main jet (A, **Figure 26**) and the primary nozzle (**Figure 27**).

10. Remove the secondary main jet (B, **Figure 26**) and the needle holder (**Figure 28**).

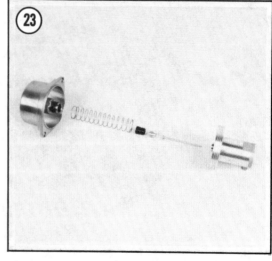

Tilt the carburetor to the side and catch the needle jet as it slides out of the tube.

11. Carefully push out the float pin (**Figure 29**).

12. Lift the float and needle valve (**Figure 30**) out of the main body.

13. Do not remove the slow air jet as it is pressed into place. Remove the black plastic plug that covers it (A, **Figure 31**).

> *NOTE*
> *Prior to removing the pilot screw, record the number of turns necessary until the screw lightly seats. Record the number of turns for all 4 carburetors as they must be reinstalled into the same exact setting.*

6

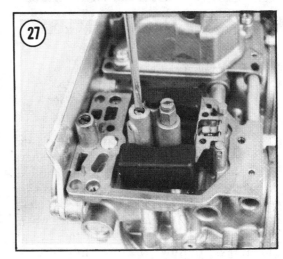

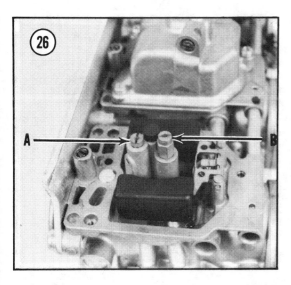

14. Remove the pilot screw (B, **Figure 31**).

> *NOTE*
> *Further disassembly is neither necessary nor recommended. If throttle or choke shafts or butterflies are damaged, take the body to your dealer for replacement.*

15. Clean all parts, except rubber or plastic parts, in a good grade of carburetor cleaner. This solution is available at most automotive or motorcycle supply stores, in a small, resealable tank with a dip basket, for just a few dollars (**Figure 32**). If it is tightly sealed when not in use, the solution will last for several cleanings. Follow the manufacturer's instructions for correct soak time (usually about 1/2 hour).

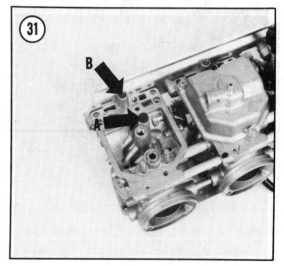

> *NOTE*
> *It is recommended that one carburetor be cleaned at a time to avoid interchanging of parts.*

16. Remove the parts from the cleaner and blow dry with compressed air. Blow out the jets with compressed air. *Do not* use a piece of wire to clean them as minor gouges in a jet can alter flow rate and upset the fuel/air mixture.

17. Make sure the air jets (**Figure 33**) are clean.

18. Repeat Steps 1-17 for the other 3 carburetors; note that Steps 1 and 2 are performed only on specific carburetors, as indicated.

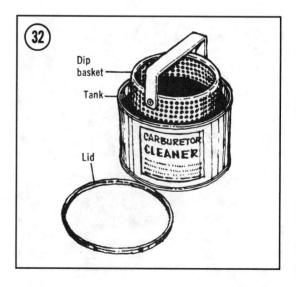

19. Assemble by reversing these disassembly steps, noting the following.

20. Replace any O-rings and gaskets that appear to be damaged or deteriorated. If they have become hardened their ability to seal is greatly reduced.

21. Screw the pilot screw into the exact same position (same number of turns) as recorded in Step 14.

22. When installing the diaphragm on the accelerator pump make sure the 2 tabs on the diaphragm align with the notches in the float bowl (**Figure 34**). Inspect the condition of the diaphragm for cracks and hardening; ensure that the rod is not bent.

23. Assemble the vacuum cylinder. Insert the jet needle into the vacuum cylinder (**Figure 35**) and screw in the needle set screw (**Figure 36**). Push in the full open stopper (**Figure 37**).

24. Be sure to install the small O-ring (**Figure 38**) on the No. 1 carburetor air cutoff valve.

25. After assembly and installation are completed, adjust the carburetors as described under *Pilot Screw Adjustment* in this chapter and *Carburetor Synchronization* in Chapter Three.

Separation/Assembly

1. Remove the carburetor assembly as described under *Carburetor Removal/Installation* in this chapter.

2. Unhook the choke relief spring from the shaft of the No. 2 and 3 carburetors (**Figure 39**).

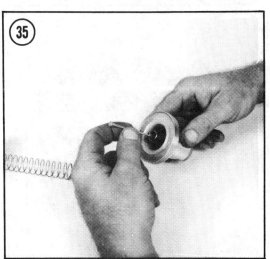

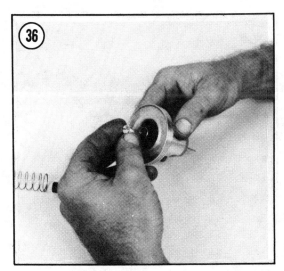

NOTE
The carburetors are numbered in the same sequence as the engine cylinders. The No. 1 carburetor is located on the left-hand side and No. 2, 3 and 4 continue from left to right.

NOTE
Loosen the locknut and turn the adjuster screw in until it seats. Record the number of turns so it can be adjusted to the same position. Record all 3 different carburetor settings.

3. Loosen the synchronization adjuster screw locknuts; loosen the adjuster screw until it is under no tension. Perform this on all carburetors except carburetor No. 2 which has no adjuster screw.

4. Remove the screws securing the rear bracket and remove the rear bracket (**Figure 40**).

5. Remove the screws securing the front bracket and remove the front bracket (**Figure 41**).

CAUTION
Pull the carburetors apart horizontally in the same plane. Avoid damage to the fuel and air vent pipes and the choke linkage that join the 2 subassemblies.

6. Carefully pull the carburetor subassemblies (No. 1 and 2, and No. 3 and 4) apart in the middle.

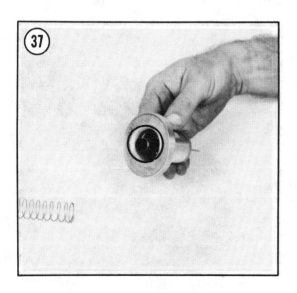

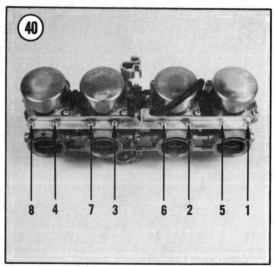

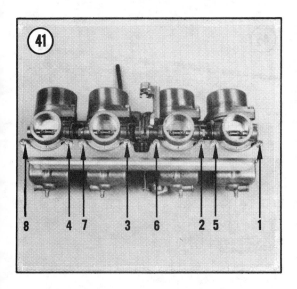

6

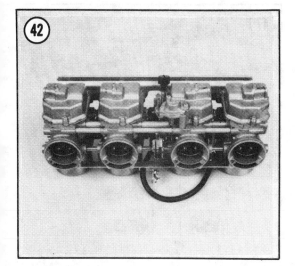

7. Further disassembly is not recommended and should be entrusted to a Honda dealer or carburetor specialist.

8. Assemble the subassemblies by performing the following steps.

9. Apply a light coat of oil to *new O-rings* on the fuel pipes and install them and the air vent pipe.

10. Assemble the 2 subassemblies and install the front bracket and screws—leave the screws loose at this time. Set the carburetor assembly on a flat surface with the float bowls up (**Figure 42**). Press the 2 subassemblies together and tighten the screws in 2 or 3 steps to a final torque of 3-4 ft.-lb. (4-6 N•m). Use the torque pattern shown in **Figure 41**.

11. Install the rear bracket using the same sequence as used in Step 10. Tighten the screws in 2 or 3 steps to a final torque of 2-3 ft.-lb. (2.8-4.2 N•m). Use the torque pattern shown in **Figure 40**.

> *NOTE*
> *Make sure the carburetors are properly aligned and that the choke shaft (*Figure 43) *operates smoothly. If not, loosen the screws and correctly align the carburetor subassemblies.*

12. Turn the synchronizing adjuster screws back to their original position as noted in Step 3.

13. Open the throttle slightly by pressing on the throttle linkage (**Figure 44**). It must

operate smoothly and return completely with no drag or hesitation. If it does not operate smoothly the carburetors are not properly aligned. Repeat Steps 10 and 11 and check for bent or damaged linkage.

14. Hook the choke relief spring onto the shaft (**Figure 39**). Make sure the choke valve operation is smooth by closing the choke linkage (**Figure 45**). It must close smoothly with no drag or hesitation. If it does not, the carburetors are not properly aligned. Repeat Steps 10 and 11 and check for bent or damaged linkage.

CARBURETOR ADJUSTMENTS

Float Adjustment

The carburetor assembly has to be removed and partially disassembled for this adjustment.

1. Remove the carburetor assembly as described under *Carburetor Removal/ Installation* in this chapter.

2. Remove the screws (**Figure 46**) securing the float bowls to the main bodies and remove them. In order to use a float level gauge it is necessary to remove all float bowls for gauge clearance.

3. Measure the distance from the bottom of the float to the float bowl gasket surface (**Figure 47**). The correct height is 0.61 in. (15.5 mm). Use a float level gauge as shown in **Figure 48**.

4. Adjust by carefully adjusting the tang on the float arm.

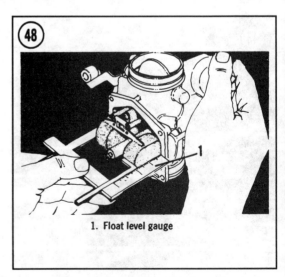

1. Float level gauge

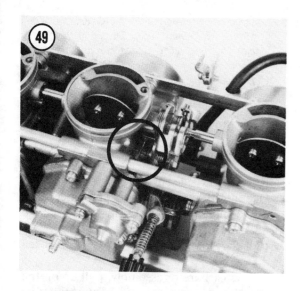

CAUTION
The floats on all 4 carburetors must be adjusted to exactly the same height to maintain the same fuel/air mixture to all 4 cylinders.

5. If the float level is set too high, the result will be a rich fuel/air mixture. If it is set too low, the mixture will be too lean.

6. Reassemble and install the carburetors by reversing the steps.

Needle Jet Adjustment

The needle jet is *non-adjustable* on all CB750 models.

Accelerator Pump Adjustment (No. 2 Carburetor Only)

1. Remove the carburetor assembly as described under *Carburetor Removal/ Installation* in this chapter.

2. Measure the distance between the accelerator pump rod and the adjusting arm (**Figure 49**). The correct clearance is 0-0.0016 in. (0-0.4 mm).

NOTE
The throttle valve must be in the closed position.

3. Adjust by carefully bending the adjusting arm.

4. Measure the distance between the adjusting arm and the stopper (**Figure 50**) on the carburetor body. The correct clearance is 0.12-0.13 in. (3.1-3.3 mm).

5. Adjust by carefully bending the adjusting arm.

Pilot Screw Adjustment

NOTE
The pilot jet is pre-set at the factory and adjustment is not necessary unless the carburetor has been overhauled or someone has misadjusted it.

1. For the preliminary adjustment, carefully turn the pilot screw on each carburetor (A, **Figure 51**) in until it seats lightly and then back it out as follows:

    a. Carburetor model No. VB2A—1 1/2 turns

b. Carburetor model No. VB42C—1 3/4 turns

2. Start the engine and let it reach normal operating temperature. Stop-and-go driving for approximately 10 minutes is sufficient.

3. Turn the engine off and connect a portable tachometer following the manufacturer's instructions. The bike's tach is not accurate enough at a low rpm.

4. Start the engine and adjust the idle speed to 1,000 +/-100 rpm. Use the throttle adjust screw (B, **Figure 51**).

NOTE
***Figure 51** is shown with the carburetor assembly removed for clarity; do not remove it to perform this adjustment.*

5. Turn *each* pilot screw (A, **Figure 51**) *out* 1/2 turn from the initial setting in Step 1.

6. If engine idle speed increases by 50 rpm or more, turn *each* pilot screw *out* by an additional 1/2 turn until the idle speed drops by 50 rpm or less.

7. Readjust the idle speed; refer to Step 4.

8. *On the No. 1 carburetor only*, turn the pilot screw *in* until the engine speed drops 50 rpm.

NOTE
The carburetors are numbered in the same sequence as the engine cylinders. The No. 1 carburetor is located on the left-hand side and No. 2, 3 and 4 go from left to right.

9. *On the No. 1 carburetor only*, turn the pilot screw *out* from the position in Step 8 by the following amount:

a. Carburetor model No. VB2A—3/8 turn

b. Carburetor model No. VB42C—3/4 turn

10. Readjust the idle speed. Refer to Step 4.

11. Repeat Steps 8-10 on carburetor No. 2, then on No. 3 and then on the No. 4 carburetor.

12. After all adjustments are completed, readjust the idle speed. Open and close the throttle a couple of times; check for variation in idle speed. Readjust if necessary.

WARNING
With the engine idling, move the handlebar from side to side. If the idle speed increases during this movement, the throttle cables may need adjusting or they may be incorrectly routed through the frame. Correct this problem immediately. Do not ride the bike in this unsafe condition.

13. Disconnect the portable tachometer.

Choke Adjustment — All Models

1. Remove the side covers, seat and fuel tank.

2. Operate the choke knob and check for smooth operation of the cable and choke mechanism.

3. Pull the knob all the way *up* to the closed position.

4. At the carburetor assembly, pull up on the choke lever to make sure it is at the end of its travel, thus closing the choke valves. If you can move the choke lever an additional amount it must be adjusted.

5. To adjust, loosen the cable clamping screw and move the cable sheath *up* until the choke lever is fully closed. Hold the choke lever in this position and tighten the cable clamping screw securely.

6. Push the choke knob all the way *down* to the fully open position.

7. At the carburetor assembly, check that the choke lever is fully open by checking for free play between the cable and the choke lever. The cable should move slightly as there should be no tension on it.

8. If proper adjustment cannot be achieved using this procedure the cable has stretched and must be replaced.

9. The choke knob should remain in whatever position it is placed from fully closed to fully open. If it does not, pull up on the rubber cover and turn the adjuster. Look down onto the knob and turn it either clockwise to increase resistance or counterclockwise to decrease resistance.

10. Reinstall the fuel tank, seat and side covers.

Rejetting the Carburetors

Do not try to solve a carburetion problem by rejetting if all the following conditions hold true:

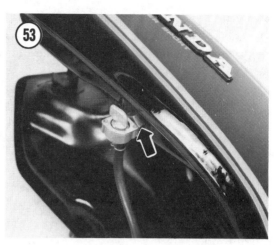

1. The engine has held a good tune in the past with the current jetting and needle positions.

2. The engine has not been modified.

3. The motorcycle is being operated in the same geographical region under the same general climatic conditions as in the past.

4. The motorcycle was and is being ridden at average highway speeds.

If those conditions all hold true, the chances are that the problem is due to a malfunction in the carburetion or in another component that needs to be adjusted or repaired. Changing the carburetion probably won't solve the problem.

Rejetting the carburetors may be necessary if any of the following conditions hold true:

1. A nonstandard type of air filter element is being used.

2. A nonstandard exhaust system is being used.

3. Any of the top end components in the engine (pistons, valves, compression ratio, etc.) have been modified.

4. The motorcycle is in use at considerably higher or lower altitudes, or in a markedly hotter or colder climate, than in the past.

5. The motorcycle is being operated at considerably higher speeds than before and changing to colder spark plugs does not solve the problem.

6. Someone has changed the jetting or needle positions in your motorcycle.

7. The motorcycle has never held a satisfactory engine tune.

If jetting the carburetors is needed, check with a Honda dealer for recommendations as to the sizes of jets to install.

FUEL SHUTOFF VALVE

Removal/Installation

1. Turn the fuel shutoff valve to the OFF position (**Figure 52**).

2. Remove the fuel line from the valve.

3. Install a longer piece of fuel line to the valve and place the loose end into a clean, approved gasoline container. If the fuel is kept clean, it can be reused.

4. Turn the valve to the RES position and open the fuel filler cap. This will speed up the flow of fuel. Drain the tank completely.

5. Remove the fuel shutoff valve by unscrewing the locknut (**Figure 53**) from the tank.

NOTE
Figure 53 is shown with the fuel tank removed for clarity. It is not necessary to remove it for this procedure.

6. After removing the valve, insert a corner of a clean shop rag into the opening in the tank to stop the dribbling of fuel onto the engine and frame.

7. Refer to *Fuel Shutoff Valve and Filter Removal/Installation* in Chapter Three for cleaning procedure.

8. Install by reversing these removal steps. Do not forget to install the washer between the valve and the tank. Check for leakage after installation is completed.

FUEL TANK

Removal/Installation

1. Place the bike on the centerstand.
2. Hinge up the seat and remove it.
3. Remove the right- and left-hand side covers (**Figure 54**).
4. Disconnect the battery negative lead (**Figure 55**).
5. Remove the bolt (**Figure 56**) securing the rear of the tank; pull the tank to the rear and remove it.
6. Install by reversing these steps.

Sealing (Pin Hole Size)

This procedure requires the use of a non-petroleum, non-flammable solvent.

If you feel unqualified to accomplish it, take the tank to your dealer and let him seal the tank.

> *WARNING*
> *Before attempting any service on the fuel tank be sure to have a fire extinguisher rated for gasoline or chemical fires within reach. Do not smoke or allow anyone to smoke or work where there are any open flames (i.e. water heater or clothes dryer gas pilots). The work area must be well-ventilated.*

1. Remove the tank as described in this chapter.
2. Mark the spot on the tank where the leak is visible with a grease pencil.
3. Turn the fuel shutoff valve to the RESERVE position and blow the interior of the tank completely dry with compressed air.
4. Turn the fuel shutoff valve to the OFF position and pour about 1 qt. (1 liter) of non-petroleum based solvent into the tank; install the fuel filler cap and shake the tank vigorously one or 2 minutes. This is used to remove all fuel residue.
5. Drain the solvent into a safe, storable container. This solution may be reused.

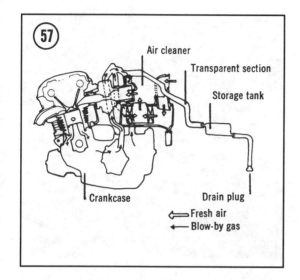

57

Air cleaner

Transparent section

Storage tank

Crankcase

Drain plug

⇦ Fresh air
⟵ Blow-by gas

6. Remove the fuel shutoff valve by unscrewing the fitting from the tank. If necessary, plug the tank with a cork or tape it closed with duct tape. Thoroughly clean the surrounding area with ignition contact cleaner so the tape will stick securely.

7. Again blow the tank interior completely dry with compressed air.

8. The following steps are best done out of doors as the fumes are very strong and flammable. Pour the sealant into the tank (a silicone rubber base sealer like Pro-Tech Fuel Tank Sealer, or equivalent, may be used). This is available at most motorcycle supply stores.

CAUTION
Do not spill the sealant onto the painted surface of the tank as it will destroy the finish.

6

9. Position the tank so that the point of the leak is located at the lowest part of the tank. This will allow the sealant to accumulate at the point of the leak.

10. Let tank set in this position for at least 48 hours.

11. After the sealant has dried, install the fuel shutoff valve, turn it to the OFF position and refill the tank with fuel.

12. After the tank has been filled, let it sit for at least 2 hours and recheck the leak area.

13. Install the tank on the motorcycle.

CRANKCASE BREATHER SYSTEM (U.S.)

In order to comply with air pollution standards, the Honda CB750 is equipped with a crankcase breather system. The system shown in **Figure 57** is used to draw out blow-by gases generated in the crankcase and recirculate them into the fuel/air mixture and thus into the engine to be burned.

Inspection

Make sure all clamps are tight (**Figure 58**) on hoses from the engine and the storage tank (**Figure 59**). Check the hoses for deterioration and replace if necessary.

Remove the plug (**Figure 60**) from the drain hose and drain out all residue. This

58

59

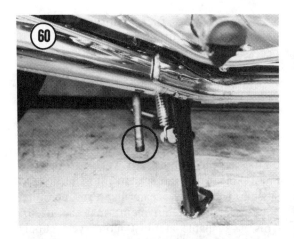

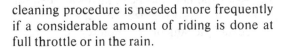

cleaning procedure is needed more frequently if a considerable amount of riding is done at full throttle or in the rain.

NOTE
Be sure to install the plug and clamp.

EXHAUST SYSTEM

The exhaust system consists of either 4 exhaust pipes and 4 mufflers or 4 exhaust pipes, 2 collectors and 2 mufflers, depending on the model.

Removal/Installation

1. Place the bike on the centerstand.
2. Remove the nuts and lockwashers (**Figure 61**) securing the exhaust pipe flanges to the cylinder head.
3A. On models with 4 mufflers, remove the bolt and nut (**Figure 62**) securing the mufflers to the frame.
3B. On models with 2 mufflers, remove the bolts and nuts (**Figure 63**) securing the muffler to the footpeg.
4. Remove the exhaust system by pushing it forward to clear the exhaust port studs and remove it. Repeat for the other side.
5. Install by reversing these removal steps, noting the following.
6. Install new gaskets into each exhaust port in the cylinder head.
7. Tighten the rear bolt(s) only finger-tight at first until the exhaust flange nuts are securely tightened; then tighten them completely. This will minimize an exhaust leak at the cylinder head. Be sure the split keepers are correctly installed into the recesses in the cylinder head.
8. Start the engine and check for leaks.

TABLE 1 CARBURETOR SPECIFICATIONS

Carburetor model number	
Model CB750K	VB42A or VB42C
Model CB750K-LTD	VB42A
Model CB750C	VB42A or VB42C
Model CB750F	VB42C
Main jet number	
Primary—all models	No.68
Secondary	
Models CB750K, K-LTD, and C	No. 102
Model CB750F	No.98
Jet needle clip setting	Non-adjustable
Pilot screw opening	
Initial opening (see *Pilot Screw Adjustment* in text for additional opening)	
Model CB750K (carb. No. VB42A)	1½ turns
Model CB750K (carb. No. VB42C)	1¾ turns
Models CB750K-LTD, C, and F	1½ turns
Idle speed—all models	1,000 ± 100 rpm
Fast idle speed—all models	2,000 ± 500 rpm (after break-in)

6

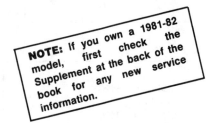
NOTE: If you own a 1981-82 model, first check the Supplement at the back of the book for any new service information.

ELECTRICAL SYSTEM

The electrical system includes the following systems:

    a. Charging system
    b. Ignition system
    c. Lighting system
    d. Directional signals
    e. Horn

Table 1 and **Table 2** are located at the end of this chapter.

CHARGING SYSTEM

The charging system consists of the battery, alternator and voltage regulator/rectifier (**Figure 1**).

Alternating current generated by the alternator is rectified to direct current. The voltage regulator maintains the voltage to the battery and additional electrical load (lights, ignition, etc.) at a constant voltage regardless of variations in engine speed and load.

Charging System Output Test

Whenever a charging system trouble is suspected, make sure the battery is good before going any further. Clean and test the battery as described under *Battery Testing* in Chapter Three. Warm up engine prior to performing the test. To test the charging system, connect a 0-15 DC voltmeter to the battery as shown in **Figure 2**. Connect the positive voltmeter terminal to the positive battery terminal and the negative voltmeter terminal to ground.

NOTE
Do not disconnect either the positive or negative battery cables; they are to remain in the circuit as is.

Connect a 0-10 DC ammeter in line with the main fuse connectors (fusible link). Loosen the screws securing the fusible link (**Figure 3**) and remove the fusible link. Install an inline fuse/fuse holder (available at most

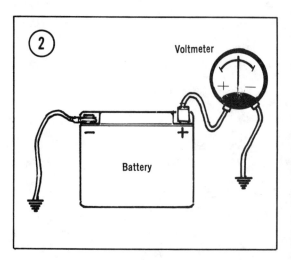

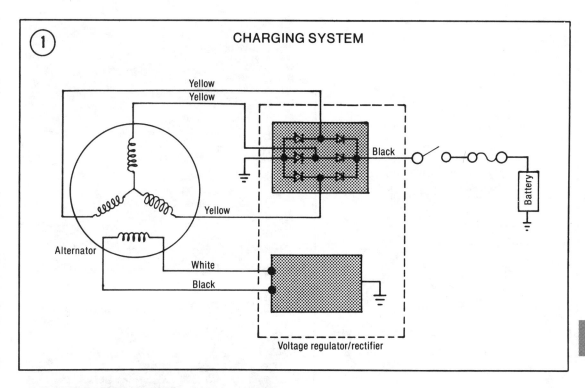

CHARGING SYSTEM

Yellow
Yellow
Black
Battery
Yellow
Alternator
White
Black
Voltage regulator/rectifier

7

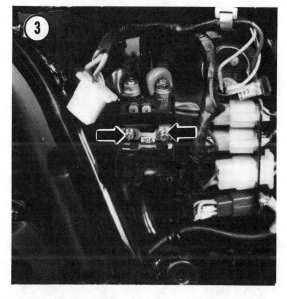

CAUTION
Do not try to test the system by connecting an ammeter between the positive battery terminal and the starter cable. The ammeter will burn out when the electric starter is operated.

NOTE
During the test if the needle of the ammeter reads in the opposite direction on the scale, reverse the polarity of the test terminals.

Start the engine and run at 5,000 rpm. Minimum charging current should be 0 amperes. Voltage should read 14.5 volts.

NOTE
All test measurements are to be made with the headlight on high beam.

If the charging current is considerably lower than specified, check the alternator and voltage regulator/rectifier. Less likely is the possibility that the voltage is too high; in that case, the voltage regulator is probably at fault.

Test the separate charging system components as described under the appropriate headings in this chapter.

auto supply or electronic supply stores) along with the ammeter as shown in **Figure 4**. Use alligator clips (**Figure 5**) on the test leads for good electrical connections.

CAUTION
In order to protect the ammeter, always run the test with the fuse in line in the circuit.

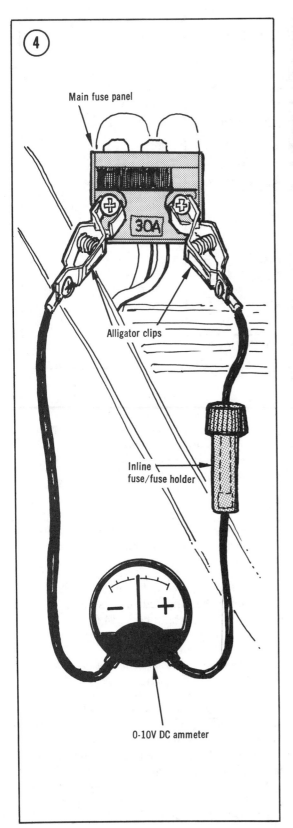

④

Main fuse panel

30A

Alligator clips

Inline
fuse/fuse holder

0-10V DC ammeter

⑤

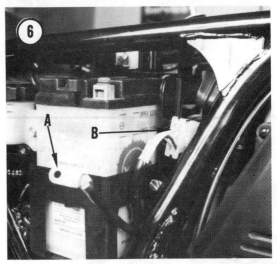

⑥

A

B

⑦

HONDA

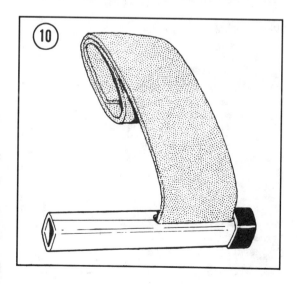

BATTERY

For complete battery information, refer to *Battery* in Chapter Three.

ALTERNATOR

An alternator is a form of electrical generator in which a magnetized field called a rotor revolves within a set of stationary coils called a stator. As the rotor revolves, alternating current is induced in the stator. The current is then rectified and used to operate the electrical accessories on the motorcycle and for charging the battery. The rotor is an electromagnet and receives its electricity through 2 brushes connected to the stator wiring harness and located within the alternator cover.

Removal/Installation

1. Place the bike on the centerstand.
2. Remove the right-hand side cover and disconnect the battery negative lead (A, **Figure 6**).
3. Disconnect the alternator electrical connector (B, **Figure 6**).
4. Remove the electrical harness from the clips on the engine (**Figure 7**).

> *NOTE*
> *Figure 7 is shown with the engine removed for clarity.*

5. Remove the bolts (**Figure 8**) securing the alternator cover and remove the cover and the gasket.
6. Remove the 17 mm bolt (**Figure 9**) securing the alternator rotor.

> *NOTE*
> *If necessary, use a strap wrench (**Figure 10**) to keep the rotor from turning while removing the bolt, or shift the transmission into gear and hold the rear brake on.*

7. Rotor removal requires a special 2-piece rotor puller (**Figure 11**), Honda part No. 07933-4250000. Screw the inner part of the puller into the threaded hole in the crankshaft. Screw it in until it completely stops (**Figure 12**).

7

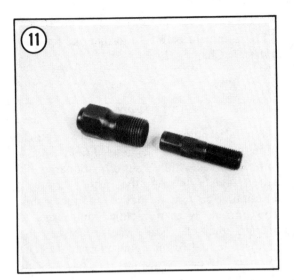

CAUTION
Do not use any other type or configuration
of rotor puller other than that shown in
Figure 11. *If any other type is used either*
the rotor and/or the crankshaft may be
damaged.

8. Screw the outer part of the puller into the
alternator rotor (**Figure 13**) until it stops on
the inner part. Turn the outer rotor puller with
a 19 mm wrench until it is free.
9. Remove the rotor from the crankshaft.
Remove the rotor puller parts from the rotor
and the crankshaft (**Figure 14**).
10. Install by reversing these removal steps.
Tighten the rotor bolt to 58-72 ft.-lb. (80-100
N•m) and route the electrical harness as
shown in **Figure 7**.

Brush Inspection/Replacement

Inspect the length of both brushes within
the stator housing (**Figure 15**). The brushes
must be replaced if worn to the scribe line.
Always replace both brushes as a set.
1. Remove the Phillips screws (A, **Figure 16**)
securing the holder in place.
2. Remove the bolts and nuts (B, **Figure 16**)
securing the brush assembly and replace with
new brushes.

Stator Testing

1. Inspect the right-hand side cover and
disconnect the alternator electrical connector

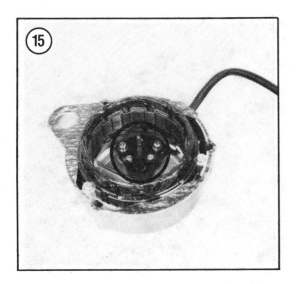

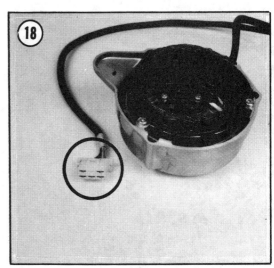

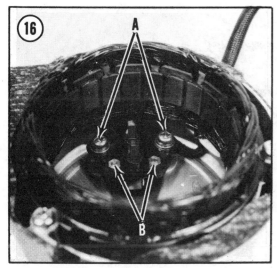

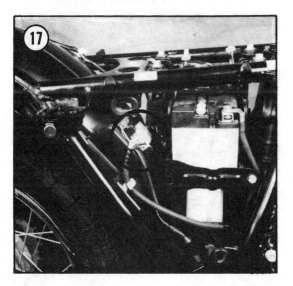

7

(**Figure 17**). This connector contains 5 wires —3 yellow, one black and one white.

2. Use an ohmmeter and check continuity between each yellow terminal (**Figure 18**). The specified resistance between all yellow terminals is 0.41-0.51 ohms. Replace the stator if any yellow terminal shows no continuity to any other. This would indicate an open in the winding.

NOTE
Prior to replacing the stator with a new one, check the electrical wires to and within the terminal connector for any opens or poor connections.

3. Use an ohmmeter and check for continuity between all 5 terminals to ground. Replace the stator if any of the terminals show continuity to ground. This would indicate a short within a winding.

Rotor Testing

1. Clean the 2 slip rings with contact cleaner and a clean shop rag to remove any carbon deposits.

2. Use an ohmmeter and check for continuity between the 2 slip rings. There is no factory specified resistance; some resistance should be present (approximately 3.5-5.5 ohms). If there is very high resistance (infinity reading on the scale) this indicates there is an open and the rotor should be replaced.

3. Use an ohmmeter and check for continuity between each slip ring and the center core which is the ground. The reading should be infinity for each ring. Replace the rotor if either ring shows continuity to ground which would indicate a short within a winding.

VOLTAGE REGULATOR/RECTIFIER

Removal/Installation

1. Remove the right- and left-hand side covers.
2. Disconnect the negative battery lead (**Figure 19**).
3. Disconnect all 4 electrical connectors (**Figure 20**) and pull them carefully out of the way.
4. Remove the nuts (**Figure 21**) securing the voltage regulator/rectifier in place. Remove it and the 2 electrical connectors and wires.
5. Install by reversing these removal steps.

Testing

To test the voltage regulator/rectifier, disconnect the 2 electrical connectors from the harness. One terminal contains 3 wires—1 green, 1 black and 1 red/white (**Figure 22**). The other contains 5 wires—3 yellow, one black and one white—and is attached to the voltage regulator/rectifier wires on the left-hand side (**Figure 23**).

Make the following measurements using an ohmmeter and refering to **Figure 24**.

1. Connect either ohmmeter lead to the green rectifier lead. Connect the other ohmmeter lead to each of the yellow leads. These 3 measurements must be the same, either all very high resistance (2,000 ohms minimum) or very low resistance (5-40 ohms). If one or more differ, the voltage regulator/rectifier is bad and the entire unit must be replaced.

2. Reverse ohmmeter leads and repeat Step 1. This time, the readings must also be the same, but just the opposite from the measurements in Step 1. For example, if all readings in Step 1 were low, all readings in this step must be high and vice versa. Replace the voltage regulator/rectifier if these measurements are not correct.

3. Connect either ohmmeter lead to the red/white voltage regulator/rectifier lead. Connect the other ohmmeter lead to each of the yellow leads. These 3 measurements must be the same, either all very high or all very low. Replace the voltage regulator/rectifier if these measurements are not correct.

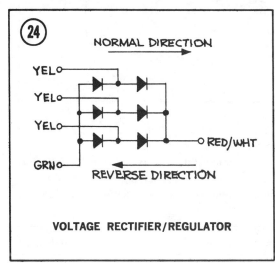

VOLTAGE RECTIFIER/REGULATOR

Voltage Regulator Performance Test

Connect a voltmeter across the battery (**Figure 25**). Start the engine and let it idle; increase engine speed until the voltage going to the battery reaches 14.0-15.0 volts. At this point, the voltage regulator/rectifier should prevent any further increase in voltage. If this does not happen and voltage increases above specifications the voltage regulator/rectifier must be replaced.

IGNITION SYSTEM

The ignition system consists of 2 ignition coils, 2 spark units, a pulse generator, and 4 spark plugs.

System Operation

All model CB750's are equipped with a fully transistorized ignition system. This capacitor discharge ignition (CDI) system uses no breaker points. The system provides a longer life for components and delivers a more efficient spark throughout the entire speed range of the engine. Ignition timing is maintained for a long time without periodic adjustment.

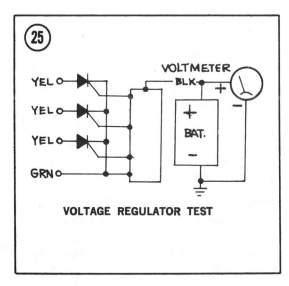

VOLTAGE REGULATOR TEST

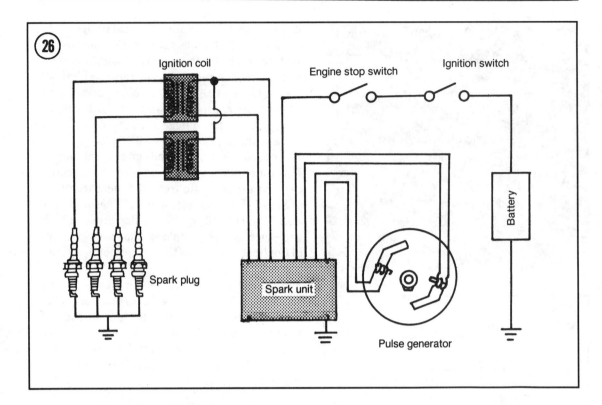

Alternating current from the alternator is rectified to direct current and is used to charge the capacitor. As the piston approaches the firing position, a pulse from the pulse generator pick-up coil is used to trigger the silicone-controlled rectifier. The rectifier in turn allows the capacitor to discharge quickly into the primary circuit of the ignition coil, where the voltage is stepped up in the secondary circuit to a value sufficient to fire the spark plug of the No. 1 and No. 4 cylinders, causing the plugs to fire. The same sequence of events happens to No. 2 and 3 cylinders and is controlled by the rotation of the puse generator's driven rotor.

NOTE
The plugs will fire at the same time (No. 1 and 4 or No. 2 and 3) but only one of the cylinders will be at TDC on the compression stroke. The other cylinder is on the exhaust stroke and the spark in that cylinder has no effect on it.

CDI Precautions

Certain measures must be taken to protect the transistorized ignition system. Damage to the semi-conductors in the system may occur if the following precautions are not observed:

1. Never connect the battery backwards. If the battery polarity is wrong, damage will occur to the voltage regulator/rectifier, alternator and ignition unit.

2. Do not disconnect the battery when the engine is running. A voltage surge will occur which will damage the voltage regulator/rectifier and possibly burn out the lights.

3. Keep all connections between the various units clean and tight. Be sure that the wiring connectors are pushed together firmly.

4. Do not substitute another type of ignition coil(s) or battery.

5. The spark units are mounted with a rubber vibration isolator. Always be sure that the isolator is in place when replacing a spark unit.

CDI Troubleshooting

Problems with the transistorized ignition system are usually the production of a weak spark or no spark at all.

1. Check all connections to make sure they are tight and free of corrosion.

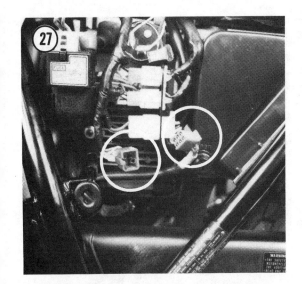

2. Check the ignition coils as described under *Ignition Coil Testing* in this chapter.

3. Check the pulse generator pick-up coil assembly with an ohmmeter. The coil resistance should be 530 ohms +/-50 ohms at 68° F (20° C). Refer to **Figure 27**. For cylinders No. 1 and 4 check between the blue leads and for No. 2 and 3 check between the yellow leads.

4. If the ignition coil and pick-up coil check out okay, the spark unit is at fault and must be replaced.

Spark Unit Replacement

1. Remove the seat and the right- and left-hand side covers.

2. Disconnect the battery negative lead.

3. Disconnect the electrical connector (**Figure 28**) going to the spark units.

4. Remove the bolts securing the spark units to the frame and remove them. Refer to **Figure 29** or **Figure 30** for location.

5. Install by reversing these removal steps.

Spark Unit Testing

Tests may be performed on the unit but a good one may be damaged by someone unfamiliar with the test equipment. To play it safe, have the tests performed by a dealer or substitute a known good unit for a suspected one.

IGNITION COIL

There are 2 ignition coils; the one on the left-hand side fires the No. 1 and 4 cylinders and the one on the right-hand side fires the No. 2 and 3 cylinders.

Removal/Installation

1. Remove the seat and the right-hand side cover.
2. Disconnect the battery negative lead.
3. Remove the left-hand side cover and the bolt securing the fuel tank. Slide the tank to the rear and remove it.
4. Disconnect the coil primary electrical wire connectors (black and black/white—left-hand coil; yellow and black/white—right-hand coil). See A, **Figure 31**.
5. Disconnect the spark plug connectors from the plugs (**Figure 32**).
6. Remove the 2 bolts (B, **Figure 31**) securing the coils to the frame and remove them.
7. Install by reversing these removal steps. Be sure to install the ground strap onto the front mounting bolt (B, **Figure 31**).
8. Make sure to route the spark plug wires to the correct cylinder. Refer to **Figure 33**.

Testing

The ignition coil is a form of transformer which develops the high voltage required to

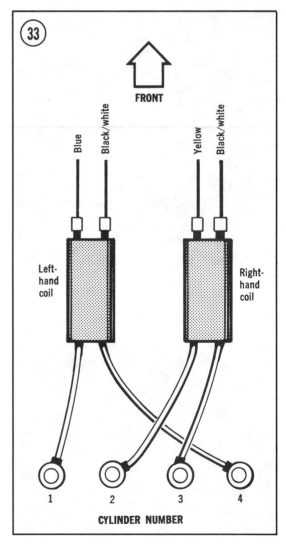

jump the spark plug gap. The only maintenance required is that of keeping the electrical connections clean and tight and occasionally checking to see that the coil is mounted securely.

Replace any coil if the spark plug lead exhibits visible damage and/or if the coil cases are damaged in any way.

PULSE GENERATOR

Replacement

1. Remove the right- and left-hand side covers.

2. Disconnect the battery negative lead (**Figure 34**).

3. Disconnect the pulse generator electrical connector (red) containing 4 wires (2 yellow and 2 blue). Refer to **Figure 35**.

4. Remove the screws (**Figure 36**) securing the ignition cover and remove the cover and the O-ring.

5. Remove the bolts (**Figure 37**) securing the left-hand crankcase cover and remove the cover and gasket.

6. Remove the bolts, or Phillips screws (**Figure 38**), securing the pulse generator to the cover.

7. Turn the crankcase cover over and remove the bolt and strap (**Figure 39**) securing the electrical harness in place and remove it.

8. Install by reversing these removal steps. Be sure to install the rubber grommet (A, **Figure**

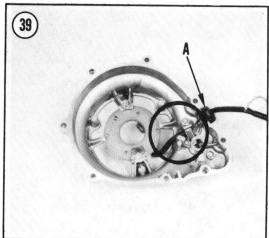

39) correctly into the backside of the crankcase cover.

9. Check and adjust the ignition timing. Refer to *Ignition Timing* in Chapter Three.

IGNITION ADVANCE MECHANISM

The ignition advance mechanism advances the ignition (fires the spark plugs sooner) as engine speed increases. If it does not advance properly and smoothly, the ignition will be incorrect at high engine rpm. It must be inspected periodically to make certain it operates freely.

1. Remove the ignition advance mechanism as described under *Ignition Advance Mechanism Removal/Installation* in Chapter Four.

2. Inspect the pivot points (A, **Figure 40**) of each weight. It must pivot freely to maintain proper ignition advance. Apply lightweight grease to the pivot pins.

3. Inspect the pivot cam (B, **Figure 40**) operation on the shaft. It must rotate smoothly.

4. Make sure the centrifugal advance weight return springs (C, **Figure 40**) completely retract the weights. If not, replace the advance unit.

SPARK PLUGS

The spark plugs recommended by the factory are usually the most suitable for your machine. If riding conditions are mild, it may

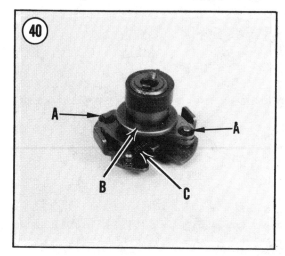

be advisable to go to spark plugs one step hotter than normal. Unusually severe riding conditions may require slightly colder plugs. See Chapter Three for details.

STARTING SYSTEM

The starting system consists of the starter motor, starter solenoid and the starter button.

The layout of the starting system is shown in **Figure 41**. When the starter button is pressed, it engages the solenoid switch that closes the circuit. The electricity flows from battery to the starter motor.

CAUTION
Do not operate the starter for more than 5 seconds at a time. Let it rest approximately 10 seconds, then use it again.

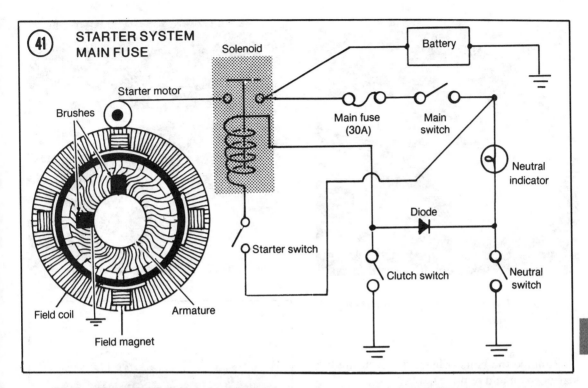

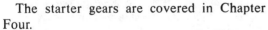

The starter gears are covered in Chapter Four.

Table 1 lists possible starter problems, probable causes and the most common remedies.

STARTER

Removal/Installation

1. Place bike on the centerstand.

2. Turn the ignition switch to the OFF position.

3. Remove the left- and right-hand side covers.

4. Disconnect the battery negative lead.

5. Disconnect the black electric starter cable from the solenoid (**Figure 42**).

Figure 43 and *Figure 44* are shown with the carburetor assembly removed for

clarity. It is not necessary to remove them for this procedure.

6. Remove the bolts (**Figure 43**) securing the starter cover and remove it.

7. Remove the bolts (**Figure 44**) securing the starter in place. Pull the starter to the right and remove it.

8. Install by reversing these removal steps.

9. When installing the cover, make sure the oil pressure switch wire is properly positioned in the rubber grommet (A, **Figure 45**) and that the starter cable is positioned in the notch (B, **Figure 45**).

Disassembly/Inspection/Assembly

Refer to **Figure 46** for this procedure.

The overhaul of a starter motor is best left to an expert. This section shows how to determine if the unit is defective.

1. Remove the starter motor case screws and separate the case.

NOTE
Write down how many thrust washers are used and install the same number when reassembling the starter.

2. Clean all grease, dirt and carbon dust from the armature, case and end covers.

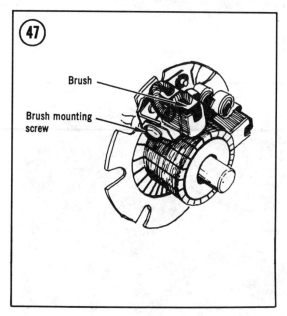

Brush

Brush mounting screw

CAUTION
Do not immerse brushes or the wire windings in solvent or the insulation might be damaged. Wipe the windings with a cloth lightly moistened with solvent and dry thoroughly.

3. Remove the screws (**Figure 47**) securing the brushes in their holders and remove both brushes. Measure the length of the brush with a vernier caliper (**Figure 48**). If the length is 0.30 in. (7.5 mm) or less, it must be replaced. Replace both brushes as a set even though only one may be worn to this dimension.

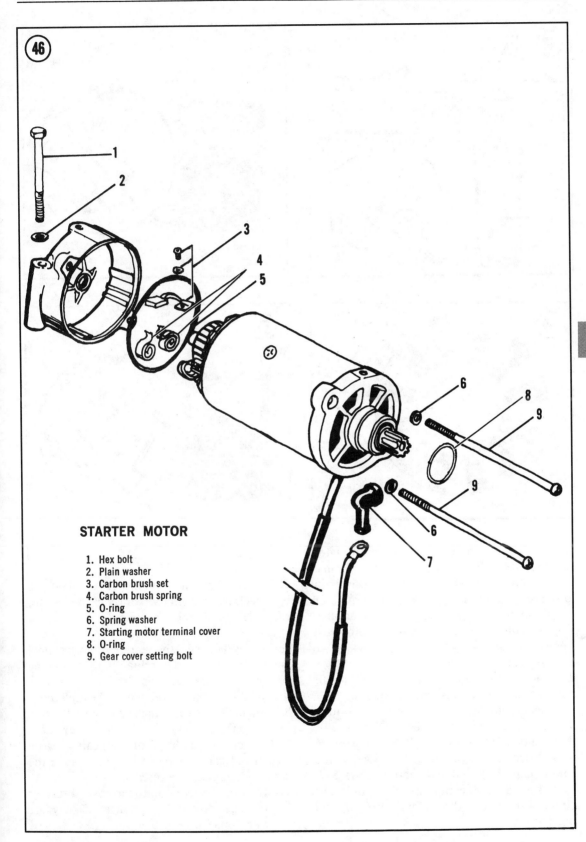

46

STARTER MOTOR

1. Hex bolt
2. Plain washer
3. Carbon brush set
4. Carbon brush spring
5. O-ring
6. Spring washer
7. Starting motor terminal cover
8. O-ring
9. Gear cover setting bolt

7

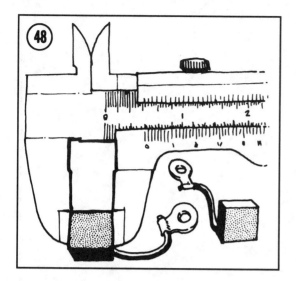

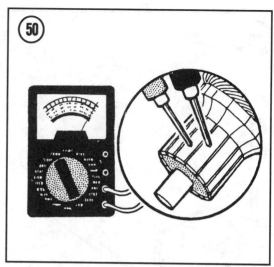

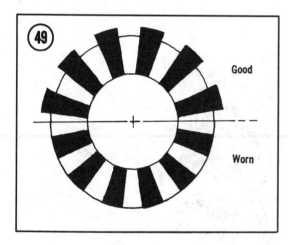

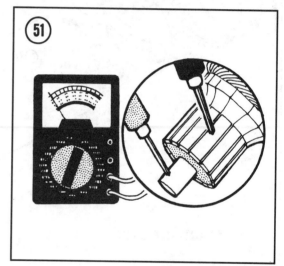

4. Inspect the condition of the commutator (**Figure 49**). The mica in the normal commutator is also shown; the copper is worn to the level of the mica. A worn commutator can be undercut, but it requires a specialist. Take the job to a Honda dealer or motorcycle electrical repair shop.

5. Inspect the commutator bars for discoloration. If a pair of bars are discolored, grounded armature coils are indicated.

6. Use an ohmmeter and check for continuity between the commutator bars (**Figure 50**); there should be continuity between pairs of bars. Also check continuity between the commutator bars and the shaft (**Figure 51**); there should be no continuity. If the unit fails either of these tests the armature is faulty and must be replaced.

7. Use an ohmmeter and inspect the field coil by checking continuity between the starter cable terminal and the motor case; there should be no continuity. Also check continuity between the starter cable terminal and each brush wire terminal; there should be continuity. If the unit fails either of these tests the case/field coil assembly must be replaced.

8. Assemble the case; make sure that the line marks on the case and cover align (**Figure 52**).

9. Inspect the condition of the gears (**Figure 53**). If they are chipped or worn, remove the circlip and replace the gear.

10. Inspect the front and rear cover bearings for damage. Replace the starter if they are worn or damaged.

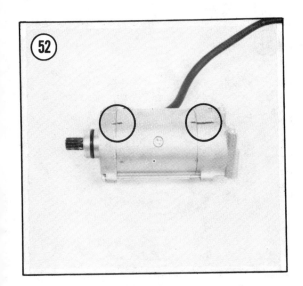

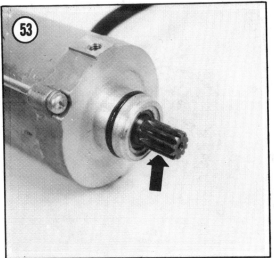

Starter Solenoid Removal/Installation

1. Turn the ignition switch to the OFF position. Disconnect the negative battery lead.
2. Remove the left-hand side cover and disconnect the electrical connector (A, **Figure 54**).
3. Slide off the rubber protective boot and disconnect the 2 electrical wires from the large terminals (B, **Figure 54**).
4. Remove the solenoid from the frame along with the main fuse holder that is attached to it.
5. Install by reversing these removal steps.

LIGHTING SYSTEM

The lighting system consists of the headlight, taillight/brakelight combination, directional signals, warning lights and speedometer and tachometer illumination lights. **Table 2** lists replacement bulbs for these components.

Headlight Replacement (U.S., Canada)

1. Remove the mounting screws (**Figure 55**) on each side of the headlight housing.
2. Pull the trim bezel and headlight unit out and disconnect the electrical connector from the backside (**Figure 56**).
3. Remove the retaining screws (A, **Figure 57**) and the adjusting bolt, nut and spring (B, **Figure 57**). Remove the inner rim and remove the sealed beam.

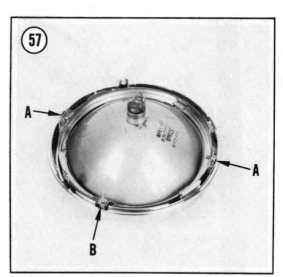

4. Install by reversing these removal steps. Be sure to install the sealed beam unit with the TOP mark facing up.

5. Adjust the headlight as described in this chapter.

Headlight Replacement (U.K.)

U.K. models use a prefocused headlamp bulb and a city (pilot) lamp. To replace either bulb:

1. Unscrew the mounting screws from the headlight rim and remove the rim from the housing.

2. Pull the city lamp out of the housing (**Figure 58**). Insert a new bulb and push it back into the housing.

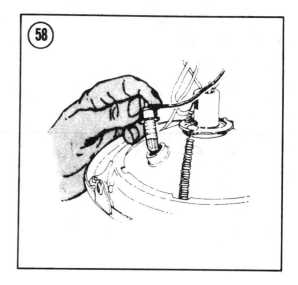

3. Disconnect the spring that holds the headlamp socket in place (**Figure 59**). Remove the old bulb from the socket. Install a new bulb (**Table 2**), making sure the offset pins line up with their respective slots so that the prefocusing will not be disturbed. Note also that the socket can be installed only one way. Reconnect the spring.

> *NOTE*
> *Do not touch the glass portion of the bulb with your fingers. Should you do so, wipe the bulb clean before installing it. Grease or oil from your fingers will shorten the life of the bulb.*

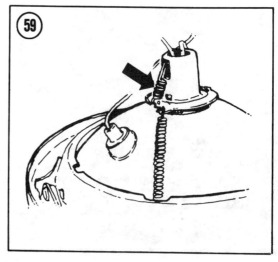

4. Install the headlamp unit in the housing, install the rim and screw in and tighten the mounting screws.

Headlight Adjustment

Adjust the headlight horizontally and vertically according to Department of Motor Vehicle regulations in your area.

To adjust the headlight horizontally, turn the screw (**Figure 60**). Screwing it in turns the light toward the right-hand side of the rider and loosening it will direct the light to the left-hand side. For vertical adjustment, unscrew the front side reflex reflector, loosen the mounting bolt (**Figure 61**) on each side and position the headlight correctly. Retighten the bolts and reinstall the reflex reflectors.

Taillight Replacement

Remove the screws securing the lens (**Figure 62** or **Figure 63**) and remove it. Wash out the inside and outside of the lens with a mild detergent and wipe dry. Wipe off the reflective base surrounding the bulb with a soft cloth. Replace the bulbs and install the lens; do not overtighten screws or the lens may crack.

Directional Signal Light Replacement

Remove the screws (**Figure 64**) on the backside of the base and remove the lens from the front. Wash the inside and outside of the lens with a mild detergent. Replace the bulb(s). Install the lens; do not overtighten the screws as that may crack the lens.

Speedometer and Tachometer
Illumination Light Replacement

1. Remove the headlight as described under *Headlight Replacement* in this chapter.

2. Disconnect the speedometer and tachometer drive cables (A, **Figure 65**).

3. Disconnect the instrument cluster electrical connector inside the headlight housing (**Figure 66**). The connector contains 8 wires — one orange, one blue, one brown/white, one light green/red, one blue/red, one black/brown, one green and one light blue.

4. Remove the nuts and washers (B, **Figure 65**) securing the instrument cluster and remove it.

5. Remove the Phillips screws (**Figure 67**) on the top cover and separate the assembly.

6. Turn the lower assembly over and remove the cap nuts (**Figure 68**) securing the back cover and remove it.

> *CAUTION*
> *Do not leave the instruments upside down any longer than necessary as the damping fluid may leak out.*

> *NOTE*
> **Figure 67** and **Figure 68** are shown with the instrument cluster installed for clarity. It must be removed for this procedure.

7. Remove the nuts on the mounting bracket and separate the tachometer and speedometer assemblies.

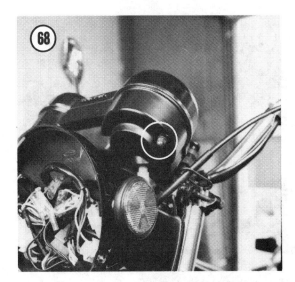

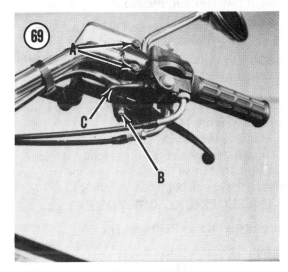

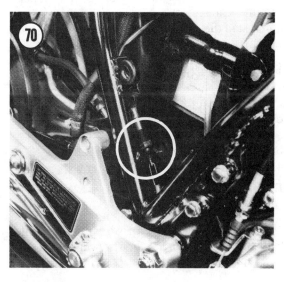

8. Remove the light bulb holder(s) and replace the defective bulb(s).

9. Install by reversing these removal steps.

Indicator Light Replacement (High Beam, Oil Pressure, Neutral Indicator and Turn Signal Indicator)

Perform Steps 1-5 of *Speedometer and Tachometer Illumination Light Replacement* in this chapter. Replace the defective bulb(s).

SWITCHES

Front Brake Light Switch Replacement

Remove the bolts (A, **Figure 69**) securing the front master cylinder and remove it from the handlebar. Turn it upside down and remove the Phillips screw (B, **Figure 69**). Remove the switch (C, **Figure 69**) and disconnect the electrical wires from the switch.

> *CAUTION*
> *If any brake fluid spills out of the coupling when the switch is removed, wipe it up. Wash any brake fluid off of painted or plated surfaces immediately, as it will destroy the finish. Use soapy water and rinse completely.*

Install the new switch and bleed the brake if any brake fluid was lost. Refer to *Bleeding the System* in Chapter Ten.

Rear Brake Light Switch Replacement

1. Remove the right-hand side cover.

2. Unhook the spring from the brake arm (**Figure 70**).

3. Unscrew the switch housing and locknut from the bracket.

4. Pull up the rubber boot and remove the electrical wires.

5. Replace the switch; reinstall and adjust as described under *Rear Brake Light Switch Adjustment*, in this chapter.

Rear Brake Light Switch Adjustment

1. Turn the ignition switch to the ON position.

2. Depress the brake pedal. The light should come on just as the brake begins to work.

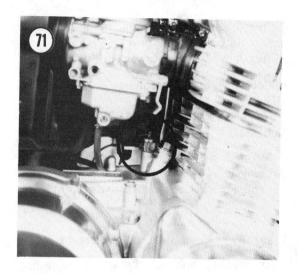

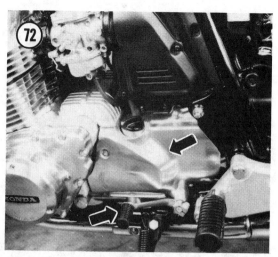

3. To make the light come on earlier, hold the switch body and turn adjusting locknut *clockwise* as viewed from the top. Turn *counterclockwise* to delay the light.

> *NOTE*
> *Some riders prefer the light to come on a little early. This way, they can tap the pedal without braking to warn drivers who follow too closely.*

Oil Pressure Switch Replacement

1. Pull back the rubber boot and remove the screw securing the electrical connector (**Figure 71**).
2. Unscrew the switch from the upper crankcase.
3. Install the switch. Apply Locktite Lock N' Seal to the threads prior to installation. Tighten to 11-14 ft.-lb. (15-20 N•m).
4. Install the electrical wire; make sure all electrical connections are free of oil prior to installation.

Neutral Indicator Switch Replacement

Remove the shift lever and left-hand rear crankcase cover (**Figure 72**). Disconnect the electrical wire and unscrew the switch (**Figure 73**).

> *NOTE*
> ***Figure 73** is shown with the engine removed and partially disassembled for clarity.*

Clutch Switch Replacement

1. Disconnect the electrical wire (A, **Figure 74**).
2. Pull back the rubber boot (B, **Figure 74**) and disconnect the clutch cable from the hand lever.
3. Remove the bolt and remove the hand lever (C, **Figure 74**).
4. Remove the switch.
5. Install by reversing these removal steps. Position the small protrusion on the switch toward the handlebar when installing it.

ELECTRICAL COMPONENTS

Turn Signal Relay Replacement

Remove the left-hand side cover and pull the flasher relay (**Figure 75**) out of the rubber mount. Transfer the wires to the new relay and install the relay in the rubber mount.

Horn Removal/Installation

1. On model CB750F only, remove the screw (**Figure 76**) and remove the plastic trim panel.
2. Disconnect horn connector(s) from electrical harness (A, **Figure 77**).
3. Remove the bolt securing horn(s) to bracket (B, **Figure 77**).
4. Installation is reverse of these steps.

Horn Testing

Disconnect the horn wires from the harness. Connect the horn wires to a 12-volt battery. If the horn is good it will sound, if not, replace it.

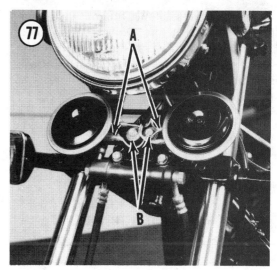

FUSES

There are 5 fuses used on the CB750. The main fuse (fusible link) is located under the left-hand side cover and all remaining fuses are located in a panel on the handlebar base.

If the main fusible link blows, disconnect the electrical connector, unscrew the Phillips screws securing the link and replace it (A, **Figure 78**). There is a spare link inside the panel (B, **Figure 78**).

The remaining fuses are accessible by removing the cover (**Figure 79**) on the handlebar base. There is one spare fuse (**Figure 80**) here also; always carry spares.

Whenever a fuse blows, find out the reason for the failure before replacing the fuse. Usually, the trouble is a short circuit in the wiring. This may be caused by a worn-through insulation or a disconnected wire shorting to the ground.

> *CAUTION*
> *Never substitute aluminum foil or wire for a fuse. Never use a higher amperage fuse than specified. An overload could result in fire and complete loss of the bike.*

WIRING DIAGRAMS

Wiring diagrams are located at the end of this book.

Table 1   STARTER TROUBLESHOOTING

Symptom	Probable Cause	Remedy
Starter does not work	Low battery	Recharge battery
	Worn brushes	Replace brushes
	Defective relay	Repair or replace
	Defective switch	Repair or replace
	Defective wiring or connection	Repair wire or clean connection
	Internal short circuit	Repair or replace defective component
Starter action is weak	Low battery	Recharge battery
	Pitted solenoid contacts	Clean or replace
	Worn brushes	Replace brushes
	Defective connection	Clean and tighten
	Short circuit in commutator	Replace armature
Starter runs continuously	Stuck solenoid	Replace solenoid
Starter turns; does not turn engine	Defective starter clutch	Replace starter clutch

TABLE 2 REPLACEMENT BULBS

Bulb	U.S. & Canada	U.K.
Headlight	12V 50/65W	12V 50/65W
Tail/stop	12V 8/27W (SAE 1157)	12V 7/23W
Directionals	12V 23W (SAE 1034/1073)	12V 24W
Instrument/indicators	12V 3.4W (SAE 57)	12V 3W
Pilot (city)	— — — —	12V 6W

NOTE: If you own a 1981-82 model, first check the Supplement at the back of the book for any new service information.

FRONT SUSPENSION AND STEERING

This chapter describes repair and maintenance procedures for the front wheel, forks and steering components.

Torque specifications (**Table 1**) are found at the end of the chapter.

FRONT WHEEL

Removal

1. Place wooden blocks under the crankcase to lift the front wheel off the ground.
2. Partially unscrew the speedometer cable set screw (A, **Figure 1**). Pull the speedometer cable free from the hub.
3. On dual disc models, remove the Allen bolts (**Figure 2**) securing the caliper assembly to the front fork. Remove either the right- or left-hand caliper assembly; it is only necessary to remove one. Tie the caliper up to the front fork to relieve strain on the brake line.

NOTE
It is not necessary to remove the caliper on models with a single brake disc.

4. Loosen the axle clamp nuts evenly, then remove them and the lockwashers and clamps (B, **Figure 1**). There are 2 on each side.
5. Pull the wheel down and forward being careful not to damage the studs on the fork end.

CAUTION
*Do not set the wheel down on the disc surface as it may get scratched or warped. Set the wheel on 2 blocks of wood (**Figure 3**).*

NOTE
Insert a piece of wood in the caliper(s) in place of the disc(s). That way, if the brake lever is inadvertently squeezed, the piston will not be forced out of the cylinder. If this does happen, the caliper might have to be disassembled to reseat the piston and the system will have to be bled. By using the wood, bleeding the brake is not necessary when installing the wheel.

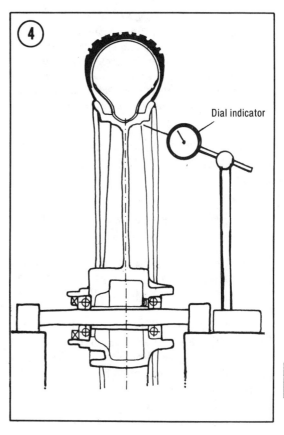

Dial indicator

Inspection

Measure the axial and radial runout of the wheel with a dial indicator as shown in **Figure 4**. The maximum axial and radial runout for both the wire spoke type and the ComStar wheel is 0.08 in. (2.0 mm). If the runout exceeds this dimension, check the wheel bearing condition.

On models with wire wheels, some of this condition can be corrected as described under *Spoke Adjustment* in this chapter.

On models with the ComStar wheels, if the runout exceeds this dimension the wheel will have to be replaced as it cannot be serviced. Inspect the condition of the ComStar wheel for signs of cracks, fractures, dents or bends. If it is damaged in any way, it must be replaced.

WARNING
Do not try to repair any damage to a ComStar wheel as it will result in an unsafe riding condition.

Check axle runout as described under *Front Hub Inspection* in this chapter.

Installation

1. Make sure the axle bearing surfaces of the fork slider and the lower clamps are free from dirt or small burrs.
2. Remove the wood piece(s) from the caliper(s).
3. Position the wheel in place, carefully inserting the disc between the pads.
4. Install the axle clamps with the "F" mark or arrow (**Figure 5**) facing forward. Install the lockwashers and nuts, finger-tight only at this time.
5. Position the speedometer housing so that the cable inlet is at the 3 o'clock position.
6. Tighten the front axle clamp nut first and then the rear nut to 13-18 ft.-lb. (18-25 N•m).

WARNING
*The clamp nuts must be tightened in this manner and to this torque value. After installation is complete, there will be a slight gap (**Figure 6**) at the rear, with **no gap** at the front. If done incorrectly, the studs could fail, resulting in loss of control of the bike when riding.*

7. Install the speedometer cable into the speedometer housing. Tighten the cable set screw.

NOTE
Slowly rotate the wheel while inserting the cable so it will engage properly.

8. On dual disc models, carefully install the caliper assembly that was removed onto the disc. Tighten the bolts to 22-29 ft.-lb. (30-40 N•m).

9. On dual disc models, measure the distance between the outside surface of the disc and the left-hand caliper holder with a flat feeler gauge. The clearance must be 0.028 in. (0.7 mm) or more. If clearance is insufficient, loosen the axle holder nuts and pull the left-hand fork leg out until this dimension is achieved. Tighten the nuts by repeating Step 6.

10. After the wheel is completely installed, rotate it several times and apply the brakes a couple of times to make sure it rotates freely and that the brake pads are against the disc(s).

FRONT HUB

Disassembly

Refer to **Figure 7** for this procedure.

1. Remove the front wheel as described in this chapter.

2. Remove the axle nut and spacer (**Figure 8**) from the right-hand side of the wheel.

3. Withdraw the axle from the left-hand side and remove the speedometer housing (**Figure 9**).

4. Remove the flange bolts (A, **Figure 10**) securing the brake disc and remove the disc(s).

5. Remove the dust seal (A, **Figure 11**) and unscrew the bearing retainer (B, **Figure 11**).

6. Remove the speedometer drive dog (B, **Figure 10**).

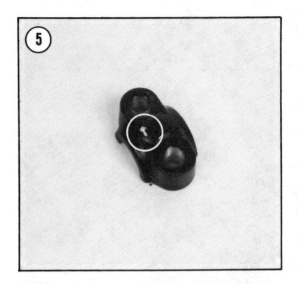

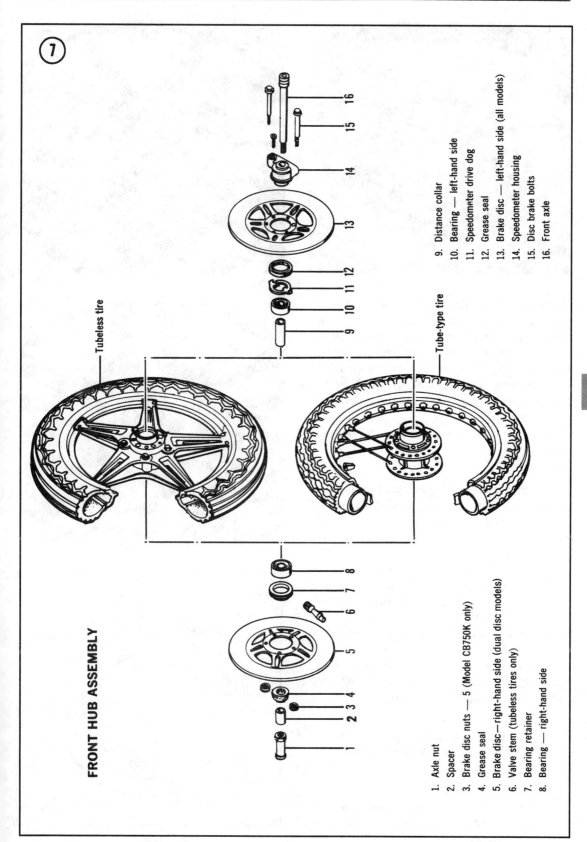

FRONT HUB ASSEMBLY

Tubeless tire

Tube-type tire

1. Axle nut
2. Spacer
3. Brake disc nuts — 5 (Model CB750K only)
4. Grease seal
5. Brake disc—right-hand side (dual disc models)
6. Valve stem (tubeless tires only)
7. Bearing retainer
8. Bearing — right-hand side
9. Distance collar
10. Bearing — left-hand side
11. Speedometer drive dog
12. Grease seal
13. Brake disc — left-hand side (all models)
14. Speedometer housing
15. Disc brake bolts
16. Front axle

8

7. To remove the right- and left-hand bearings and distance collar, insert a soft aluminum or brass drift into one side of the hub. Push the distance collar over to one side and place the drift on the inner race of the lower bearing. Tap the bearing out of the hub with a hammer, working around the perimeter of the inner race.

8. Remove the other bearing in the same manner.

Inspection

1. Do not clean sealed bearings. If non-sealed bearings are installed, throroughly clean them in solvent and dry with compressed air. Do not let the bearing spin while drying.

2. Clean the inside and the outside of the hub with solvent. Dry with compressed air.

3. Turn each bearing by hand (**Figure 12**). Make sure bearings turn smoothly. On non-sealed bearings, check the balls for evidence of wear, pitting or excessive heat (bluish tint). Replace bearings if necessary; always replace as a complete set. When replacing, be sure to take your old bearings along to ensure a perfect matchup.

> *NOTE*
> *Some axial play is normal, but radial play should be negligible. The bearings should turn smoothly.*

> *NOTE*
> *Fully sealed bearings are available from many good bearing specialty shops. Fully*

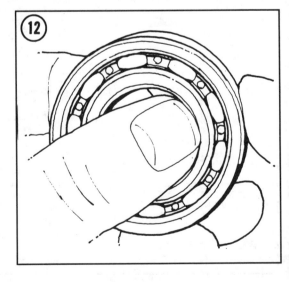

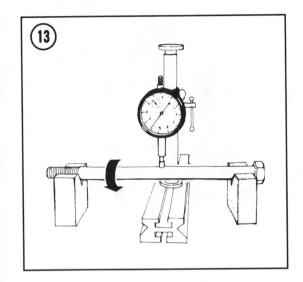

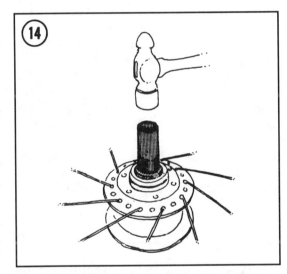

sealed bearings provide better protection from dirt and moisture that may get into the hub.

4. Check the axle for wear and straightness. Use V-blocks and a dial indicator as shown in **Figure 13**. If the runout is 0.01 in. (0.2 mm) or greater, the axle should be replaced.

Assembly

1. On non-sealed bearings, pack the bearings with a good quality bearing grease. Work the grease in between the balls thoroughly; turn the bearing by hand a couple of times to make sure the grease is distributed evenly inside the bearing.
2. Blow any dirt or foreign matter out of the hub prior to installing the bearings.
3. Install the right-hand bearing and press the distance collar into place.
4. Install the left-hand bearing.

> *CAUTION*
> *Tap the bearings squarely into place and tap on the outer race only. Use a socket (**Figure 14**) that matches the outer race diameter. Do not tap on the inner race or the bearing might be damaged. Be sure that the bearings are completely seated.*

> *NOTE*
> *Install the bearings with the sealed side facing outward.*

5. Screw the bearing retainer into the right-hand side securely. Lock it into place by staking it (**Figure 15**) with a center punch and hammer.

> *NOTE*
> *Prior to installing the bearing retainer, inspect the condition of the threads; replace if necessary.*

6. Install the dust seal.
7. Install the speedometer drive gear.
8. Lubricate the inside of the oil seal with grease.
9. Pack the speedometer drive gear housing with multipurpose grease. Align the tangs of the drive gear and install it.

8

10. Install the brake disc(s) and tighten the flange bolts to 20-24 ft.-lb. (27-33 N•m).

11. Install the front axle from the left-hand side. Slide on the spacer and screw on the axle nut. Tighten the nut to 40-47 ft.-lb. (55-65 N•m).

WHEELS

Wheel Balance

An unbalanced wheel is unsafe. Depending on the degree of unbalance and the speed of the motorcycle, the rider may experience anything from a mild vibration to a violent shimmy which may even result in loss of control.

On spoke type wheels, the balance weights are applied to the spokes on the light side of the wheel to correct this condition.

On models equipped with ComStar wheels, weights are attached to the rim. A kit of Tape-A-Weight, or equivalent, may be purchased from most motorcycle supply stores. This kit contains test weights and strips of adhesive-backed weights that can be cut to the desired weight and attached directly to the rim.

> *NOTE*
> *Be sure to balance the wheel with the brake disc(s) in place as they affect the balance.*

Before you attempt to balance the wheel, check to be sure that the wheel bearings are in good condition and properly lubricated and that the brakes do not drag. The wheel must rotate freely.

1. Remove the wheel as described under *Front Wheel Removal* in this chapter or *Rear Wheel Removal* in Chapter Nine.

2. Mount the wheel on a fixture such as the one in **Figure 16** so it can rotate freely.

3. Give the wheel a spin and let it coast to a stop. Mark the tire at the lowest point.

4. Spin the wheel several more times. If the wheel keeps coming to rest at the same point, it is out of balance.

5. On spoke type wheels, attach a weight to the upper (or light) side of the wheel at the spoke (**Figure 17**). Weights come in 4 sizes: 5,

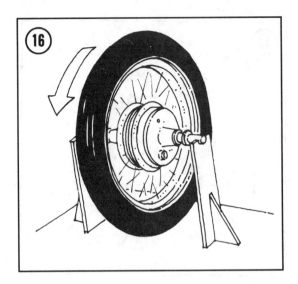

10, 15 and 20 grams. They are crimped onto the spoke with ordinary gas pliers.

6. On ComStar wheels, tape a test weight to the upper (or light) side of the wheel.

7. Experiment with different weights until the wheel, when spun, comes to rest at a different position each time. On wire spoke wheels tighten the weights so they won't be thrown off.

8. On ComStar wheels, remove the test weight and install the correct size adhesive-backed or clamp-on weight (**Figure 18**).

Spoke Adjustment (Wire Spoke Type Wheels)

Spokes loosen with use and should be checked periodically. If all appear loose, tighten all spokes on one side of the hub, then tighten all the spokes on the other side. One-half to one turn should be sufficient; do not overtighten. If you have a torque wrench, tighten the spokes to 22-43 in.-lb. (2.5-5.0 N•m).

After tightening spokes, check rim runout to be sure you haven't pulled the rim out of shape.

One way to check rim runout is to mount a dial indicator on the front fork so that it bears on the rim. If you don't have a dial indicator, improvise as shown in **Figure 19**. Adjust position of bolt until it just clears rim. Rotate rim and note whether clearance increases or

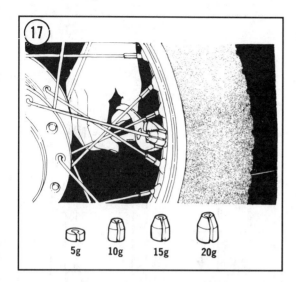

5g   10g   15g   20g

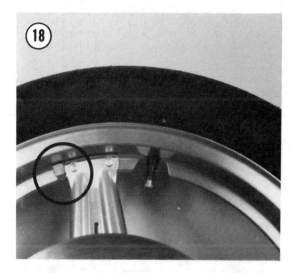

decreases. Mark the tire with chalk or crayon at areas that produce significantly large or small clearance. Clearance must not change by more than 0.08 in. (2 mm).

To pull rim out, tighten spokes which terminate on the same side of hub and loosen spokes which terminate on the opposite side of hub. See **Figure 20**. In most cases, only a slight amount of adjustment is necessary to true a rim. After adjustment, rotate rim and make sure another area has not been pulled out of true. Continue adjustment and checking until runout does not exceed 0.08 in. (2 mm)

Wheel Alignment

1. Measure the width of the 2 tires at their widest points.
2. Subtract the smaller dimension from the larger.
3. Make an alignment tool out of wood, approximately 7 feet long, with an offset equal to one half of the dimension obtained in Step 2. See D in **Figure 21**.
4. If the wheels are not aligned as in A and C, **Figure 21**, the rear wheel must be shifted to correct the situation.
5. Adjust the rear wheel with the chain adjuster bolts (**Figure 22**) until the wheels align.

NOTE
After this procedure is completed, refer to
Drive Chain Adjustment *in Chapter*

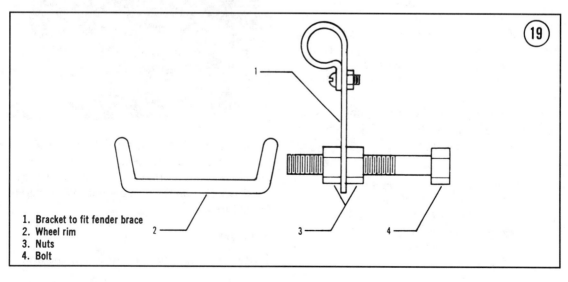

1. Bracket to fit fender brace
2. Wheel rim
3. Nuts
4. Bolt

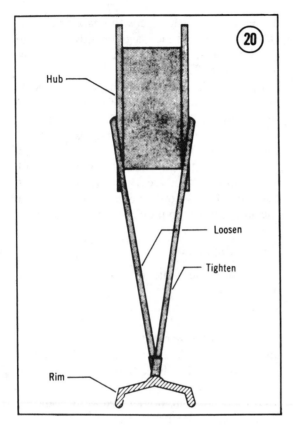

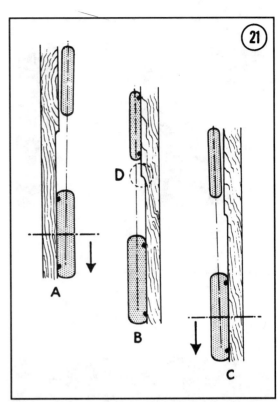

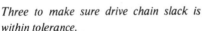

Three to make sure drive chain slack is within tolerance.

TIRE CHANGING

The rim of the ComStar wheel is aluminum and the exterior appearance can easily be damaged. Special care must be taken with tire irons when changing a tire to avoid scratches and gouges to the outer rim surface. Insert scraps of leather between the tire iron and the rim to protect the rim from gouges. Honda offers rim protectors (part No. 07772-0020200) for this purpose that are very handy to use.

Some models are factory equipped with tubeless tires and wheels designed specifically for use with tubeless tires.

> *WARNING*
> *Do not install tubeless tires on wheels designed for use only with tube-type tires. Personal injury and tire failure may result from rapid tire deflation while riding. Wheels for use with tubeless tires are so marked.*

Tire removal and installation are basically the same for tube and tubeless tires; where differences occur, they are noted. Tire repair is different and is covered in separate procedures.

Removal

1. Remove the valve core to deflate the tire.

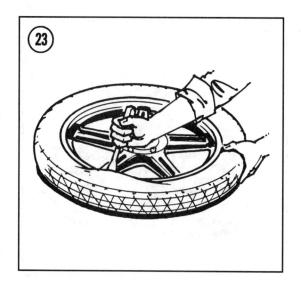

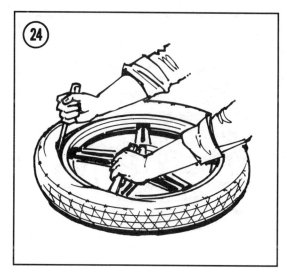

2. Press the entire bead on both sides of the tire into the center of the rim. Lubricate the beads with soapy water.

NOTE
When performing the following steps on models with Comstar wheels, insert scraps of leather between the tire iron and the rim to protect the rim from damage.

3. Insert the tire iron under the bead next to the valve (**Figure 23**). Force the bead on the opposite side of the tire into the center of the rim and pry the bead over the rim with the tire iron.

4. Insert a second tire iron next to the first to hold the bead over the rim. Then work around the tire with the first tire iron, prying the bead over the rim (**Figure 24**). On tube-type tires be careful not to pinch the inner tube with the tire irons.

5. On tube-type tires, remove the valve stem from the hole in the rim and remove the tube from the tire.

NOTE
Step 6 is required only if it is necessary to completely remove the tire from the rim, such as for tire replacement.

6. Stand the tire upright. Insert the tire iron between the second bead and the side of the rim that the first bead was pried over (**Figure 25**). Force the bead on the opposite side from the tire iron into the center of the rim. Pry the second bead off the rim, working around as with the first.

7. On tubeless tires, inspect the condition of the rubber O-ring seal where the valve stem seats against the inner surface of the wheel. Replace if it's starting to deteriorate or has lost its resiliency. This is a common location for air loss.

Installation

1. Carefully inspect the tire for any damage, especially inside.

2. A new tire may have balancing rubbers inside. These are not patches and should not be disturbed. A colored spot near the bead indicates a lighter point on the tire. This spot should be placed next to the valve stem (**Figure 26**).

8

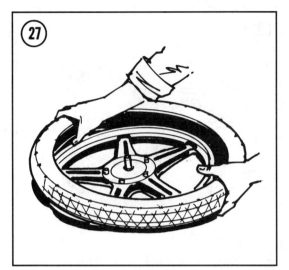

3. On tube-type tires, inflate the tube just enough to round it out. Too much air will make installation difficult. Place the inner tube inside the tire.

4. Lubricate both beads of the tire with soapy water.

5. Place the backside of the tire into the center of the rim and insert the valve stem through the stem hole in the wheel. The lower bead should go into the center of the rim and the upper bead outside. Work around the tire in both directions (**Figure 27**). Use a tire iron for the last few inches of bead (**Figure 28**).

6. Press the upper bead into the rim opposite the valve (**Figure 29**). Pry the bead into the rim on both sides of the initial point with a tire iron, working around the rim to the valve (**Figure 30**).

7. On tube-type tires, wiggle the valve stem to be sure the tube is not under the bead. Set the valve squarely in its hole before screwing in the valve nut to hold it against the rim.

8. Check the bead on both sides of the tire for even fit around the rim.

9. On tube-type tires, inflate the tire slowly to seat the beads in the rim. It may be necessary to bounce the tire to complete the seating. Inflate to the required pressure. Balance the wheel as previously described.

10. On tubeless tires, bounce the wheel several times, rotating it each time. This will force the tire beads against the rim flanges. After the tire beads are in contact with the rim evenly, inflate the tire to seat the beads.

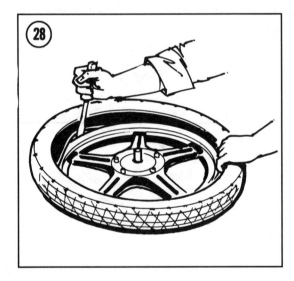

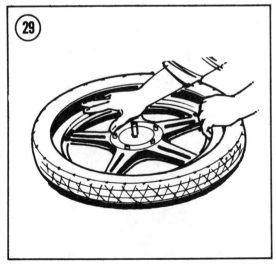

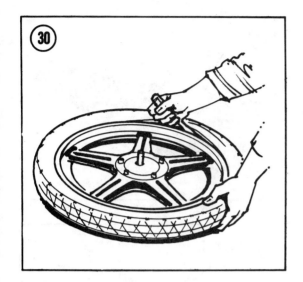

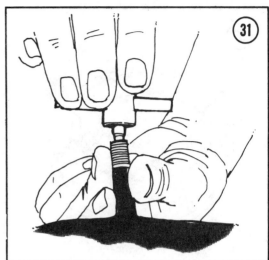

NOTE
If you are unable to get an air-tight seal this way, install an inflatable band around the circumference of the tire. Slowly inflate the band until the beads are seated against the rim flanges, then inflate the tire. If you still encounter trouble, deflate the inflation band and the tire. Apply additional lubricant to the beads and repeat the inflation procedure. Also try rolling the tire back and forth while inflating it.

11. On tubeless tires, inflate the tire to more than the recommended inflation pressure for the initial seating of the rim flanges. Once the beads are seated correctly, deflate the tire to the correct pressure.

WARNING
Never exceed 56 psi (4.0 kg/cm^2) inflation pressure as the tire could burst causing severe injury. Never stand directly over the tire while inflating it.

TIRE REPAIRS
(TUBE-TYPE TIRES)

Every rider eventually experiences trouble with a tire or tube. Repairs and replacement are fairly simple and every rider should know the techniques.

Patching a motorcycle tube is only a temporary fix. A motorcycle tire flexes too much and could rub a patch right off. However, a patched tire will get you far enough to buy a new tube.

Tire Repair Kits

Tire repair kits can be purchased from motorcycle dealers and some auto supply stores. When buying, specify that the kit you want is for motorcycles.

There are two types of tire repair kits:
a. Hot patch
b. Cold patch

Hot patches are stronger because they actually vulcanize to the tube, becoming a part of it. However, they are far too bulky to carry for roadside repairs and the strength is unnecessary for temporary repair.

Cold patches are not vulcanized to the tube; they are simply glued to it. Though not as strong as hot patches, cold patches are still very durable. Cold patch kits are less bulky than hot and more easily applied under adverse conditions. A cold patch kit containing everything necessary tucks in easily with your emergency tool kit.

Tube Inspection

1. Install the valve core into the valve stem (**Figure 31**) and inflate the tube slightly. Do not overinflate.

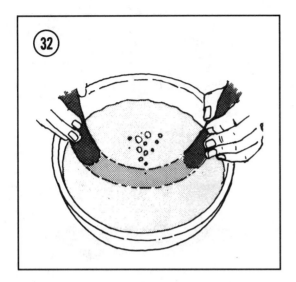

2. Immerse the tube in water a section at a time. See **Figure 32**. Look carefully for bubbles indicating a hole. Mark each hole and continue checking until you are certain that all holes are discovered and marked. Also make sure that the valve core is not leaking; tighten it if necessary.

> *NOTE*
> *If you do not have enough water to immerse sections of the tube, try running your hand over the tube slowly and very close to the surface. If your hand is damp, it works even better. If you suspect a hole anywhere, apply some saliva to the area to verify it* **(Figure 33)**.

3. Apply a cold patch using the techniques described under *Cold Patch Repair*, following.

4. Dust the patch area with talcum powder to prevent it from sticking to the tire.

5. Carefully check inside the tire casing for glass particles, nails or other objects which may have damaged the tube. If inside of tire is split, apply a patch to the area to prevent it from pinching and damaging the tube again.

6. Check the inside of the rim. Make sure the rim band is in place, with no spoke ends protruding, which could puncture the tube.

7. Deflate tube prior to installation in the tire.

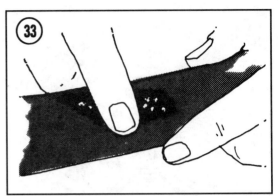

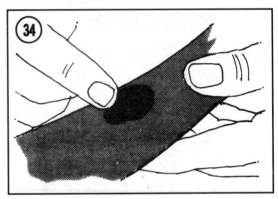

Cold patch repair

1. Remove the tube from the tire as described under *Tire Removal* in this chapter.

2. Roughen area around hole slightly larger than the patch; use a cap from tire repair kit or pocket knife. Do not scrape too vigorously or you may cause additional damage.

3. Apply a small quantity of special cement to the puncture and spread it evenly with a finger **(Figure 34)**.

4. Allow cement to dry until tacky—usually 30 seconds or so is sufficient.

5. Remove the backing from the patch.

> *CAUTION*
> *Do not touch the newly exposed rubber with your fingers or the patch will not stick firmly.*

6. Center the patch over hole. Hold the patch firmly in place for about 30 seconds to allow the cement to set **(Figure 35)**.

7. Dust the patched area with talcum powder to prevent sticking.

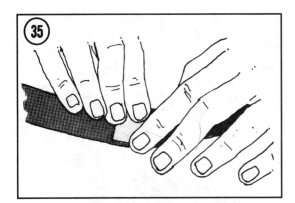

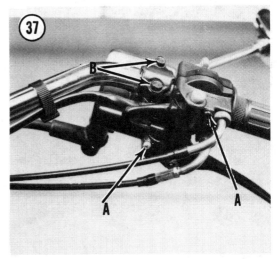

TIRE REPAIRS
(TUBELESS TIRES)

Patching a tubeless tire on the road is very difficult. If both beads are still in place against the rim, a can of pressurized tire sealant may inflate the tire and seal the hole. The beads must be against the wheel for this method to work. Another solution is to carry a spare inner tube that could be temporarily installed and inflated. This will enable you to get to a service station where the tire can be correctly repaired. Be sure that the tube is designed for use with a tubeless tire.

Honda (and the tire industry) recommends that the tubeless tire be patched from the inside. Therefore, do not patch the tire with an external type plug. If you find an external patch on a tire, it is recommended that it be patch-reinforced from the inside.

Due to the variations of material supplied

with different tubeless tire repair kits, follow the instructions and recommendations supplied with the repair kit.

Honda recommends that the valve stem be replaced each time the tire is removed from the wheel.

HANDLEBAR

Removal/Installation

1. Remove the rear view mirrors, seat and fuel tank.
2. Remove the right-hand side cover and disconnect the negative lead from the battery (**Figure 36**).
3. Remove the screws (A, **Figure 37**) securing the right-hand handlebar switch assembly and remove the electrical wires from the clip on the handlebar.

> *CAUTION*
> *Cover the frame with a heavy cloth or plastic tarp to protect it from accidental spilling of brake fluid. Wash any brake fluid off of any painted or plated surface immediately, as it will destroy the finish. Use soapy water and rinse thoroughly.*

4. Remove the bolts (B, **Figure 37**) securing the master cylinder and lay it over the frame. Keep the master cylinder in the upright position to minimize the loss of brake fluid. It is not necessary to remove the hydraulic brake line.

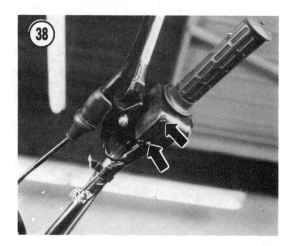

5. Remove the screws (**Figure 38**) securing the left-hand handlebar switch assembly and remove the electrical wires from the clips on the handlebar.

6. Slacken the clutch cable (**Figure 39**) and disconnect the cable from the clutch hand lever.

7. Loosen the clutch bracket bolt and slide off the clutch lever assembly.

8. Remove the throttle assembly and lay it over the frame; be careful not to kink the throttle cables.

9. Remove the screws (**Figure 40**) securing the fuse panel cover and remove the cover.

10. Remove the Allen bolts (**Figure 41**) securing the handlebar holder/fuse panel and move the holder up and out of the way.

11. Remove the handlebar.

12. Install by reversing these removal steps, noting the following.

13. Tighten the Allen bolts securing the handlebar holder/fuse panel to 13-18 ft.-lb. (18-25 N•m).

NOTE
*Align the punch mark on the handlebar with the top of the handlebar lower holder (**Figure 42**).*

14. When installing all assemblies, align the punch mark on the handlebar with the split on the mounting bracket (**Figure 43**).

NOTE
Apply a light coat of multipurpose grease to the throttle grip area on the handlebar prior to installation.

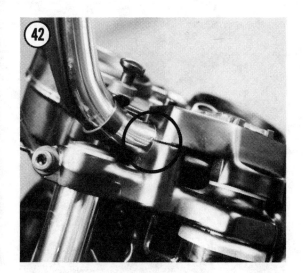

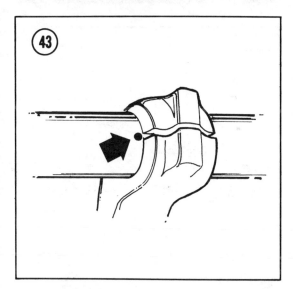

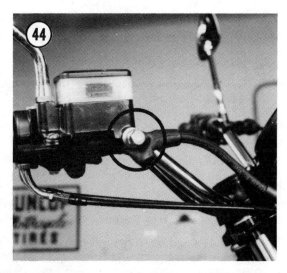

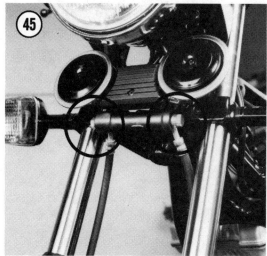

> *WARNING*
> *After installation is completed, make sure the brake lever **does not** come in contact with the throttle grip assembly when it is pulled on fully.*

15. Adjust the clutch and throttle operation as described in Chapter Three.

STEERING HEAD

Disassembly

1. Remove the front wheel as described in this chapter.

2. Remove the caliper assembly(ies) as described under *Front Caliper Assembly Removal* in Chapter Ten.

3. Remove the union bolt (**Figure 44**) securing the brake hose from the master cylinder to the fitting. Remove the union bolt(s) (**Figure 45**) securing the caliper hose(s) to the fitting and remove the hoses.

4. Disconnect all electrical leads (**Figure 46**) to the front brake light switch.

5. Remove the fuel tank.

6. Remove the handlebar as described in this chapter.

7. Remove the headlight, front directional lights and horn(s).

8. Remove the tachometer and speedometer cables (**Figure 47**) from the instrument cluster.

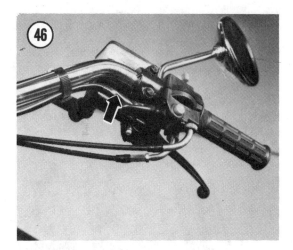

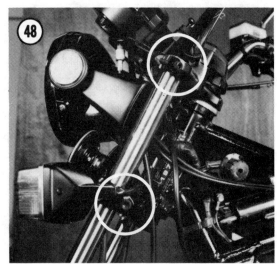

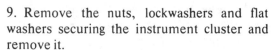

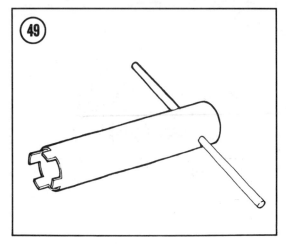

9. Remove the nuts, lockwashers and flat washers securing the instrument cluster and remove it.

10. Loosen the pinch bolts (**Figure 48**) on the upper and lower fork bridges.

11. Remove the fork and front fender assembly.

12. Remove the steering stem head nut and washer.

13. Remove the upper fork bridge.

14. Remove the bearing adjusting nut with a pin spanner, provided in the factory tool kit or use an easily improvised unit (**Figure 49**).

15. Remove the upper bearing cover.

16. Pull the steering stem out of the frame. The upper and lower bearings are assembled roller bearings—don't worry about catching any loose ball bearings.

Inspection

1. Clean the bearing races in the steering head and both roller bearings with solvent.

2. Check for broken welds on the frame around the steering head.

3. Check the bearings for pitting, scratches or discoloration, indicating wear or corrosion. Replace them in sets.

4. Check upper and lower races in the steering head. See *Headset Bearing Race Removal/Installation* in this chapter if races are pitted, scratched or badly worn.

5. Check steering stem for cracks.

Steering Head Bearing Races

The headset and steering stem bearing races are pressed into place. Because they are easily

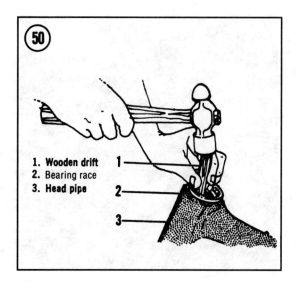

1. Wooden drift
2. Bearing race
3. Head pipe

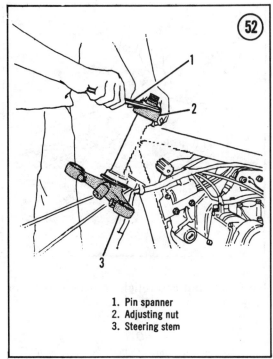

1. Pin spanner
2. Adjusting nut
3. Steering stem

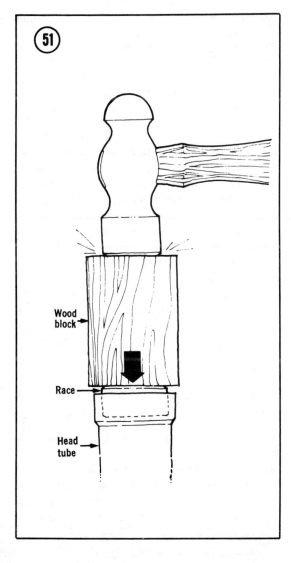

Wood
block

Race

Head
tube

bent, do not remove them unless they are worn and require replacement.

Headset Bearing Race Removal/Installation

To remove a headset outer race, insert a hardwood stick into the head tube and carefully tap the race out from the inside (**Figure 50**). Tap all around the race so that neither the race nor the head tube are bent. To install a race, fit it into the end of the head tube. Tap it into place slowly and squarely with a block of wood (**Figure 51**).

Steering Head Assembly

1. Make sure the steering head bearings are properly seated. Coat them with wheel bearing grease.
2. Thoroughly pack the bearings with wheel bearing grease.
3. Install the dust seal and lower bearing onto the steering stem.
4. Insert the steering stem into the head tube. Hold it firmly.
5. Install the upper bearing and upper bearing cover.
6. Install the bearing adjuster nut (**Figure 52**) and torque to 22-29 ft.-lb. (30-40 N•m). Then

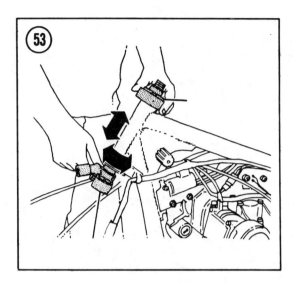

loosen the nut and retighten it to 9-17 in.-lb. (1.0-2.0 N•m).

> *NOTE*
> *The adjuster nut should be just tight enough to remove play, both horizontal and vertical (Figure 53), yet loose enough so that the assembly will turn to both lock positions under its own weight after an initial assist.*

7. Continue assembling by reversing *Disassembly* Steps 1-11. Note the following.

8. Tighten the bolts to the following torque specifications:
   a. Upper fork bridge bolts: 7-9 ft.-lb. (9-13 N•m)
   b. Lower fork bridge bolts: 22-29 ft.-lb. (30-40) N•m)
   c. Steering stem nut: 58-87 ft.-lb. (80-120 N•m)
   d. Brake system union bolts: 18-25 ft.-lb. (25-35 N•m)

9. After the total assembly is completed, check the stem for looseness or binding; readjust if necessary.

10. Bleed the front brake as described under *Bleeding the System* in Chapter Ten.

Steering Stem Adjustment

If play develops in the steering system, it may only require adjustment. However, don't take a chance on it. Disassemble the stem and look for possible damage. Then reassemble the stem and adjust as described in Step 6 of *Steering Head Assembly* in this chapter.

FRONT FORK

The Honda front suspension consists of a spring-controlled, hydraulically damped telescopic fork. Before suspecting major trouble, drain the fork oil and refill it with the proper type and quantity; refer to *Front Fork Oil Change* in Chapter Three. If you still have trouble, such as poor damping, tendency to bottom out or top out, or leakage around the rubber seals, then follow the service procedures in this section.

To simplify fork service and to prevent the mixing of parts, the fork legs should be removed, serviced and reinstalled individually.

Removal/Installation

1. Remove the front wheel as described in this chapter.

2. Remove the bolts securing the caliper(s) and remove them from the fork slider. Remove the brake hose from the retainer on the fork (**Figure 54**). Do not remove the brake hose from the caliper(s). Tie the caliper(s) up to the frame to relieve the strain on the hose(s).

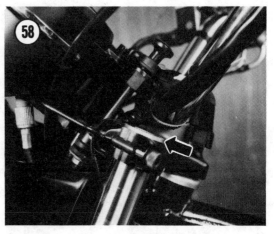

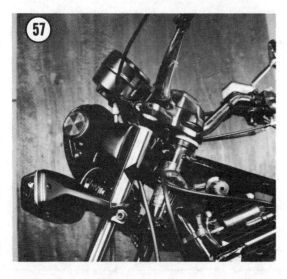

8

NOTE
Insert a piece of wood in the caliper(s) in place of the disc. That way, if the brake lever is inadvertently squeezed, the piston will not be forced out of the cylinder. If it does happen, the caliper might have to be disassembled to reseat the piston and the system will have to be bled. By using the wood, bleeding the brake is not necessary when installing the wheel.

3. Remove the bolts (**Figure 55**) securing the front fender and remove the fender.
4. Loosen the upper and lower fork clamp bolts (**Figure 56**).
5. Remove the fork tube (**Figure 57**). It may be necessary to slightly rotate the tube while removing it.
6. Install by reversing these removal steps, noting the following.
7. The top surface of each fork tube must be flush with the top of the upper fork bridge (**Figure 58**). The cap bolt will stick up past this surface.
8. Tighten the bolts to the following torque specifications:

   a. Upper fork bridge bolts: 7-9 ft.-lb. (9-13 N•m)
   b. Lower fork bridge bolts: 22-29 ft.-lb. (30-40 N•m)
   c. Caliper mounting bolts: 22-29 ft.-lb. (30-40 N•m)

Disassembly

Refer to **Figure 59** for this procedure.
1. Hold the fork tube in a vise with soft jaws. Keep the slider end lower than the top end.

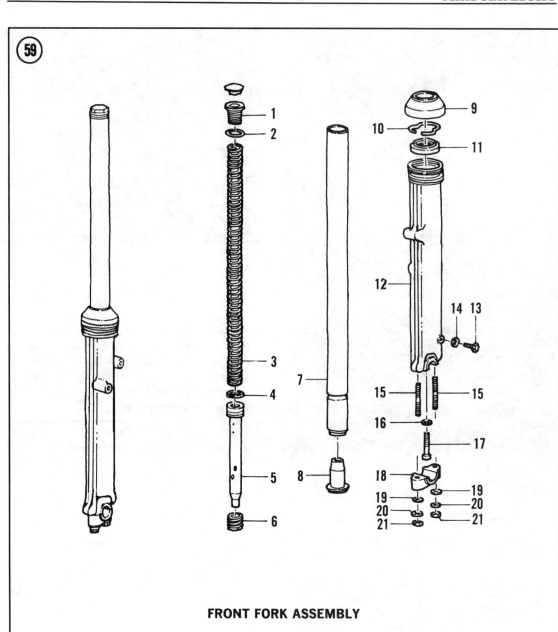

FRONT FORK ASSEMBLY

1. Top bolt	12. Slider
2. Flat washer	13. Drain bolt
3. Spring	14. Washer
4. Piston ring	15. Lower studs
5. Dampener rod	16. Sealing washer
6. Rebound spring	17. Allen bolt
7. Upper fork tube	18. Axle clamp
8. Oil lock piece	19. Washer
9. Dust seal	20. Lockwasher
10. Snap ring	21. Nut
11. Oil seal	

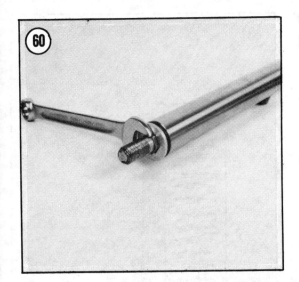

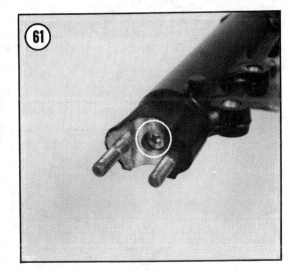

> *WARNING*
> *Be careful when removing the top bolt as the spring is under pressure.*

2. Remove the top bolt from the fork. Use a 17 mm Allen wrench or insert the head of a 17 mm bolt into the socket and turn it with a 17 mm open-end wrench (**Figure 60**).

3. Remove the flat washer and spring.

4. Remove the fork from the vise and pour the oil out and discard it. Pump the fork several times by hand to expel most of the oil.

5. Clamp the slider in a vise with soft jaws.

6. Remove the 6 mm Allen bolt (**Figure 61**) at the bottom of the slider and pull the fork tube out of the slider.

7. Remove the oil lock piece, damper rod and rebound spring.

8. If oil has been leaking from the top of the slider, remove the snap ring and oil seal (**Figure 62**).

> *CAUTION*
> *Use a dull screwdriver blade to remove the oil seal. Do not damage the outer or inner surface of the slider.*

> *NOTE*
> *It may be necessary to slightly heat the area on the slider around the oil seal prior to removal. On models with black painted sliders, use a rag soaked in hot water—do not apply heat or the finish will be damaged.*

Inspection

1. Thoroughly clean all parts in solvent and dry. Check the fork tube for signs of wear or galling.

2. Check the dampener rod for straightness. **Figure 63** shows one method. The rod should be replaced if the runout is 0.01 in. (0.2 mm) or greater.

3. Carefully check the dampener valve and the piston ring for wear or damage (**Figure 64**).

4. Inspect the oil seals for scoring and nicks and loss of resiliency. Replace if their condition is questionable.

5. Measure the uncompressed length of the spring with a square as shown in **Figure 65**. Replace the spring if it is 19.4 in. (492.6 mm) or shorter.

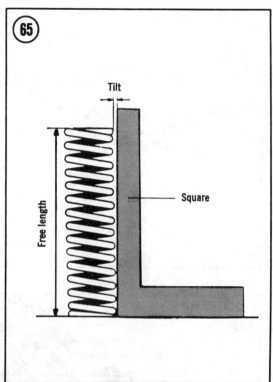

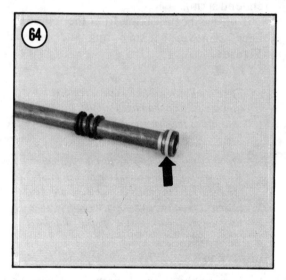

6. Check the upper fork tube exterior for scratches and straightness. If bent or scratched, it should be replaced.

7. Check the lower slider for dents or exterior damage that may cause the upper fork tube to hang up during riding conditions. Replace if necessary.

8. Check the O-ring on the top spring seat (**Figure 66**); replace if necessary.

9. Any parts that are worn or damaged should be replaced. Simply cleaning and reinstalling unserviceable components will not improve performance of the front suspension.

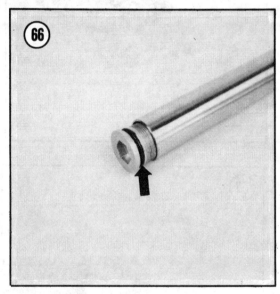

Assembly

1. If removed, install the oil seal and snap ring (**Figure 62**).

NOTE
Make sure the seal seats squarely and fully in the bore of the slider.

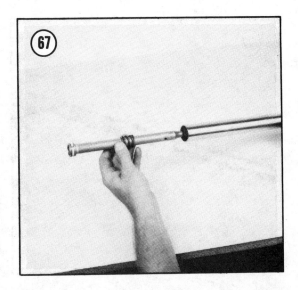

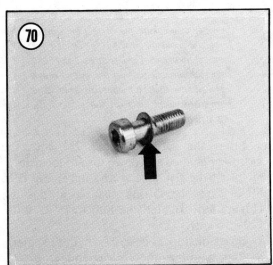

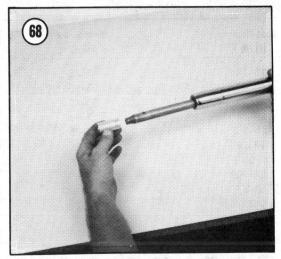

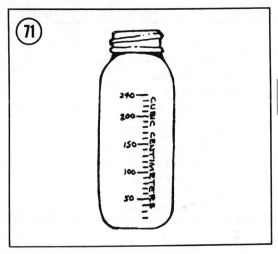

8

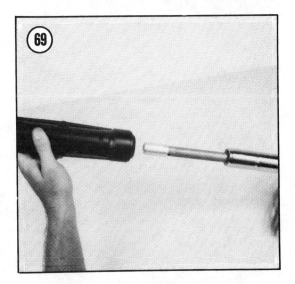

2. Insert the damper rod into the fork tube (**Figure 67**) and install the oil lock piece (**Figure 68**).

3. Apply a light coat of oil to the outside of the fork tube and install it into the slider (**Figure 69**). Apply Loctite Lock N' Seal to the threads and the underside of the bolt head (**Figure 61**). Install it and tighten to 6-9 ft.-lb. (8-12 N•m).

NOTE
*Make sure the sealing washer (**Figure 70**) is in place on the bolt prior to installing it. Without it there will be an oil leak.*

4. Fill each fork tube with 5.8-6.0 oz. (172.5-177.5 cc) of Dexron ATF (automatic transmission fluid) or SAE 10W fork oil.

NOTE
*In order to measure the correct amount of fluid, use a plastic baby bottle. These have measurements in fluid ounces (oz.) and cubic centimeters (cc) on the side (**Figure 71**). Many fork oil containers have a semi-transparent strip on the side of the bottle to aid in measuring.*

5. Insert the spring (**Figure 72**) with the narrow or tapered end down toward the axle.
6. Install the flat washer and upper cap bolt. Make sure the O-ring seal is in position (**Figure 66**). Tighten the bolt to 15-22 ft.-lb. (20-30 N•m).
7. Install the fork as described in this chapter.
8. Repeat for the other fork assembly.

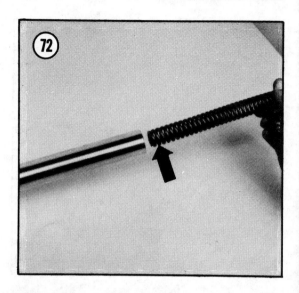

TABLE 1 FRONT SUSPENSION AND STEERING TORQUE SPECIFICATIONS

Item	Foot Pounds (ft.-lb.)	Newton Meters (N•m)
Front axle clamp nuts	13–18	18–25
Front axle nut	40–47	55–65
Caliper mounting bolts	22–29	30–40
Brake disc flange bolts	20–24	27–33
Brake system union bolts	18–25	25–35
Handlebar holder/fuse panel bolts	13–18	18–25
Upper fork bridge bolts	7–9	9–13
Lower fork bridge bolts	22–29	30–40
Steering stem nut	58–87	80–120
Front fork 6mm Allen bolt (bottom of slider)	6–9	8–12
Front fork cap bolt	15–22	20–30
Wheel spokes	22–43 in.-lb.	2.5–5.0

REAR SUSPENSION

This chapter includes repair and replacement procedures for the rear wheel and rear suspension components.

Refer to **Table 1** for rear suspension torque specifications. **Table 1** and **Table 2** are located at the end of this chapter.

WHEEL

Removal/Installation

1. Place the bike on the centerstand or block up the engine so that the rear wheel clears the ground.

2. Loosen the drive chain adjusting locknuts and adjuster bolts (**Figure 1**).

3. On drum brake models, remove the cotter pin and nut (A, **Figure 2**) securing the brake torque link. Unscrew the rear brake adjusting nut (B, **Figure 2**) and disconnect the brake rod.

4. Remove the cotter pin and loosen the rear axle nut (A, **Figure 3**). Discard the cotter pin; never reuse a cotter pin.

5. Pivot the chain adjusters down (B, **Figure 3**).

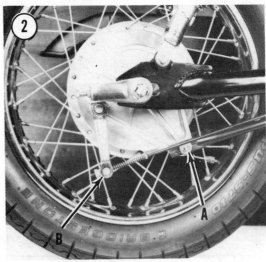

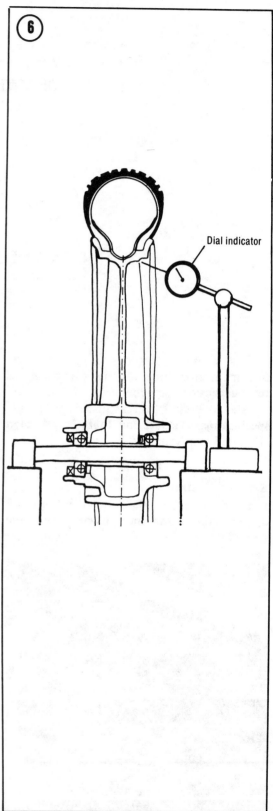

Dial indicator

6. Push the wheel forward until the drive chain is loose.

7. On disc brake models, withdraw the axle to the left enough to remove the caliper assembly from it.

NOTE
*Tie the caliper assembly up to the rear grab bar with wire or Bungee cord (**Figure 4**). This will take the strain off the brake hose.*

8. Withdraw the axle, remove the drive chain from the rear sprocket and remove the wheel.

NOTE
*Never set a wheel with a brake disc attached onto the brake disc, as it may get damaged. Place the outer edge of the wheel on wooden blocks (**Figure 5**).*

NOTE
Insert a piece of wood in the caliper in place of the disc. That way, if the brake pedal is inadvertently pushed, the piston will not be forced out of the cylinder. If this does happen, the caliper might have to be disassembled to reseat the piston and the system will have to be bled. By using the wood, bleeding the brake is not necessary when installing the wheel.

9. Install by reversing these removal steps, noting the following.

10. Adjust the drive chain as described under *Drive Chain Adjustment* in Chapter Three.

NOTE
On drum brake models, prior to tightening the axle nut, install the brake torque link and tighten the nut to 13-18 ft.-lb (18-25 N•m). Install a new cotter pin.

11. Tighten the axle nut to 58-72 ft.-lb. (80-100 N•m) and install a new cotter pin.

12. After the wheel is installed, completely rotate it and apply the brake several times to make sure it rotates freely and that the brakes work properly. On disc brake models, make sure the brake pads are against the disc.

13. On drum brake models, adjust the rear brake as described under *Rear Brake Pedal Free Play (Drum Type)* in Chapter Three.

Inspection

Measure the axial and radial runout of the wheel with a dial indicator as shown in **Figure 6**. The maximum axial and radial runout for both the wire spoke type wheel and the ComStar wheel is 0.08 in. (2.0 mm). If the runout exceeds this dimension, check the wheel bearing condition.

On models with wire spoke wheels, some of this condition can be corrected as described under *Spoke Adjustment* in Chapter Eight.

On models with the ComStar wheels, if the runout exceeds this dimension the wheel will have to be replaced as it cannot be serviced. Inspect the ComStar wheel for signs of cracks, fractures, dents or bends. If it is damaged in any way, it must be replaced.

WARNING
Do not try to repair any damage to a ComStar wheel as it will result in an unsafe riding condition.

Check axial runout as described under *Rear Hub Inspection* in this chapter.

REAR HUB

Disassembly

Refer to **Figure 7** for this procedure.

1. Remove the rear wheel as described in this chapter.

2. On drum brake models, pull the brake assembly (**Figure 8**) straight up and out of the wheel.

3. On disc brake models, remove the nuts (A, **Figure 9**) securing the brake disc and remove it.

4. Remove the axle spacer (**Figure 10**).

5. Unscrew the bearing retainer (**Figure 11**) and dust seal from the driven flange and remove them.

6. Remove the driven flange assembly (**Figure 12**) from the left-hand side of the wheel. Remove the rubber dampers (A, **Figure 13**).

7. On drum brake models, unscrew the bearing retainer on the left-hand side and the dust seal.

8. Turn the wheel over and unscrew the right-hand bearing retainer (B, **Figure 9**) and dust seal.

9

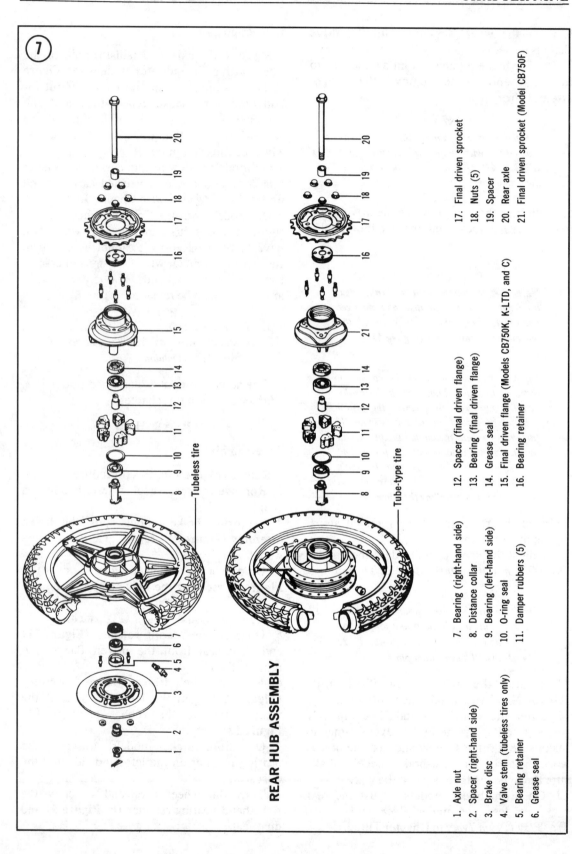

⑦

REAR HUB ASSEMBLY

1. Axle nut
2. Spacer (right-hand side)
3. Brake disc
4. Valve stem (tubeless tires only)
5. Bearing retainer
6. Grease seal
7. Bearing (right-hand side)
8. Distance collar
9. Bearing (left-hand side)
10. O-ring seal
11. Damper rubbers (5)
12. Spacer (final driven flange)
13. Bearing (final driven flange)
14. Grease seal
15. Final driven flange (Models CB750K, K-LTD, and C)
16. Bearing retainer
17. Final driven sprocket
18. Nuts (5)
19. Spacer
20. Rear axle
21. Final driven sprocket (Model CB750F)

Tubeless tire

Tube-type tire

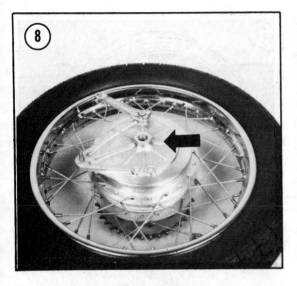

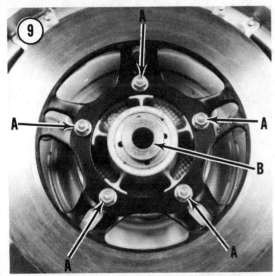

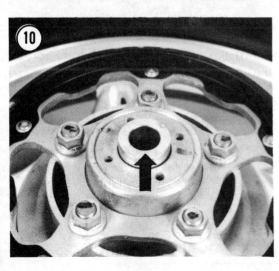

9. To remove the left-hand bearing (B, **Figure 13**) and distance collar, insert a soft aluminum or brass drift into the right-hand side of the hub. Push the distance collar over to one side and place the drift on the inner race of the left-hand bearing. Tap the bearing out of the hub with a hammer, working around the perimeter of the inner race.

10. Remove the distance collar and tap out the right-hand bearing in the same manner.

11. Remove the bearing from the driven flange.

Inspection

1. Do not clean sealed bearings. If non-sealed bearings are installed, throughly clean them in solvent and dry with compressed air. Do not let the bearing spin while drying.

2. Clean the inside and outside of the hub with solvent. Dry with compressed air.

3. Turn each bearing by hand (**Figure 14**). Make sure bearings turn smoothly. On non-sealed bearings, check the balls for evidence of wear, pitting or excessive heat (bluish tint). Replace bearings if necessary; always replace as a complete set. When replacing the bearings, be sure to take your old bearings along to ensure a perfect matchup.

> *NOTE*
> *Fully sealed bearings are available from many good bearing specialty shops. Fully sealed bearings provide better protection from dirt and moisture that may get into the hub.*

4. Check the axle for wear and straightness. Use V-blocks and a dial indicator as shown in **Figure 15**. If the runout is 0.01 in. (0.2 mm) or greater, the axle should be replaced.

Assembly

1. On non-sealed bearings, pack the bearings thoroughly with a good quality bearing grease. Work the grease in between the balls thoroughly; turn the bearing by hand a couple of times to make sure the grease is distributed evenly inside the bearing.

2. Blow any dirt or foreign matter out of the hub prior to installing the bearings.

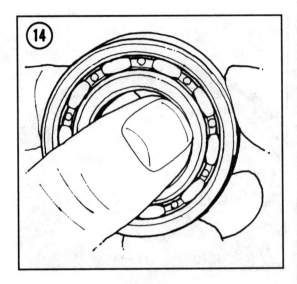

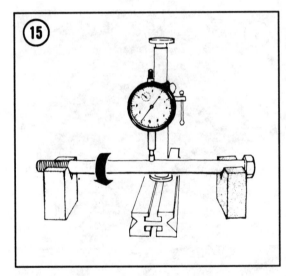

3. Install the right-hand bearing and bearing retainer.

4. Install the distance collar, left-hand bearing and bearing retainer.

> *CAUTION*
> *Tap the bearings squarely into place and tap only on the outer race. Use a socket (**Figure 16**) that matches the outer race diameter. Do not tap on the inner race or the bearing will be damaged. Be sure to tap the bearings until they seat completely.*

> *NOTE*
> *Install the bearings with the sealed side facing outward.*

NOTE
Prior to installing the bearing retainer, inspect the condition of the threads; replace the retainer(s) if necessary.

5. After the bearing retainers have been screwed in securely, lock them into place by staking them (**Figure 17**) with a center punch and hammer.

6. Install the axle spacer (**Figure 10**).

7. On disc brake models, install the brake disc and tighten the nuts (A, **Figure 9**) to 20-24 ft.-lb. (27-33 N•m).

8. On drum brake models, install the brake assembly into the hub.

9. Install the driven flange assembly (**Figure 12**). Make sure it is completely seated into the hub. If the driven sprocket nuts were loosened during disassembly, tighten them to the following specifications:

a. Disc brake models: 40-47 ft.-lb. (55-65 N•m)

b. Drum brake models: 58-72 ft.-lb. (80-100 N•m)

10. Install the rear wheel as described in this chapter.

DRIVEN FLANGE ASSEMBLY

Disassembly/Assembly

Refer to **Figure 7** for this procedure.

1. Remove the rear wheel as described in this chapter.

2. Pull the driven flange assembly (**Figure 18**) up and out of the wheel hub.

NOTE
If it is difficult to remove, tap on the backside of the sprocket (from the opposite side of the wheel, through the spokes) with the wooden handle of a hammer. Tap evenly around the perimeter until it is free.

3. To remove the sprocket from the assembly, remove the flange nuts (**Figure 19**) and remove the sprocket.

4. If the bearing needs replacing, refer to Step 5 of *Rear Hub Disassembly* in this chapter.

5. Install the sprocket and tighten the flange bolts to the following torque specifications:

a. Disc brake models: 40-47 ft.-lb. (55-65 N•m)

b. Drum brake models: 58-72 ft.-lb. (80-100 N•m)

6. To install the bearing, refer to *Rear Hub Assembly* in this chapter.

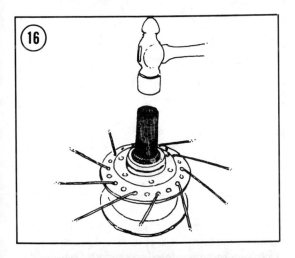

Inspection

1. Visually inspect the rubber dampers (**Figure 20**) for signs of damage or deterioration. Replace if necessary as a complete set.

2. Inspect the flange assembly housing for cracks or damage; replace if necessary.

3. Inspect the teeth of the sprocket. If the teeth are visibly worn (**Figure 21**), replace with a new sprocket.

4. If the sprocket requires replacement, also inspect the condition of the drive chain and the drive sprocket. They may also be worn and need replacing. Refer to *Drive Chain Adjustment* in Chapter Three.

DRIVE CHAIN

Removal/Installation

> *CAUTION*
> *The drive chain is manufactured as a continuous closed loop with no master link. Do not cut it with a chain cutter as this will result in future chain failure and possible loss of control under riding conditions.*

1. Remove the mufflers as described under *Exhaust System Removal/Installation* in Chapter Six.

2. Remove the rear wheel as described in this chapter.

3. Remove the rear swing arm as described in this chapter.

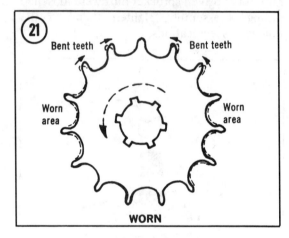

4. Perform Steps 1-7 under *Drive Sprocket Removal* in Chapter Five. Remove the drive chain from the drive sprocket and remove it.

5. Install by reversing these removal steps.

WHEEL BALANCING

For complete information refer to *Wheel Balancing* in Chapter Eight.

TIRE CHANGING

Refer to *Tire Changing* in Chapter Eight.

REAR SWING ARM

In time, the bushings (or bearings) will wear and the swing arm will become loose on the pivot shaft. This will cause loss of high speed stability.

Refer to **Figure 22** for this procedure.

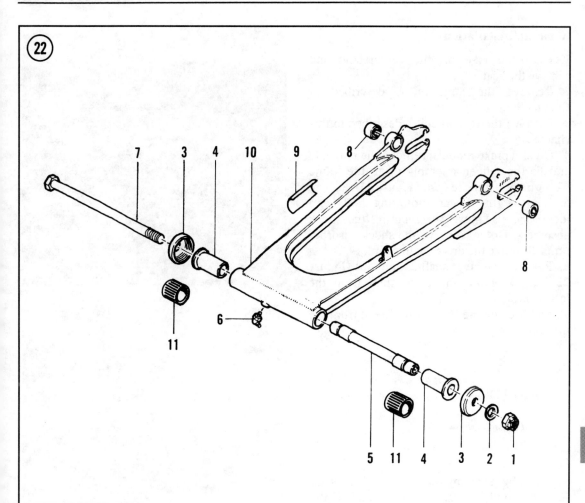

REAR SWING ARM ASSEMBLY

1. Locknut
2. Washer
3. Dust seal cap
4. Pivot bushing (1979)
5. Pivot collar
6. Grease fitting
7. Pivot shaft
8. Rubber bushing
9. Decal
10. Swing arm
11. Needle bearing (1980-on)

Removal/Installation

1. Place the bike on the centerstand and remove the seat.

2. Remove the mufflers as described in Chapter Six.

3. Remove the rear wheel as described in this chapter.

4. On disc brake models, remove the rear axle and tie the caliper assembly up to the frame with wire or a Bungee cord (**Figure 23**).

5. Remove the lower mounting bolts and lockwashers (**Figure 24**) securing the shock absorbers. Do not remove the shock absorber units. Remove the drive chain guard.

6. Remove the pivot shaft 24 mm nut (**Figure 25**) and withdraw the pivot shaft from the left-hand side.

7. Pull back on the swing arm, free it from the drive chain and remove it.

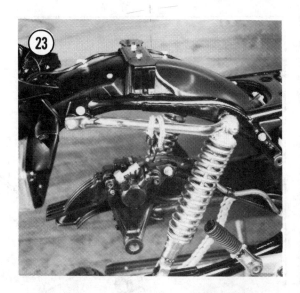

> *NOTE*
> *Don't lose the caps on each side of the pivot points; they will fall off when the swing arm is removed.*

8. Install by reversing these removal steps. Be sure to install the caps onto the end of the pivot prior to installation.

> *NOTE*
> *Be sure to slip the swing arm through the drive chain—the chain **must** be on the inside of the swing arm.*

9. Tighten the swing arm pivot bolt nut to 40-51 ft.-lb. (55-70 N•m). Tighten the upper shock absorber nut to 14-22 ft.-lb. (20-30 N•m).

10. Adjust the drive chain as described in Chapter Three. On drum brake models, adjust the rear brake as described in Chapter Three.

11. If the swing arm was disassembled for inspection, it must be lubricated as described under *Rear Swing Arm Bushings or Bearings Lubrication* in Chapter Three.

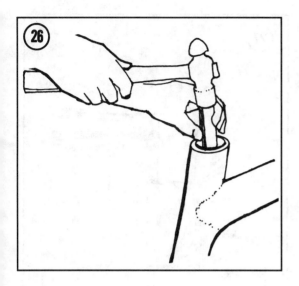

Inspection

1. Remove the rear brake torque arm from the swing arm.
2. Remove both dust seal caps and withdraw the pivot collar.
3. On 1979 models, measure the outside diameter of the pivot collar with a micrometer at both ends. If the diameter is 0.843 in. (21.4 mm) or less at either end, the pivot collar must be replaced.

> *NOTE*
> *If the pivot collar is replaced, the bushings at each end must be replaced at the same time.*

4A. On 1979 models, measure the inside diameter of the bushings at both ends. If the dimension is 0.854 in. (21.7 mm) or greater, both bushings must be replaced.

> *NOTE*
> *Always replace both bushings evn though only one may be worn.*

4B. On models since 1980, the roller bearings wear very slowly and the wear is difficult to measure. Turn the bearing by hand; make sure they rotate smoothly. Check the rollers for evidence of wear, pitting or color change (bluish tint) indicating heat from lack of lubrication.
5. Prior to assembly, coat all parts with a good grade multipurpose grease. Thoroughly work

the grease into the needle bearings on models so equipped.
6. Install the brake torque link onto the swing arm.
7. After installation on the motorcycle, lubricate as described under *Rear Swing Arm Bushings or Bearings Lubrication* in Chapter Three.

Rear Swing Arm Bushing or Bearing Replacement

The swing arms on 1979 models are equipped with a nylon bushing at each end. Since 1980 they are equipped with needle bearings at each end. The bushings or bearings will be damaged when removed, so don't remove them unless absolutely necessary.

> *NOTE*
> *The standard nylon bushings can be replaced with more stable, better quality bronze bushings. These are available from Ontario Moto Tech Corp., 6850 Vineland Ave., Unit 16, North Hollywood, CA 91605 and retail for approximately $20 a set. The needle bearings will not fit into older bushing type swing arms as the bearings have a 2 mm larger OD.*

1. Secure the swing arm in a vise with soft jaws.
2. Tap the bushing or needle bearings out with a soft aluminum or brass drift from the opposite end (**Figure 26**).
3. Repeat for the other end.
4. Thoroughly clean out the inside of the swing arm with solvent and dry with compressed air.
5. Apply oil to the inside and outside of the bushing or needle bearing prior to installation.
6. Tap the new bushing or needle bearings into place slowly and squarely with a wood block (**Figure 27**). Make sure they are properly seated.

> *CAUTION*
> *Never reinstall a bushing or needle bearing that has been removed. During removal it becomes slightly damaged and is no longer true to alignment. If installed, it will damage the sleeve and create an unsafe riding condition.*

SHOCK ABSORBERS

The rear shocks are spring controlled and hydraulically damped. Spring preload can be adjusted on all models. On model CB750F, since 1980, they are gas charged and have an additional adjustment at the top as well as at the bottom.

The shock damper unit is sealed and cannot be serviced. Service is limited to removal and replacement of the damper unit and/or the spring.

WARNING
Do not try to dismantle the gas charged damper unit or apply any form of heat to it. If the unit is heated in any way it will result in an extremely dangerous explosion.

NOTE
Check local regulations before discarding gas-charged units as it may be illegal to dispose of them in your household trash.

Spring Preload Adjustment
(Non-gas Charged)

The spring preload can be adjusted to 5 positions by rotating the cam ring at the base of the spring (**Figure 28**). Rotate *clockwise to increase* preload and *counterclockwise to decrease* preload.

NOTE
Use the spanner wrench furnished in the factory tool kit for this adjustment.

Both cams must be indexed to the same detent or it will result in an unsafe riding condition.

Gas Charged Shock Adjustments

These shocks have 3 adjustments for rider and cargo variations. The spring preload should be adjusted first. This adjustment is the same as in the previously described *Spring Preload Adjustment.* Next adjust the rebound dampening adjuster located at the top of the shock (**Figure 29**) to one of the 3 positions. Use the same spanner wrench used in spring preload adjustment.

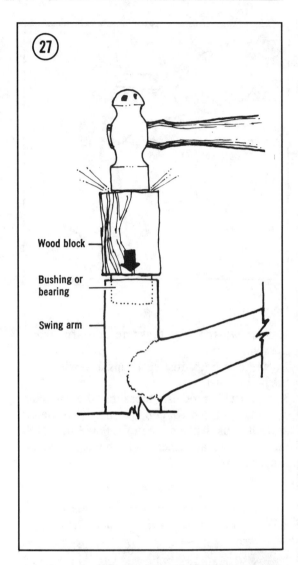

Wood block

Bushing or bearing

Swing arm

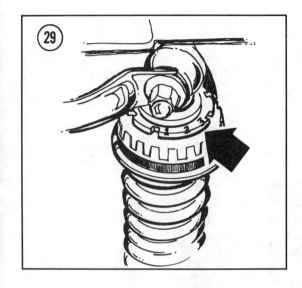

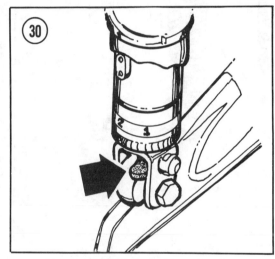

The last adjustment is the compression damper adjustment located at the base of the shock (**Figure 30**). Move the lever to either of the 2 positions.

Refer to **Table 2** for factory-recommended settings.

All of the previous settings must be indexed to the same detents for both shocks or it will result in an unsafe riding condition.

Removal/Installation

Removal and installation of the rear shocks is easier if each shock is done separately. The remaining unit will support the rear of the bike and maintain the correct relationship between the top and bottom shock mounts.

1. Place the bike on the centerstand; remove the seat and both side covers.
2. Adjust both shocks to their softest setting, *completely counterclockwise.*
3. Remove the mufflers as described under *Exhaust System Removal/Installation* in Chapter Six.
4. Remove grab bar rear mounting bolt (A, **Figure 31**).
5. Remove the upper acorn nut, lockwasher and washer (B, **Figure 31**).
6. Remove the grab bar.
7. Remove the lower shock mounting bolt and washer (C, **Figure 31**).
8. Pull the unit straight off the upper bolt and remove it.
9. Repeat for the other side.
10. Install by reversing these removal steps. Tighten the upper mounting nut to 14-22 ft.-lb. (20-30 N•m) and the lower bolt to 22-29 ft.-lb. (30-40 N•m)

> *NOTE*
> *Install the grab bar on the outside surface of the shock.*

Disassembly/Inspection/Assembly (Non-gas Filled Units Only)

Refer to **Figure 32** for this procedure.

> *WARNING*
> *Without the proper tool, this procedure can be dangerous. The spring can fly loose, causing injury. For a small bench fee, a dealer can do the job for you.*

9

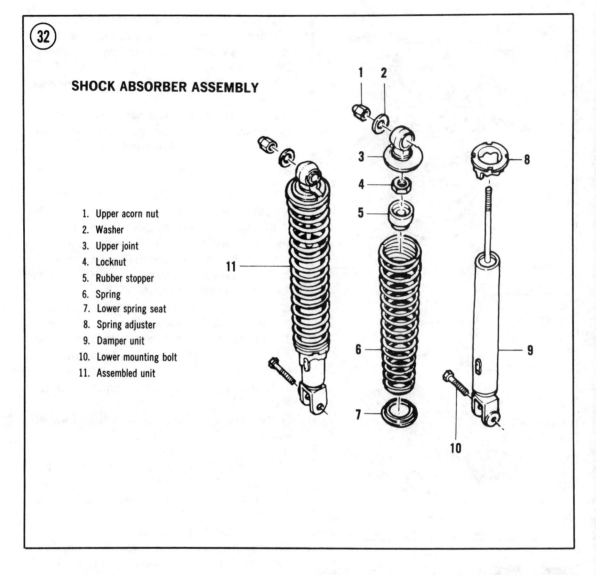

③②

SHOCK ABSORBER ASSEMBLY

1. Upper acorn nut
2. Washer
3. Upper joint
4. Locknut
5. Rubber stopper
6. Spring
7. Lower spring seat
8. Spring adjuster
9. Damper unit
10. Lower mounting bolt
11. Assembled unit

NOTE
Take the gas filled units to your dealer for disassembly.

1. Install the compression tool as shown in **Figure 33**. This is a special tool and is available from a Honda Dealer. It is the Shock Absorber Compressor tool, part No. 07959-3290001.

2. Compress the spring just enough to remove the locknut.

3. Clamp the upper joint in a vise equipped with soft jaws.

4. Loosen the locknut and unscrew the upper joint.

5. Release the spring tension and remove the shock from the compression tool.

6. Slide off the spring and measure the spring free length (**Figure 34**). The spring must be replaced if it has sagged to the service limit of 9.5 in. (237.2 mm) or less.

7. Check the damper unit for leakage and make sure the damper rod is straight.

8. Assembly is the reverse of these disassembly steps. Note the order of the parts shown in **Figure 32**.

NOTE
Apply Loctite Lock N' Seal to the threads prior to installing the upper joint. Tighten the locknut securely.

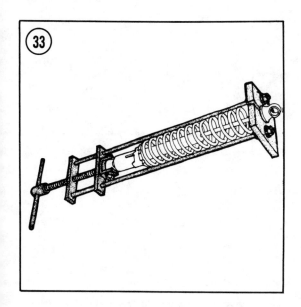

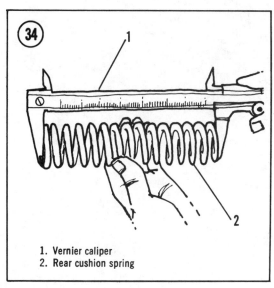

1. Vernier caliper
2. Rear cushion spring

TABLE 1 REAR SUSPENSION TORQUE SPECIFICATIONS

Item	Foot Pounds (ft.-lb.)	Newton Meters (N·m)
Rear axle nut	58–72	80–100
Rear swing arm pivot nut	40–51	55–70
Shock absorbers		
Upper mounting nut	14–22	20–30
Lower mounting bolt	22–29	30–40
Brake torque link bolt and nut		
All models	13–18	18–25
Drive sprocket nuts		
Model CB750F	40–47	55–65
Models CB750K, CB750K-LTD, and CB750C	58–72	80–100
Brake disc attachment nuts	20–24	27–33

9

TABLE 2 SHOCK ABSORBER SETTINGS (GAS CHARGED)

Conditions			
Rider(s) **Luggage**	**Riding Conditions**	**Rebound Damper Adjuster**	**Compression Damper Adjuster**
One	City riding or smooth road	1	1
One	Highway or winding road	2	1
One	Rough road	3	1
One/two	City riding or smooth road	1	2
One/two or luggage	Highway or winding road	2	2
One/two or luggage	Rough road	3	2

NOTE: If you own a 1981-82 model, first check the Supplement at the back of the book for any new service information.

CHAPTER TEN

BRAKES

The front brake system consists of either a single or dual disc depending on different models. The rear brake is either a single disc or drum type, again depending on different models.

There are slight differences in the caliper assemblies between the 2 models; where these differences occur they are identified. Be sure you follow the correct procedure for your particular model.

Refer to **Table 1** for torque specifications and **Table 2** for specifications and wear limits on all brake components. **Table 1** and **Table 2** are located at the end of this chapter.

FRONT DISC BRAKE(S)

The front disc brake(s) is actuated by hydraulic fluid and is controlled by a hand lever. As the brake pads wear, the brake fluid level drops in the reservoir and automatically adjusts for wear.

When working on hydraulic brake systems, it is necessary that the work area and all tools be absolutely clean. Any tiny particles of foreign matter and grit in the caliper assembly or the master cylinder can damage the components. Also, sharp tools must not be used inside the caliper or on the piston. If there is any doubt about your ability to correctly and safely carry out major service on the brake components, take the job to a Honda dealer or brake specialist.

FRONT MASTER CYLINDER

Removal/Installation

1. Remove the rear view mirror.

CAUTION
Cover the fuel tank and instrument cluster with a heavy cloth or plastic tarp to protect them from accidental brake fluid spills. Wash any brake fluid off any painted or plated surfaces immediately, as it will destroy the finish. Use soapy water and rinse completely.

2. Pull back the rubber boot and remove the union bolt (**Figure 1**) securing the brake hose to the master cylinder and remove the brake hose. Tie brake hose up and cover it to prevent the entry of foreign matter.
3. Remove the clamping bolts and clamp (A, **Figure 2**) securing the master cylinder to the handlebar and remove the master cylinder.
4. Install by reversing these removal steps, noting the following.
5. Install the clamp with the notch relief facing down. Align the lug with the line on the switch housing (B, **Figure 2**) and tighten the upper bolt first, then the lower.
6. Install the brake hose onto the master cylinder. Be sure to place a sealing washer on each side of the fitting and install the union bolt. Tighten the bolt to 18-25 ft.-lb. (25-35 N•m).

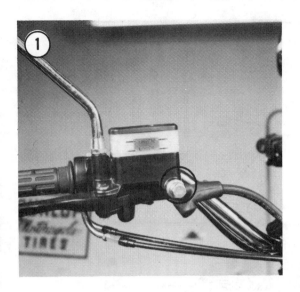

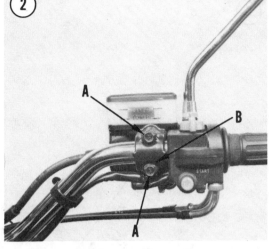

7. Bleed the brake as described in this chapter.

Disassembly

Refer to **Figure 3** for this procedure.

1. Remove the front master cylinder as described in this chapter.

2. Remove the bolt, washer and nut securing the brake lever and remove it.

3. Remove the screws securing the cover (**Figure 4**) and remove the cover, gasket and diaphragm; pour out the brake fluid and discard it. *Never reuse brake fluid.*

4. Remove the rubber boot from the area where the hand lever actuates the internal piston.

5. Using circlip pliers (**Figure 5**) remove the internal circlip from the body.

6. Remove the stop plate, secondary cup and piston assembly.

7. Remove the primary cup and spring.

Inspection

1. Clean all parts in denatured alcohol or fresh brake fluid. Inspect the cylinder bore and piston contact surfaces for signs of wear and damage. If either part is less than perfect, replace it.

2. Check the end of the piston for wear caused by the hand lever and check the pivot bore in the front-hand lever. Replace the piston if the secondary cup requires replacement.

3. Make sure the passages in the bottom of the brake fluid reservoir are clear. Check the reservoir cap and diaphragm for damage and deterioration and replace as necessary.

4. Inspect the condition of the threads in the bores for the brake line.

5. Check the front-hand lever pivot lug for cracks.

6. Measure the cylinder bore (**Figure 6**). The cylinder bore must not exceed 0.5533 in. (14.055 mm). Replace the master cylinder if it exceeds this dimension.

7. Measure the outside diameter of the piston with a micrometer. If the dimension is 0.5490 in. (13.945 mm) or less the piston assembly must be replaced.

Assembly

1. Soak the new cups in fresh brake fluid for at least 15 minutes to make them pliable. Coat the inside of the cylinder with fresh brake fluid prior to the assembly of parts.

> *CAUTION*
> *When installing the piston assembly, do not allow the cups to turn inside out as they will be damaged and allow brake fluid leakage within the cylinder bore.*

2. Install the spring, primary cup and piston assembly into the cylinder together. Install the spring with the tapered end facing toward the primary cup.

10

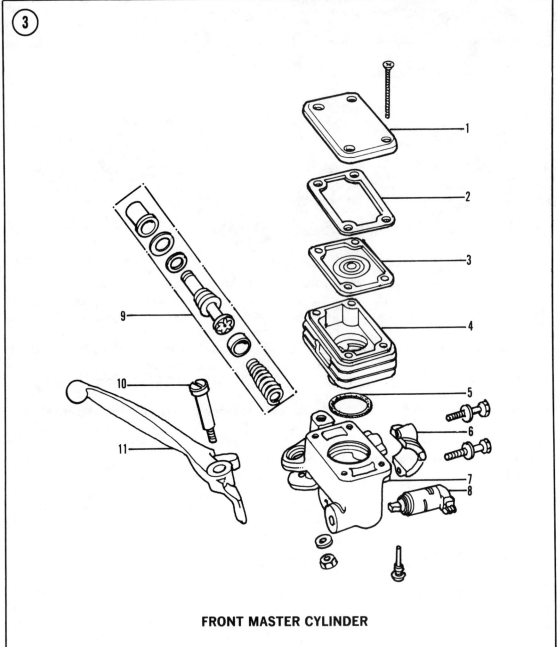

FRONT MASTER CYLINDER

1. Cover
2. Gasket
3. Diaphragm
4. Reservoir
5. Seal
6. Clamp
7. Master cylinder body
8. Brake light switch
9. Piston assembly
10. Lever bolt
11. Lever

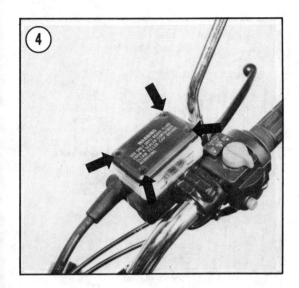

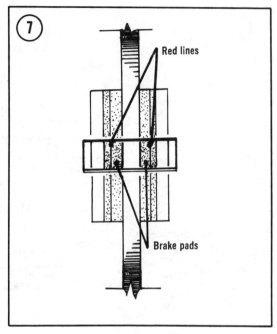

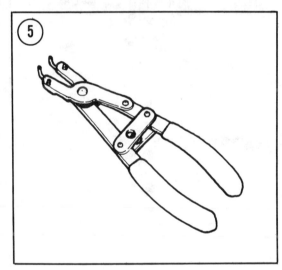

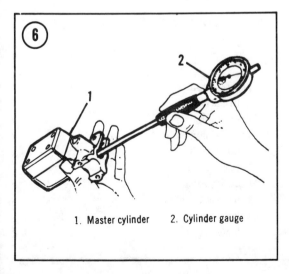

1. Master cylinder   2. Cylinder gauge

NOTE
Be sure to install the primary cup with the open end in first, toward the spring.

3. Install the stop plate and circlip. Slide in the rubber boot.

4. If the brake fluid reservoir was removed from the master cylinder body, inspect the condition of the O-ring. Replace if necessary.

5. Install the diaphragm, gasket and cover. Do not tighten the cover screws at this time as fluid will have to be added later.

6. Install the brake lever onto the master cylinder body.

7. Install the front master cylinder as described in this chapter.

FRONT BRAKE PAD REPLACEMENT

There is no recommended mileage interval for changing the friction pads in the disc brake. Pad wear depends greatly on riding habits and conditions. The pads should be checked for wear every 600 miles (1,000 km) and replaced when the wear indicator (**Figure 7**) reaches the edge of the brake disc. Always replace all pads (2 per disc) at the same time.

Refer to **Figure 8** for single disc models or **Figure 9** for dual disc models.

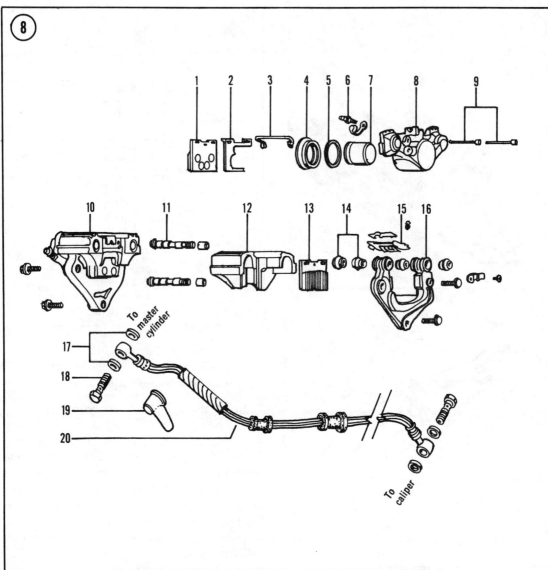

⑧

FRONT CALIPER ASSEMBLY — SINGLE DISC MODELS

1. Brake pad (outer)
2. Shim
3. Pin clip
4. Boot seal
5. Oil seal
6. Bleeder valve
7. Caliper piston
8. Caliper A
9. Brake pad retaining clips (2)
10. Caliper (assembled)
11. Caliper shaft (2)
12. Caliper B
13. Brake pad (inner)
14. Caliper shaft boots
15. Caliper cover
16. Caliper carrier
17. Sealing washer
18. Union bolt
19. Protective cap
20. Brake hose

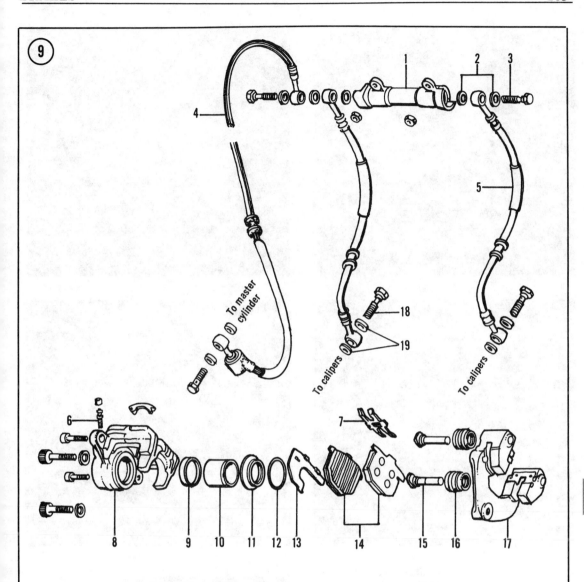

FRONT CALIPER ASSEMBLY—DUAL DISC MODELS

1. Fitting
2. Sealing washers
3. Union bolt
4. Brake hose — from master cylinder
5. Brake hose — from fittings to caliper (right- and left-hand side)
6. Bleeder valve
7. Brake pad spring
8. Caliper
9. Seal
10. Caliper piston

11. Boot
12. O-ring
13. Shim
14. Brake pads
15. Caliper pins (2)
16. Dust covers (2)
17. Caliper bracket
18. Union bolt
19. Sealing washers

1A. On single disc models, remove the caliper cover (**Figure 10**) and pull up and remove the clip (**Figure 11**). Remove the pins securing the pads in place (**Figure 12**), remove the pads (**Figure 13**) and discard them.

1B. On dual disc models, remove the Allen bolts (**Figure 14**) securing the caliper cover and remove it. Remove both pads and the shim (**Figure 15**).

2. Clean the pad recess and end of the piston with a soft brush. Do not use solvent, wire brush or any hard tool which would damage the cylinder or piston.

3. Lightly coat the end of the piston and the backs of the new pads (not the friction material) with disc brake lubricant.

NOTE
Check with your dealer to make sure the friction compound of the new pad is compatible with the disc material. Remove any roughness from backs of new pads with a fine cut file; blow them clean with compressed air.

4. Remove the cap from the master cylinder and slowly push the piston into the caliper while checking the reservoir to make sure the brake fluid does not overflow. Remove fluid, if necessary, prior to it overflowing. The piston should move freely. If it does not and there is any evidence of it sticking in the cylinder, the caliper should be removed and serviced as described under *Caliper Rebuilding* in this chapter.

5. Push the caliper to the right and push the piston in to allow the new pads to be installed.

6A. On single disc models, install the new pads with the anti-rattle shim on the outboard pad next to the piston (**Figure 13**). Insert the pins with the holes (**Figure 12**) facing upward to enable the insertion of the clip. Install the clip (**Figure 11**). Install the caliper cover.

6B. On dual disc models, install the new pads and shim with the arrow facing *up* (**Figure 15**). Install the caliper cover and Allen bolts; tighten the bolts to 11-14 ft.-lb. (15-20 N•m).

NOTE
Torque the bolts evenly in 2 or 3 steps to the final torque.

7. Carefully remove any rust or corrosion from the disc.

8. Block the motorcycle up so that the front wheel is off the ground. Spin the front wheel and activate the brake lever as many times as it takes to refill the cylinder in the caliper and correctly locate the pads.

9. Refill the reservoir with fluid if necessary and reinstall the top cap.

WARNING
Use brake fluid clearly marked DOT 3. Others may vaporize and cause brake failure. Always use the same brand name; do not intermix, as many are not compatible.

WARNING
Do not ride the motorcycle until you are sure the brake is operating correctly with full hydraulic advantage. If necessary, bleed the brakes as described under **Bleeding the System** *in this chapter.*

10. Bed the pads in gradually for the first 50 miles (80 km) by using only light pressure as much as possible. Immediate hard application will glaze the new friction pads and greatly reduce the effectiveness of the brake.

FRONT CALIPER(S)

Removal/Installation

Refer to **Figure 8** for single disc models or **Figure 9** for dual disc models.

It is not necessary to remove the front wheel in order to remove either or both caliper assemblies.

1. Remove the brake pads as described in this chapter.

2. Remove the brake line from the caliper (**Figure 16**). To prevent the loss of brake fluid, cap the end of the brake line and tie the end of it up to the forks. Be sure to cap or tape the ends to prevent the entry of moisture and dirt.

3A. On single disc models, loosen the caliper bolts (**Figure 17**) gradually in several steps. Push on the caliper while removing these bolts to push the piston back into the caliper. Remove caliper "A." To remove caliper "B,"

10

remove the 2 bolts (**Figure 18**) securing it and the caliper carrier to the fork and remove them.

3B. On dual disc models, remove the Allen bolts (A, **Figure 19**) and push on the caliper to push the piston back into the caliper. Remove caliper "A." Remove the bolt securing the speedometer cable and remove the clamp. To remove caliper "B," remove the Allen bolts (B, **Figure 19**) securing it and the caliper carrier to the fork and remove them.

4. Install by reversing these removal steps. Tighten the bolts (Allen and hex head) securing both the caliper assemblies "A" and "B" to 22-29 ft.-lb. (30-40 N•m) on all models.

5. Install the brake hose onto the caliper. Be sure to place a sealing washer on each side of the fitting and install the union bolt. Tighten the bolt to 18-25 ft.-lb. (25-35 N•m).

6. Bleed the brake as described in this chapter.

WARNING
Do not ride the motorcycle until you are sure that the brakes are operating properly.

Caliper Rebuilding

If the caliper leaks, the caliper should be rebuilt. If the piston sticks in the cylinder, indicating severe wear or galling, the entire unit should be replaced. Rebuilding a leaky caliper requires special tools and experience.

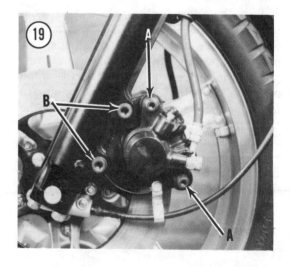

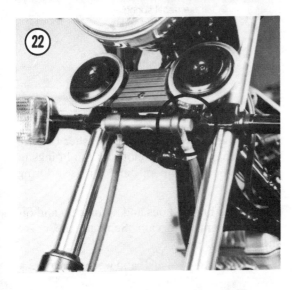

Caliper service should be entrusted to a Honda dealer or brake specialist. Considerable money can be saved by removing the caliper yourself and taking it in for repair.

The factory recommends that the piston fluid seal and dust seal be replaced every other time the pads are replaced.

FRONT BRAKE HOSE REPLACEMENT

There is no factory-recommended replacement interval but it is a good idea to replace all brake hoses every 4 years or when they show signs of cracking or damage.

Refer to **Figure 8** for single disc models or **Figure 9** for dual disc models.

> *CAUTION*
> *Cover the front wheel, fender and fuel tank with a heavy cloth or plastic tarp to protect it from accidental spilling of brake fluid. Wash any brake fluid off of any painted or plated surface immediately, as it will destroy the finish. Use soapy water and rinse completely.*

1. Remove the union bolt (**Figure 20**) securing the brake hose to the caliper and remove the hose. Drain the brake fluid from the hose and discard it—*never* reuse brake fluid. On dual disc models, repeat for the other caliper.

2A. On single disc models, remove the union bolt (**Figure 21**) securing the brake hose to the master cylinder and remove the hose from the clamps on the forks.

2B. On dual disc models, remove the union bolt (**Figure 22**) securing the left-hand brake hose to the fitting. Remove the union bolt (**Figure 23**) securing the right-hand lower hose and upper hose to the fitting and remove them. Remove the union bolt (**Figure 24**) securing the upper hose to the master cylinder and remove it.

3. Install new hoses, sealing washers and union bolts in the reverse order of removal. Be sure to install new sealing washers in the correct positions; refer to **Figure 8** or **Figure 9**. Tighten all union bolts to 18-25 ft.-lb. (25-35 N•m).

4. Refill the master cylinder with fresh brake fluid clearly marked DOT 3 only. Bleed the brake as described in this chapter.

10

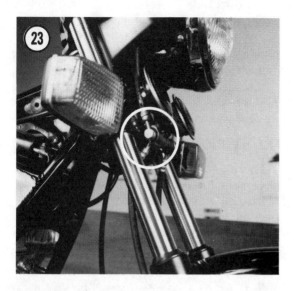

WARNING
Do not ride the motorcycle until you are
sure that the brakes are operating properly.

REAR DRUM BRAKE

Disassembly

Refer to **Figure 25** for this procedure.

1. Remove the rear wheel as described under *Rear Wheel Removal/Installation* in Chapter Nine.

2. Pull the brake assembly straight up and out of the brake drum.

3. Loosen the clamping bolt and remove the brake arm (A, **Figure 26**).

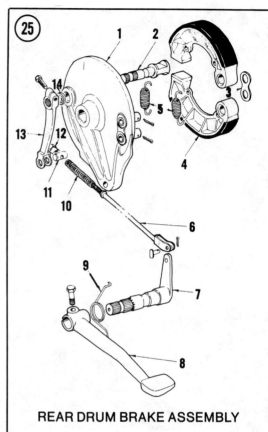

REAR DRUM BRAKE ASSEMBLY

1. Rear brake panel
2. Rear brake cam
3. Rear brake anchor pin washer
4. Rear brake shoe components
5. Brake shoe spring
6. Rear brake rod components
7. Rear brake spindle components
8. Rear brake pedal
9. Brake pedal spring
10. Rear brake rod spring
11. Rear brake arm joint
12. Rear brake adjusting nut
13. Rear brake arm
14. Brake cover dust seal

4. Remove the cotter pins and washer (**Figure 27**). Place a clean shop cloth on the linings to protect them from oil and grease during removal.

5. Pull the brake shoes and springs up and off the guide pins and cam. Separate the brake shoes and springs.

6. Remove the camshaft and wear indicator.

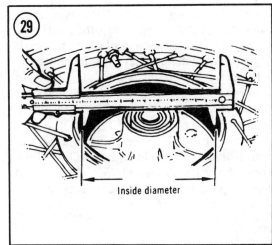

Inside diameter

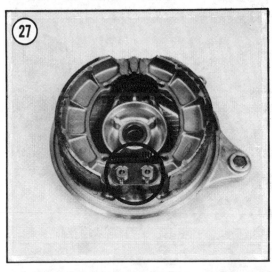

10

Inspection

1. Thoroughly clean and dry all parts except the linings.

2. Check the contact surface of the drum (**Figure 28**) for scoring. If there are grooves deep enough to snag a fingernail, the drum should be reground.

3. Measure the inside diameter of the brake drum with vernier calipers (**Figure 29**). If this dimension is 7.1 in. (181 mm) or greater, the drum must be replaced.

4. If the brake drum is turned, the linings will have to be replaced and the new ones arced to the new drum contour.

5. Check the brake linings. They should be replaced if worn within 0.08 in. (2.0 mm) of the metal shoe table (**Figure 30**).

6. Inspect the linings for imbedded foreign material. Dirt can be removed with a stiff wire brush. Check for any traces of oil or grease; if they are contaminated, they must be replaced.

7. Inspect the cam lobes and the pivot pin area of the shaft for wear and corrosion. Minor roughness can be removed with fine emery cloth.

8. Inspect the brake shoe return springs for wear. If they are stretched, they will not fully retract the brake shoes and they will drag and wear out prematurely. Replace if necessary.

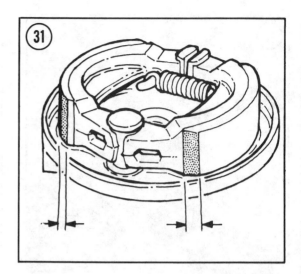

Assembly

1. Assemble the brake by reversing the disassembly steps.

2. Grease the shafts, cams and pivot posts with a light coat of molybdenum disulfide grease; avoid getting grease on the brake plate where the linings may come in contact with it.

> *NOTE*
> *If new linings are being installed, file off the leading edge of each shoe a little (**Figure 31**) so it will not grab when applied.*

3. When installing the brake arm onto the camshaft, be sure to align the dimples on the 2 parts (B, **Figure 26**).

4. Install the wheel as described under *Rear Wheel Installation* in Chapter Nine.

REAR MASTER CYLINDER

Removal/Installation

Refer to **Figure 32** for this procedure.

> *CAUTION*
> *Cover the surrounding frame with a heavy cloth or plastic tarp to protect it from accidental spilling of brake fluid. Wash any brake fluid off of any painted or plated surfaces immediately, as it will destroy the finish. Use soapy water and rinse completely.*

1. Remove the right-hand side cover (**Figure 33**).

2. Remove the brake fluid reservoir lower hose clamp (A, **Figure 34**) and pull the hose

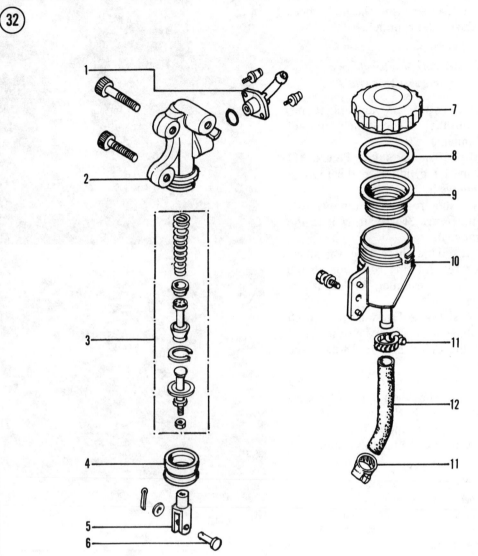

REAR MASTER CYLINDER ASSEMBLY

1. Reservoir hose fitting
2. Master cylinder body
3. Piston assembly
4. Rubber boot
5. Rod eye
6. Pin
7. Reservoir cap
8. Gasket
9. Diaphragm
10. Reservoir
11. Hose clamp
12. Reservoir hose

10

off the master cylinder. Remove the union bolts (B, **Figure 34**) securing the brake hose to the rear of the master cylinder.

> *NOTE*
> *Drain the brake fluid from both hoses and discard it — **never reuse brake fluid**.*

3. Remove the cotter pin and pivot pin (**Figure 35**) from the rod eye at the bottom of the master cylinder.

4. Remove the Allen bolts (A, **Figure 36**) securing the master cylinder to the footrest bracket and remove it.

5. To remove the reservoir, remove the flange bolt (B, **Figure 36**) securing it to the frame and remove it.

6. Install by reversing these removal steps. Inspect the brake actuating rod boot on the bottom of the master cylinder. Replace if it is cracked or deteriorated.

7. Be sure to install a sealing washer on each side of the caliper hose and install the union bolt. Tighten the union bolt to 18-25 ft.-lb. (25-35 N•m).

8. Install the master cylinder to the foot peg bracket and tighten the Allen bolts (A, **Figure 36**) to 22-29 ft.-lb. (30-40 N•m).

9. Refill the master cylinder reservoir and bleed the brake as described in this chapter.

> *WARNING*
> *Use brake fluid clearly marked DOT 3 only. Others may vaporize and cause brake failure. Always use the same brand name; do not intermix, as many brands are not compatible.*

> *WARNING*
> *Do not ride the motorcycle until you are sure that the brake is operating correctly with full hydraulic advantage.*

Disassembly

Refer to **Figure 32** for this procedure.

1. Remove the rear master cylinder as described in this chapter.

2. Remove the rubber boot.

3. Using circlip pliers (**Figure 37**), remove the circlip and pull the pushrod assembly out of the master cylinder body.

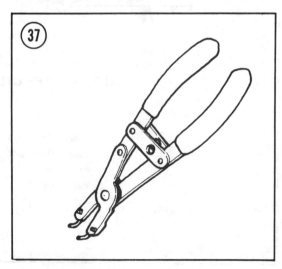

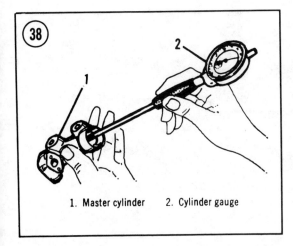

1. Master cylinder   2. Cylinder gauge

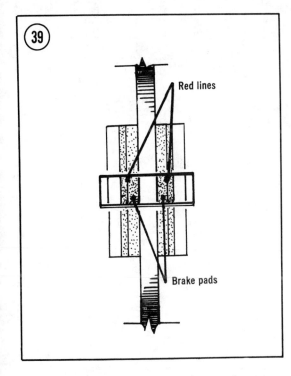

Red lines

Brake pads

4. Remove the piston assembly, primary cup and spring.

Inspection

1. Clean all parts in denatured alcohol or fresh brake fluid. Inspect the cylinder bore and piston contact surfaces for signs of wear and damage. If either part is less than perfect, replace it.

2. Check the end of the piston for wear caused by the lever and check the pivot bore in the lever. Discard the caps.

3. Make sure the passages in the bottom of the brake fluid reservoir are clear. Check the reservoir cap and diaphragm for damage and deterioration and replace as necessary.

4. Inspect the condition of the threads in the bores for the brake line and switch.

5. Measure the cylinder bore (**Figure 38**). The cylinder bore must not exceed 0.5533 in. (14.055 mm). Replace the master cylinder if it exceeds this dimension.

6. Measure the outside diameter of the piston with a micrometer. If the dimension is 0.5490 in. (13.945 mm) or less the piston assembly must be replaced.

Assembly

1. Soak the new cups in fresh brake fluid for at least 15 minutes to make them pliable. Coat the inside of the cylinder with fresh brake fluid prior to assembly.

> *CAUTION*
> *When installing the piston assembly, do not allow the cups to turn inside out as they will be damaged and allow brake fluid leakage within the cylinder bore.*

2. Install the spring with the tapered end facing out toward the primary cup. Install the primary cup with the open end in first, toward the spring.

3. Install the pushrod assembly and install the circlip.

4. Install the rubber boot, nut and rod eye.

5. Install the rear master cylinder as described in this chapter.

REAR BRAKE PAD REPLACEMENT

There is no recommended mileage interval for changing the friction pads in the disc brake. Pad wear depends greatly on riding habits and conditions. The pads should be checked for wear every 600 miles (1,000 km) and replaced when the wear indicator (**Figure 39**) reaches the edge of the disc brake. Always replace both pads at the same time.

Refer to **Figure 40** for this procedure.

1. Remove the Allen bolts (**Figure 41**) securing the caliper cover and remove it. Remove both pads and the shim (**Figure 42**).

10

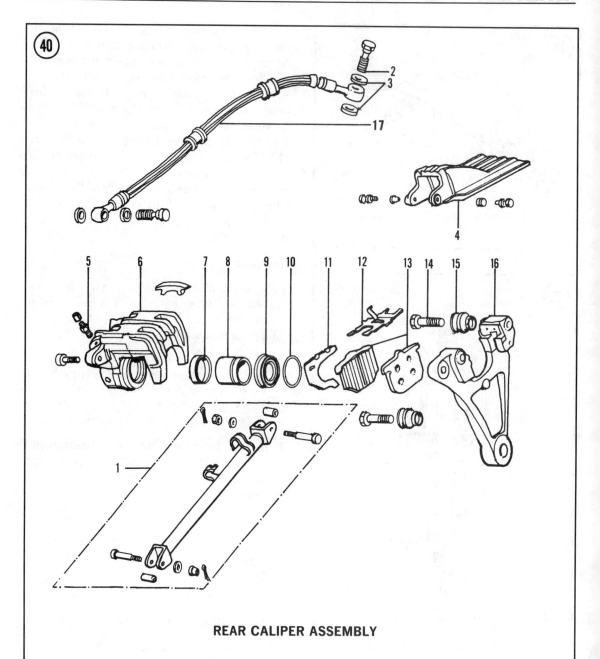

REAR CALIPER ASSEMBLY

1. Torque link assembly
2. Union bolt
3. Sealing washer
4. Dust cover
5. Bleeder valve
6. Caliper
7. Seal
8. Caliper piston
9. Dust cover
10. O-ring
11. Shim
12. Brake pad spring
13. Brake pads
14. Caliper pins (2)
15. Dust covers (2)
16. Caliper bracket
17. Brake hose

2. Clean the pad recesses and the ends of the pistons with a soft brush. Don't use solvent, a wire brush or any hard tool which would damage the cylinders or pistons.

3. Lightly coat the ends of the pistons and the backs of the new pads (not the friction material) with disc brake lubricant.

NOTE
Check with your dealer to make sure the friction compound of the new pad is compatible with the disc material. Remove any roughness from the metal backs of the pads with a fine file and blow them clean with compressed air.

4. Remove the cap from the master cylinder and slowly push the pistons into the caliper while checking the reservoir to make sure the fluid does not overflow. The pistons should move freely. If they do not and there is any evidence of them sticking in the cylinders, the caliper should be removed and serviced as described under *Caliper Rebuilding* in this chapter.

5. Push the caliper piston into the caliper (**Figure 43**) to allow the new pads to be installed.

6. Install the new pads with the anti-rattle shim on the outboard pad next to the piston (**Figure 42**). Install the shim with the arrow (**Figure 44**) in the direction of normal wheel rotation.

7. Install the caliper cover and Allen bolts; tighten the bolts to 11-14 ft.-lb. (15-20 N•m).

10

NOTE
Tighten the bolts evenly in 2 or 3 steps to the final torque.

8. Carefully remove any rust or corrosion from the disc.

9. Block the motorcycle up so that the rear wheel is off the ground. Spin the rear wheel and activate the brake pedal for as many times as it takes to refill the cylinder in the caliper and correctly locate the pads.

10. Refill the fluid in the reservoir, if necessary, and replace the top cap.

WARNING
Use brake fluid clearly marked DOT 3 only. Others may vaporize and cause brake failure. Always use the same brand name; do not intermix, as many brands are not compatible.

WARNING
*Do not ride the motorcycle until you are sure that the brake is operating correctly with full hydraulic advantage. If necessary, bleed the brakes as described under **Bleeding the System** in this chapter.*

11. Bed the pads in gradually for the first 50 miles (80 km) by using only light pressure as much as possible. Immediate hard application will glaze the new friction pads and greatly reduce the effectiveness of the brake.

REAR CALIPER

Removal/Installation

Refer to **Figure 40** for this procedure.

1. Remove the rear wheel as described under *Rear Wheel Removal/Installation* in Chapter Nine.

2. Remove the union bolt (A, **Figure 45**) securing the brake hose to the caliper. To prevent the loss of brake fluid, tie up the hose to the rear grab bar. Tape the end closed to prevent the entry of moisture and foreign matter.

3. Remove the Allen bolts and push on the caliper to push the piston into the caliper.

4. Remove the 2 brake pads and shim.

5. Remove the cotter pin and the bolt (B, **Figure 45**) securing the caliper bracket to the torque link. Remove the caliper bracket.

6. Install by reversing these removal steps. Tighten the torque link bolt and nut to 13-18 ft.-lb. (18-25 N•m) and install a new cotter pin. Tighten the caliper mounting Allen bolts to 11-14 ft.-lb. (15-20 N•m).

7. Install the brake hose onto the caliper. Be sure to place a sealing washer on each side of the fitting and install the union bolt. Tighten the bolt to 18-25 ft.-lb. (25-35 N•m).

8. Bleed the brake as described in this chapter.

WARNING
Do not ride the motorcycle until you are sure that the brakes are operating properly.

Caliper Rebuilding

Refer to *Caliper Rebuilding* as covered under *Front Disc Brakes* earlier in this chapter.

REAR BRAKE HOSE REPLACEMENT

There is no factory-recommended replacement interval, but it is a good idea to replace the brake hoses every 4 years or when they show signs of cracking or damage.

Refer to **Figure 40** for this procedure.

CAUTION
Cover the surrounding frame area with a heavy cloth or plastic tarp to protect it from accidental spilling of brake fluid. Wash

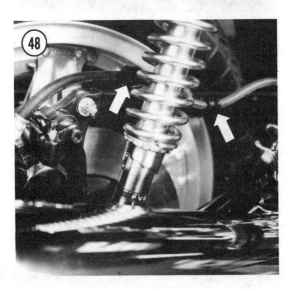

any brake fluid off of any painted or plated surface immediately, as it will destroy the finish. Use soapy water and rinse completely.

1. Remove the union bolts securing the brake hose (**Figure 46**) to the master cylinder. Drain the brake fluid from the hose and discard it. *Never* reuse brake fluid.

2. Remove the union bolt securing the brake hose (**Figure 47**) to the caliper. Remove the hose from the holder brackets and remove the hose (**Figure 48**).

3. Install the new hose, washers and union bolts in reverse order of removal. Be sure to install the sealing washers in the correct positions; refer to **Figure 40**.

4. Make sure the brake hose is positioned correctly in the holding bracket so it will not come in contact with any moving parts (shock absorber, wheel, etc.). Tighten all union bolts to 18-25 ft.-lb. (25-35 N•m).

5. Replace the hose from the reservoir to the master cylinder (**Figure 49**). Install new hose clamps.

6. Refill the master cylinder with brake fluid clearly marked DOT 3. Bleed the brake as described in this chapter.

BRAKE DISC (FRONT AND REAR)

Removal/Installation

This procedure applies to both front and rear discs.

10

1. Remove the wheel as described under *Front Wheel Removal/Installation* in Chapter Eight or *Rear Wheel Removal/Installation* in Chapter Nine.

> *NOTE*
> *Insert a piece of wood in the caliper(s) in place of the disc. This way, if the brake lever is inadvertently squeezed or depressed, the piston will not be forced out of the cylinder. If this does happen, the caliper might have to be disassembled to reseat the piston, and the system will have to be bled. By using the wood, bleeding the brake is not necessary when installing the wheel.*

2. Remove the nuts (**Figure 50**) securing the disc to the wheel. Remove the disc from the rear wheel. On the front wheel, remove the speedometer gear drive holding plate, speedometer gear drive, wheel cap and disc.

3. Install by reversing these removal steps. Torque the nuts to 20-24 ft.-lb. (27-33 N•m).

Inspection

It is not necessary to remove the disc from the wheel to inspect it. Small marks on the disc are not important, but scratches deep enough to snag a fingernail reduce braking effectiveness and increase pad wear. The disc should be replaced.

1. Measure the thickness at several points around the disc with vernier caliper or micrometer (**Figure 51**). The disc must be replaced if the thickness, at any point, is less than the following dimensions:

    a. Single front disc models: 0.24 in. (6.0 mm).

    b. Dual front disc models: 0.16 in. (4.0 mm).

    c. Rear disc: 0.24 in. (6.0 mm).

2. Check the disc runout with a dial indicator. Raise the wheel being checked and set the arm of the dial indicator against the surface of the disc (**Figure 52**) and slowly rotate the wheel while watching the indicator. If the runout is greater than 0.012 in. (0.3 mm), disc must be replaced.

3. Clean the disc of any rust or corrosion with a non-petroleum based solvent.

BLEEDING THE SYSTEM

This procedure is not necessary unless the brakes feel spongy, there has been a leak in the system, a component has been replaced or the brake fluid has been replaced.

This procedure pertains to both the front and rear brake systems. When bleeding the front system with dual discs, do one caliper at a time.

1. Remove the dust cap from the brake bleed valve.

2. Connect the length of clear tubing to the bleed valve on the caliper. See **Figure 53** for the front wheel and **Figure 54** for the rear. Place other end of the tube into a clean container. Fill the container with enough fresh brake fluid to keep the end submerged. The tube should be long enough so that a loop can be made higher than the bleed valve to prevent air from being drawn into the caliper during bleeding.

> *CAUTION*
> *Cover the fuel tank and instrument cluster or the rear frame area with a heavy cloth or plastic tarp to protect it from the accidental spilling of brake fluid. Wash any brake fluid off of any painted or plated surface immediately, as it will destroy the finish. Use soapy water and rinse completely.*

10

3. Clean the top of the master cylinder of all dirt and foreign matter. Remove the cap, diaphragm and gasket (**Figure 55**). Fill the reservoir almost to the top lip, insert the diaphragm and gasket and the cap loosely. Leave the cap in place during this procedure to prevent the entry of dirt.

> *WARNING*
> *Use brake fluid clearly marked DOT 3 only. Others may vaporize and cause brake failure. Always use the same brand name; do not intermix as many brands are not compatible.*

4. Slowly apply the brake lever or pedal several times. Pull the lever in or push the pedal down. Hold the lever or pedal in the *on* position. Open the bleed valve about one-half turn. Allow the lever or pedal to travel to its limit. When this limit is reached, tighten the

bleed screw. As the fluid enters the system, the level will drop in the reservoir. Maintain the level at about 3/8 inch from the top of the reservoir to prevent air from being drawn into the system.

> *NOTE*
> *On the front brake only, when pulling in on the brake lever, always maintain at least 3/4 inch (20 mm) distance between the back of the lever and the throttle grip. This is to prevent over-travel of the piston in the master cylinder.*

5. Continue to pump the lever or pedal and fill the reservoir until the fluid emerging from the hose is completely free of bubbles.

> *NOTE*
> *Do not allow the reservoir to empty during the bleeding operation or more air will enter the system. If this occurs, the entire procedure must be repeated.*

6. Hold the lever or pedal down, tighten the bleed valve, remove the bleed tube and install the bleed valve dust cap.
7. If necessary, add fluid to correct the level in the reservoir. It should be to the *upper* level line (**Figure 56**).
8. Install the reservoir cap.

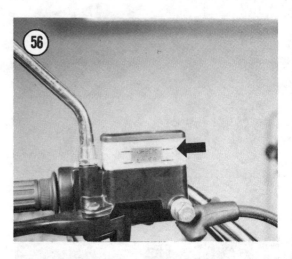

9. Test the feel of the brake lever and pedal. It should be firm and should offer the same resistance each time it's operated. If it feels spongy, it is likely that there still is air in the system and it must be bled again. When all air has been bled from the system and the fluid level is correct in the reservoir, double check for leaks and tighten all the fittings and connections.

> *WARNING*
> *Before riding the motorcycle, make certain that the brakes are operating correctly by operating the lever and pedal several times.*

TABLE 1 BRAKE COMPONENT TORQUE SPECIFICATIONS

Item	Foot Pounds (ft.-lb.)	Newton Meters (N·m)
Brake hose union bolts (all)	18–25	25–35
Master cylinder cover screws	9–17 in.-lb.	1–2
Rear master cylinder mounting bolts	22–29	30–40
Caliper mounting bolts (Allen and hex head)	22–29	30–40
Caliper cover mounting bolts	11–14	15–20
Rear caliper torque link (front and rear)	13–18	18–25
Brake disc mounting nuts	20–24	27–33

TABLE 2 BRAKE SPECIFICATIONS

Item	Specification	Wear limit
Front master cylinder		
Cylinder bore I.D.	0.5512–0.5529 in. (14.000–14.043mm)	0.554 in. (14.06mm)
Piston O.D.	0.5495–0.5506 in. (13.957–13.984mm)	0.5490 in. (13.945mm)
Rear master cylinder		
Cylinder bore I.D.	0.5512–0.5529 in. (14.000–14.043mm)	0.554 in. (14.06mm)
Piston O.D.	0.5495–0.5506 in. (13.957–13.984mm)	0.5490 in. (13.945mm)
Front caliper		
Model CB750K, K-LTD and C		
Cylinder bore I.D.	1.6870–1.6909 in. (42.850–42.950mm)	1.6896 in. (42.915mm)
Piston O.D.	1.6839–1.6859 in. (42.772–42.822mm)	1.6837 in. (42.765mm)
Model CB750F		
Cylinder bore I.D.	1.5031–1.5051 in. (38.180–38.230mm)	1.506 in. (38.24mm)
Piston O.D.	1.4999–1.5019 in. (38.098–38.148mm)	1.500 in. (38.09mm)
Rear caliper		
Cylinder bore I.D.	1.5031–1.5051 in. (38.180–38.230mm)	1.506 in. (38.24mm)
Piston O.D.	1.4999–1.5019 in. (38.098–38.148mm)	1.500 in. (38.09mm)
Front disc thickness		
Model CB750K, K-LTD and C	0.27–0.28 in. (6.9–7.1mm)	0.24 in. (6.0mm)
Model CB750F	0.19–0.20 in. (4.9–5.1mm)	0.16 in. (4.0mm)
Rear disc thickness		
Model CB750F	0.27–0.28 in. (6.9–7.1mm)	0.24 in. (6.0mm)
Disc runout—all models	— — — —	0.012 in. (0.30mm)

10

FRAME AND REPAINTING

This chapter describes procedures for completely stripping the frame. In addition, recommendations are provided for repainting the stripped frame.

This chapter also includes procedures for the kickstand, centerstand and footpegs.

KICKSTAND (SIDE STAND)

Removal/Installation

1. Place the bike on the centerstand.
2. Raise the kickstand and disconnect the return spring (A, **Figure 1**) from the frame with Vise Grips.
3. Remove the cotter pin and unbolt the kickstand from the frame (B, **Figure 1**).
4. Install by reversing these removal steps. Apply a light coat of multipurpose grease to the pivot surfaces of the frame tab and the kickstand yoke prior to installation.

CENTERSTAND

Removal/Installation

1. Block up the engine or support the bike on the kickstand.
2. Remove the rear wheel as described under *Rear Wheel Removal/Installation* in Chapter Nine.
3. Place the centerstand in the raised position and disconnect the return spring (A, **Figure 2**) from the frame peg with Vise Grips.

4. Loosen the bolts and nuts on the clamps (B, **Figure 2**) securing the pivot tube. Remove the cotter pin on the left-hand side.
5. Withdraw the tube from the right-hand side and lower the centerstand.
6. Install by reversing these removal steps. Apply a light coat of multipurpose grease to all pivoting points prior to installation.

FOOTPEGS

Remove the bolt securing the rear footpegs (**Figure 3**) to the frame or foot peg bracket.

The front footpegs are held in place with the rear lower engine mounting through bolt.

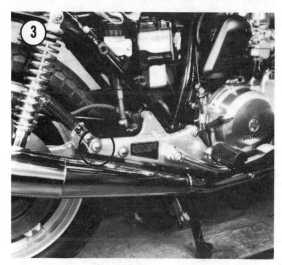

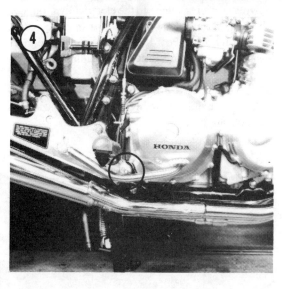

Remove the rear brake pedal and remove the self-locking nut (**Figure 4**) on the bolt; remove the through bolt and footpegs.

When installing the footpegs, make sure the locating tabs are correctly positioned. Tighten all bolts to 40-47 ft.-lb. (55-65 N•m).

FRAME

The frame does not require periodic maintenance. However, all welds should be examined immediately after any accident, even a slight one.

Component Removal/Installation

1. Disconnect the negative battery cable. Remove the fuel tank, seat and battery.
2. Remove the engine as described in Chapter Four.
3. Remove the front wheel, steering and suspension components as described in Chapter Eight.
4. Remove the rear wheel and suspension components. See Chapter Nine.
5. Remove the lighting and other electrical equipment. Remove the wiring harness. See Chapter Seven.
6. Remove the kickstand and centerstand as described in this chapter.
7. Remove the bearing races from the steering head tube as described in Chapter Eight.
8. Check the frame for bends, cracks or other damage, especially around welded joints and areas which are rusted.
9. Assemble by reversing these removal steps.

Stripping and Painting

Remove all components from the frame. Thoroughly strip off all old paint. The best way is to have it sandblasted down to bare metal. If this is not possible, you can use a liquid paint remover and steel wool and a fine, hard wire brush.

> *CAUTION*
> *The side panels, chain guard, instrument housing and, on the model CB750K, the front and rear fenders and seat support/rear spoiler are plastic (**Figure 5**). If you wish to change the color of these parts, consult an automotive paint supplier*

11

for the proper procedure. Do not use any liquid paint remover on these components as it will damage the surface. The color is an integral part of some of these components and cannot be removed.

When the frame is down to bare metal, have it inspected for hairline and internal cracks. Magnafluxing is the most common process.

Make sure that the primer is compatible with the type of paint that you are going to use for the final coat. Spray on one or two coats of primer as smoothly as possible. Let it dry thoroughly and use a fine grade of wet sandpaper (400-600 grit) to remove any flaws. Carefully wipe the surface clean and then spray the final coat. Use either lacquer or enamel and follow the manufacturer's instructions.

A shop specializing in painting will probably do the best job. However, you can do a surprisingly good job with a good grade of spray paint. Spend a few extra dollars and get a good grade of paint as it will make a difference in how well it looks and how long it will stand up. It's a good idea to shake the can and make sure the ball inside is loose when you purchase the can of paint. Shake the can as long as is stated on the can. Then immerse the can upright in a pot or bucket of *warm water (not hot–not over 120° F)*.

WARNING
Higher temperatures could cause the can to burst. **Do not** *place the can in direct contact with any flame or heat source.*

Leave the can in for several minutes. When thoroughly warmed, shake the can again and spray the frame. Several light mist coats are better than one heavy coat. Spray painting is best done in temperatures of 70° -80° F; any temperature above or below this will give you problems.

After the final coat has dried completely, at least 48 hours, any overspray or orange peel may be removed with a light application of Dupont rubbing compound (red color) and finished with Dupont polishing compound (white color). Be careful not to rub too hard and go through the finish.

Finish off with a couple of good coats of wax prior to reassembling all the components.

It's a good idea to keep the frame touched up with fresh paint if any minor rust spots or scratches appear.

An alternative to painting is powder coating. The process involves spraying electrically charged particles of pigment and resin on the object to be coated, which is negatively charged. The charged powder particles adhere to the electrically grounded object until heated and fused into a smooth coating in a curing oven. Powder coated surfaces are more resistant to chipping, scratching, fading and wearing than other finishes. A variety of colors and textures are available. Powder coating also has advantages over paint, as no environmentally hazardous solvents are used.

SUPPLEMENT

1981 AND 1982 SERVICE INFORMATION

The following supplement provides procedures unique to all 1981-1982 Honda CB750 models. All other service procedures are identical to earlier models.

The chapter headings in this supplement correspond to those in the main portion of this book. If a change is not included in the supplement, there are no changes affecting the 1981-1982 models.

CHAPTER THREE

LUBRICATION, MAINTENANCE AND TUNE-UP

PERIODIC LUBRICATION

Front Fork Oil Change

There is no factory-recommended fork oil change interval but it's a good practice to change the oil every 6,000 miles (10,000 km) or when it becomes contaminated.

1. Remove the dust cap (**Figure 1**) and *bleed off all air pressure* by depressing the valve stem (**Figure 2**).

> *NOTE*
> *Release air pressure gradually. If it is released too fast, oil will spurt out with the air. Protect your eyes and clothing accordingly.*

2. Place the bike on the centerstand.
3. Disconnect the air hose fitting from the left-hand fork cap (**Figure 3**) and then from the fitting on the right-hand fork cap (**Figure 4**). Leave the air hose in place under the fuse holder; it is not necessary to remove it unless it is to be replaced.

4. Unscrew the top fork cap/air valve assembly (**Figure 5**). Unscrew the fork cap slowly as it is under spring pressure from the fork spring.
5. Place a drain pan under the drain screw (**Figure 6**) and remove the drain screw. Allow the oil to drain for at least 5 minutes. *Never reuse the fork oil.*

> *CAUTION*
> *Do not allow the fork oil to come in contact with any of the brake components.*

6. Inspect the condition of the gasket on the drain screw; replace it if necessary. Install the drain screw.
7. Repeat for the other fork.
8. Refill each fork leg with Dexron ATF (automatic transmission fluid) or fork oil. The capacity for each fork leg is as follows:
   a. Model CB750K: 7.0 oz. (210 cc).
   b. Model CB750C, F: 8.0 oz. (245 cc).

NOTE
In order to measure the correct amount of fluid, use a plastic baby bottle. These have measurements in fluid ounces (oz.) and cubic centimeters (cc) on the side.

9. After filling each fork tube, slowly pump the fork tubes several times to expel air from the upper and lower fork chambers and to distribute the oil.

10. Inspect the condition of the O-ring seal on the top fork cap/air valve assembly; replace if necessary. Install the top fork cap/air valve assembly on each fork tube and tighten to 11-22 ft.-lb. (15-30 N•m). After the cap assemblies are tightened they must be aligned to their original position to correctly accept the air hose. If necessary, loosen the upper and lower fork bridge bolts and rotate the fork tube until alignment is correct. Retighten the upper fork bridge bolt to 7-9 ft.-lb. (9-13 N•m) and the lower to 22-29 ft.-lb. (30-40 N•m).

11. Apply a light coat of grease to new O-ring seals and install them onto the air hose fittings (**Figure 7**). Install the air hose fitting first to the right-hand side fork cap and tighten to 3-5 ft.-lb. (4-7 N•m). Install the air hose to the left-hand side fork cap and tighten the fitting to 11-15 ft.-lb. (15-20 N•m).

NOTE
Hold onto the air hose connector (attached to the top fork cap/air valve assembly) with a wrench while tightening the air hose fitting.

12. Inflate the forks to the following air pressure:

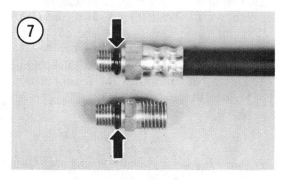

12

a. Model CB750K, C: 10-16 psi (0.7-1.1 kg/cm²).

b. Model CB750F: 11-17 psi (0.8-1.2 kg/cm²).

Do not use compressed air; only use a small hand-operated air pump like the S & W Mini-Pump (**Figure 8**) or equivalent.

> *WARNING*
> *Never use any type of compressed gas as an explosion may be lethal. Never heat the fork assembly with a torch or place it near an open flame or extreme heat as this will also result in an explosion.*

13. Road test the bike and check for leaks.

PERIODIC MAINTENANCE

Camshaft Chain
Tensioner Adjustment

In time, the camshaft chain and guide will wear and develop slack. This will cause engine noise and if neglected too long will cause engine damage. The chain tension should be adjusted every 4,000 miles (6,400 km).

> *NOTE*
> *The engine must be **cold**, at room temperature, (below 95° F/35° C) for this adjustment.*

> *NOTE*
> *In the following procedure, when the tensioner front locknut and tensioner bolt and both rear locknuts are loosened, the chain tensioners will automatically adjust to the correct tension.*

1. Remove the seat and fuel tank.

2. Remove all spark plugs (this will make it easier to turn the engine over by hand).

3. Remove the bolts (**Figure 9**) securing the alternator cover and remove the cover and gasket.

4. At the front adjuster, loosen the locknut (A, **Figure 10**) and loosen the tensioner bolt (B, **Figure 10**).

> *NOTE*
> *Steps 5 and 7 are easier done with the aid of a helper. Have the helper rotate the engine while you tighten the*

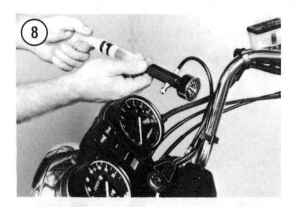

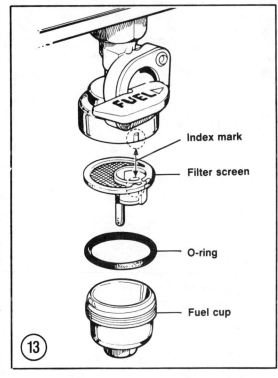

7. Have the helper rotate the crankshaft again. Use the bolt on the alternator (**Figure 11**) and a 17 mm wrench. Rotate the crankshaft *clockwise* while tightening both upper and lower locknuts.

Fuel Strainer
Removal/Cleaning/Installation (1982)

Refer to **Figure 13** for this procedure.
1. Turn the fuel shutoff valve to the OFF position.
2. Remove the fuel cup, O-ring seal and filter screen from the bottom of the fuel shutoff valve. Dispose of the fuel remaining in the fuel cup properly.
3. Clean the filter screen with a medium soft toothbrush and blow out with compressed air. Replace the filter screen if it is broken in any area.
4. Wash the fuel cup in kerosene to remove any residue or foreign matter. Thoroughly dry with compressed air.
5. Align the index marks on the filter screen and the fuel shutoff valve body.
6. Install the O-ring seal and screw on the fuel cup.
7. Hand-tighten the fuel cup and then tighten to a final torque of 2-4 ft.-lb. (3-5 N•m). Do not overtighten the fuel cup as it may be damaged.
8. Turn the fuel shutoff valve to the ON position and check for leaks.

TUNE-UP

Valve Clearance Adjustment

The valve clearance procedure and clearance for 1981-1982 models is the same for previous years. The only difference is a slightly different special tool used to hold the valve lifters in the down position for removal of the valve lifter adjusting shims. The new tool, "Valve Lifter Holder" (Honda part No. 07964-4220002), is used in the same way as the older tool but has a small handle attached to it for easier use.

GENERAL SPECIFICATIONS

Refer to **Table 1** for general specifications for all 1981-1982 models.

tensioner bolt (Step 5) and the upper and lower locknuts (Step 7).

5. Rotate the crankshaft by turning the bolt on the alternator (**Figure 11**) with a 17 mm wrench. Rotate the crankshaft *clockwise* while tightening the tensioner bolt. Tighten the locknut.
6. At the rear, loosen both the upper and lower locknuts (**Figure 12**).

NOTE
***Figure 12** is shown with the carburetor assembly removed for clarity only. Do not remove it for this procedure.*

Index mark

Filter screen

O-ring

Fuel cup

12

Table 1   GENERAL SPECIFICATIONS

Engine type	Air-cooled,4-stroke,DOHC, transverse mounted inline 4
Bore and stroke	2.44 X 2.44 in. (62.0 X 62.0 mm)
Displacement	45.7 cu.in. (749 cc)
Compression ratio	9.0 to 1
Carburetion	4 Keihin carburetors with accelerator pump on No. 2 carburetor only
Model CB750K & C	VB42A or VB42C
Model CB750F	VB42C
Ignition	Capacitor discharge ignition (CDI)
Lubrication	Wet-sump, filter, oil pump
Clutch	Wet, multi-plate (7)
Transmission	5-speed, constant velocity
Transmission ratios	
1st	2.533
2nd	1.789
3rd	1.391
4th	1.160
5th	0.964
Final reduction ratio	2.533
Drive chain	
Model CB750F & K	DID 50V or RK 50MO by 108 links
Model CB750C	DID 50V or RK 50MO by 106 links
Starting system	Electric starter only
Battery	12 Volt, 14 amp/hour
Alternator	Three phase, A.C., 0.26 kw/5000 rpm
Firing order	1-2-4-3 (No. 1 left-hand side)
Wheelbase	
Model CB750F & K	59.8 in. (1,520 mm)
Model CB750C	60.4 in. (1,535 mm)
Steering head angle	27° 30'
Trail	4.8 in. (121 mm)
Front suspension	Telescopic forks, 6.3 in. (160 mm) travel
Rear suspension	Swing arm, adjustable shock absorbers
Travel	
Models CB750F& K	4.4 in. (112 mm)
Model CB750C	4.3 in. (110 mm)
Front tire	
Model CB750K	3.50 H19 4PR
Model CB750F	3.50 S19 4PR
Model CB750C	110/90 19—62H
Rear tire	
Model CB750K	4.50 H17 4PR
Model CB750F	4.25 H18 4PR
Model CB750C	130/90 16—67H
Ground clearance	
Model CB750K	5.7 in. (145 mm)
Model CB750F	5.5 in. (140 mm)
Model CB750C	5.1 in. (130 mm)
Overall height	
Model CB750K	45.5 in. (1,155 mm)
Model CB750F	45.3 in. (1,150 mm)
Model CB750C	45.9 in. (1,165 mm)

(continued)

Table 1   GENERAL SPECIFICATIONS (continued)

Overall width (handlebar)	
Model CB750K	35.0 in. (890 mm)
Model CB750F	34.1 in. (865 mm)
Model CB750C	36.2 in. (920 mm)
Overall length	
Model CB750K	90.4 in. (2,295 mm)
Model CB750F	86.4 in. (2,195 mm)
Model CB750C	90.6 in. (2,300 mm)
Weight (dry)	
Model CB750K	516 lb. (234 kg)
Model CB750F	507 lb. (230 kg)
Model CB750C	516 lb. (234 kg)
Fuel capacity	
Model CB750K & F	5.3 U.S.gal. (20 liters, 4.3 Imp.gal.)
Model CB750C	4.4 U.S.gal. (16.5 liters, 3.6 Imp.gal.)
Oil capacity	
Oil and filter	3.5 U.S.qt. (3.7 liters, 3.1 Imp.qt.)
change	
At overhaul	4.7 U.S.qt. (4.5 liters, 3.9 Imp.qt.)
Front fork oil	Drain
capacity*	
Models CB750K	7.0 oz. (210 cc)
Models CB750F & C	8.0 oz. (245 cc)

*Capacity for each fork leg

CHAPTER SIX

FUEL AND EXHAUST SYSTEMS

CARBURETORS

Disassembly/Assembly (1982)

The disassembly and assembly procedures are the same as on previous years with the exception of the slow jet. On 1982 models the slow jet is removable for cleaning.

1. Remove the carburetor assembly as described in Chapter Six in the main body of this book.
2. Remove the screws securing the float bowl to the main body and remove the float bowl.
3. Remove the black plug covering the slow jet.
4. Unscrew the slow jet.
5. Blow out the slow jet with compressed air and inspect for damage. Replace if necessary.

6. Assemble by reversing these removal steps. Screw in the slow jet until resistance is felt, then tighten it an additional 3/4 turn.

FUEL LINE DIAPHRAGM

On models since 1981 the fuel shutoff valve can be left in the ON or RES position at all times. Vacuum from the engine opens the valve only when the engine is running and automatically closes the valve to stop the flow of fuel when the engine is shut off. The OFF position is used only when the motorcycle is stored for any length of time or when servicing the fuel system.

12

Removal/Testing/Installation

1. Remove the carburetors as described under *Carburetor Removal/Installation* in Chapter Six in the main body of this book.

2. Remove the fuel tube to the carburetors, the vacuum line (A, **Figure 14**) and the air vent tube from the carburetor assembly (leave the lines attached to the fuel line diaphragm assembly).

3. Remove the screws (B, **Figure 14**) securing the fuel line diaphragm assembly to the carburetors and remove the diaphragm assembly.

4. Place the fuel tank (removed during carburetor removal) up on a box so it is higher than the work surface of your workbench. Attach a test piece of long fuel line from the fuel shutoff valve to the fuel inlet fitting on the fuel line diaphragm.

5. Connect a portable hand vacuum pump to the vacuum hose on the fuel line diaphragm (**Figure 15**).

6. Place a suitable clean metal container under the carburetor fuel hose (the one that normally leads to the carburetors).

NOTE
If this fuel is kept clean it can be reused. If it becomes contaminated during this procedure dispose of it properly. Check with local regulations for proper disposal of gasoline.

7. Turn the fuel shutoff valve to the ON or RES position. Fuel should *not* flow from the carburetor fuel hose.

8. Apply vacuum to the diaphragm with the hand pump. Fuel *should* flow out when 0.4-0.8 in. Hg (10-20 mm Hg) of vacuum is applied.

9. If fuel does not flow the diaphragm is not operating correctly and must be replaced; it cannot be serviced.

10. Disconnect the portable hand vacuum pump.

11. Turn the fuel shutoff valve to the OFF position and remove the test fuel line from the fuel tank to the diaphragm assembly.

12. Install the fuel line diaphragm to the carburetor assembly.

13. Install the carburetors as described under *Carburetor Removal/Installation* in Chapter Six of the main body of this book.

CRANKCASE BREATHER SYSTEM (1982 U.S. MODELS)

Inspection

The inspection procedure is the same as on previous years with the exception of the location of the drain hose and cap.

Remove the right-hand side cover and remove the drain hose from the clip on the battery holding bracket. Remove the cap, drain out all residue, install the cap and reinstall the drain hose into the clip.

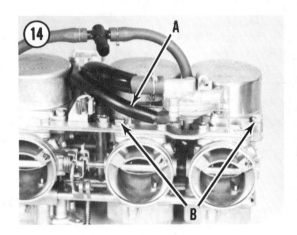

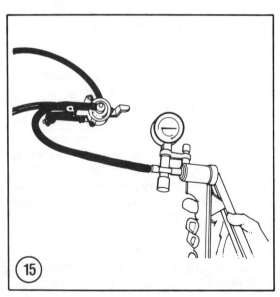

CHAPTER SEVEN

ELECTRICAL SYSTEM

VOLTAGE REGULATOR/RECTIFIER

Voltage Regulator/Rectifier Testing

To test the voltage regulator/rectifier, disconnect the 2 electrical connectors from the harness. One connector contains 3 wires—one green, one black and one white. The other connector contains 5 wires—3 yellow, one green and one red/white. Make the following measurements using an ohmmeter with a positive ground. If a negative ground ohmmeter is used reverse the test leads in the following tests.

1. Connect the negative ohmmeter lead to the green rectifier lead. Connect the positive ohmmeter lead to each of the yellow leads. These 3 measurements must be the same (0.5-50 ohms).

2. Reverse the ohmmeter leads and repeat Step 1. This time, the readings must also be the same, but just the opposite—they should read infinity.

3. Connect the positive ohmmeter lead to the red/white rectifier lead. Connect the negative ohmmeter lead to each of the yellow leads and to the green lead. These 4 measurements must be the same (0.5-50 ohms).

4. Revese the ohmmeter leads and repeat Step 3. This time, the readings must also be the same, but just the opposite—they should read infinity.

5. Connect the negative ohmmeter lead to the regulator black lead. Connect the positive ohmmeter lead to the regulator white lead and then to the green lead. The measurements should be 1-30 ohms for the white lead and 0.5-20 ohms for the green lead.

6. Connect the negative ohmmeter lead to the regulator white lead. Connect the positive ohmmeter lead to the regulator black lead and then to the green lead. The measurements should be 0.5-30 ohms for the black lead and 1-50 ohms for the green lead.

7. Connect the negative ohmmeter lead to the regulator green lead. Connect the positive ohmmeter lead to the regulator black lead and then to the white lead. The measurements should be 0.5-20 ohms for the black lead and 0.5-30 ohms for the white lead.

8. Connect the positive ohmmeter lead to the regulator black lead. Connect the negative ohmmeter lead to the regulator white lead and then to the green lead. The measurements should be 0.5-30 ohms for the white lead and 0.5-20 ohms for the green lead.

9. Connect the positive ohmmeter lead to the regulator white lead. Connect the negative ohmmeter lead to the regulator black lead and then to the green lead. The measurements should be 1-30 ohms for the black lead and 0.5-30 ohms for the green lead.

10. Connect the positive ohmmeter lead to the regulator green lead. Connect the positive ohmmeter lead to the regulator black lead and then to the white lead. The measurements should be 0.5-20 ohms for the black lead and 1-50 ohms for the white lead.

11. If the voltage regulator/rectifier fails to pass any of these tests the unit is defective and must be replaced.

12

LIGHTING SYSTEM

Headlight Replacement
(U.S., Canada and U.K.)

Models since 1981 are equipped with a quartz halogen headlight. Special handling is required as specified in this procedure.

Refer to **Figure 16** for this procedure.

1. Remove the screws (**Figure 17**) on each side securing the headlight assembly.

2. Pull out on the bottom of the headlight assembly and disengage it from the locating tab on top of the headlight housing.

3. Disconnect the electrical connector (**Figure 18**) from the headlight lens unit.

4. Remove the bulb cover, set spring and bulb assembly. Replace with a new bulb assembly—do not touch the bulb with your fingers. Assemble by reversing this sequence.

> *CAUTION*
> *Carefully read all instructions shipped with the replacement bulb. Do not touch the bulb glass with your fingers because of oil on your skin. Any traces of oil on the quartz halogen bulb will drastically reduce the life of the bulb. Clean any traces of oil from the bulb with a cloth moistened in alcohol or lacquer thinner.*

> *NOTE*
> *The headlight bulb replacement number is H4 (Phillips 12342/99 or equivalent).*

5. Install by reversing these removal steps.

6. Adjust the headlight as described under *Headlight Adjustment* in Chapter Seven of the main book.

City (Pilot)
Lamp Replacement (U.K.)

The U.K. models of the CB750 use the same headlight assembly as those for U.S. and Canada with the addition of the city (pilot) lamp.

Pull the city lamp out of the housing. Insert new bulb and push it back into the housing.

> *CAUTION*
> *The city (pilot) lamp is also a quartz type lamp. Carefully read all instructions shipped with the*

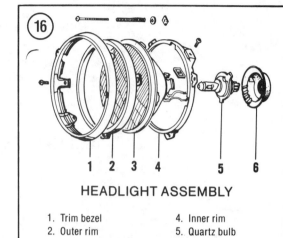

HEADLIGHT ASSEMBLY

1. Trim bezel	4. Inner rim
2. Outer rim	5. Quartz bulb
3. Headlight lens unit	6. Bulb cover

replacement bulb. Do not touch the bulb glass with your fingers because of oil on your skin. Any traces of oil on the quartz halogen bulb will drastically reduce the life of the bulb. Clean any traces of oil from the bulb with a cloth moistened in alcohol or lacquer thinner.

CHAPTER EIGHT

FRONT SUSPENSION AND STEERING

FRONT WHEEL

Removal (1982 CB750C)

Front wheel removal is the same as on all other models described in this supplement.

Installation (1982 CB750C)

During the 1982 model run, the CB750C models were equipped with two types of caliper assemblies. The only difference between the two types that relate to this procedure is the caliper-to-disc clearance required after the front wheel has been reinstalled.

Kokiko caliper assemblies are installed on bikes with the following frame serial numbers:
a. CB750C: RC011-CM204182 through CM206708.
b. CB750K: RC01E-CM301522 through CM303183.

Nisshin caliper assemblies are installed on bikes with the following frame serial numbers:
a. CB750C: RC011-CM200003 through CM204181.
b. CB750K: RC01E-CM300003 through CM301521.
c. CB750F: All models.

Installation is the same with the exception of the clearance required between the right-hand brake caliper and the brake disc.
1. Install the front wheel as described for CB750F models in this supplement.
2A. On Kokiko calipers, perform the following:
 a. With a flat feeler gauge, measure the distance between the outside surface of the right-hand disc and the rear surface of the caliper holder.
 b. The clearance must be 0.028 in. (0.7 mm) or more.
 c. If the clearance is insufficient, loosen the axle pinch bolt and pull or push the right-hand fork leg until this dimension is achieved.
 d. Tighten the axle pinch bolt to 11-18 ft.-lb. (15-25 N•m).
2B. On Nisshin calipers, perform the following:
 a. With a flat feeler gauge, measure the distance between both the inside and the outside surface of the right-hand disc and the rear surface of the caliper holder.
 b. The clearance must be 0.028 in. (0.7 mm) or more on both sides of the disc.
 c. If the clearance is insufficient, loosen the axle pinch bolt and pull or push the right-hand fork leg until this dimension is achieved on both sides of the disc.
 d. Tighten the axle pinch bolt to 11-18 ft.-lb. (15-25 N•m).

Removal (All Other Models)

1. Place a milk crate or wood block(s) under the engine or frame to support it securely with the front wheel off the ground.
2. Expand the speedometer cable set spring (**Figure 19**). Pull the speedometer cable free from the hub.

3. On one side only, remove the bolts (**Figure 20**) securing the brake caliper assembly to the front fork and tie it up to the front fork. It is necessary to remove only one of the caliper assemblies, not both.

4. Loosen the axle pinch bolt and nut (A, **Figure 21**).

5. Unscrew and withdraw the front axle (B, **Figure 21**).

6. Pull the wheel down and forward and remove it.

CAUTION
Do not set the wheel down on the disc surface as it may get scratched or warped. Set it on 2 wood blocks.

NOTE
Insert a piece of wood in both calipers in place of the brake discs. That way, if the brake lever is inadvertently squeezed, the piston will not be forced out of the cylinder. If this does happen, the caliper may have to be disassembled to reseat the piston and the system will have to be bled. By using the wood, bleeding the brake is not necessary when installing the wheel.

Installation (All Other Models)

1. Make sure the axle bearing surfaces of the fork slider and axle are free from burrs and nicks.

2. Remove the pieces of wood from the brake calipers.

3. Position the wheel into place, carefully inserting the brake disc between the brake pads.

4. Position the speedometer housing so that it is perpendicular to the left-hand fork leg.

5. Insert the front axle from the right-hand side and screw it into the left-hand fork leg.

6. Tighten the front axle to 40-47 ft.-lb. (55-65 N•m).

7. Install the pinch bolt and nut and tighten it finger-tight only.

8. Install the caliper that was removed, being careful not to damage the brake pads.

9. Tighten the caliper mounting bolts to 22-29 ft.-lb. (30-40 N•m).

10. Slowly rotate the wheel and install the speedometer cable into the speedometer housing. Install the cable set spring.

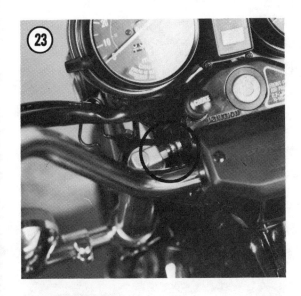

11. With a flat feeler gauge, measure the distance between the outside surface of the disc and the left-hand caliper holder. The clearance must be 0.028 in. (0.7 mm) or more. If clearance is insufficient, loosen the axle pinch bolt and pull the left-hand fork leg out until this dimension is achieved. Tighten the pinch bolt and nut to 11-18 ft.-lb. (15-25 N•m).

12. After the wheel is completely installed, rotate it several times and apply the brakes a couple of times to make sure that it rotates freely and that the brake pads are against the disc correctly.

FRONT FORK

The front suspension uses a spring controlled, hydraulically damped, air assisted telescopic fork. Disassembly should be entrusted to a Honda dealer. This fork configuration requires the use of special tools and a hydraulic press.

Before suspecting major trouble, drain the front fork oil and refill with the proper type and quantity; refer to *Front Fork Oil Change* in this supplement. If you still have trouble, such as poor damping, a tendency to bottom or top out or leakage around the rubber seals, the fork should be serviced by a dealer.

Removal/Installation

1. Remove the front wheel as described under *Front Wheel Removal/Installation* in this supplement.

2. Remove the air valve cap and *bleed off all air pressure* by depressing the valve stem (**Figure 22**).

> *NOTE*
> *Release the air pressure gradually. If released too fast, fork oil will spurt out with the air. Protect your eyes and clothing accordingly.*

3. Disconnect the air hose fitting from the left-hand fork cap (**Figure 23**) and then from the fitting on the right-hand fork cap (**Figure 24**). Leave the air hose in place under the fuse holder; it is not necessary to remove it unless it is to be replaced. Unscrew the air hose connector from the right-hand fork cap (**Figure 25**).

12

4. Remove the bolts securing the front fender and remove the fender.

5. Loosen the upper and lower fork bridge bolts (**Figure 26**).

6. Remove the fork tube. It may be necessary to slightly rotate the fork tube while pulling it down and out.

7. Install by reversing these removal steps, noting the following.

8. Install the fork tubes so that the line on the fork tube aligns with the top surface of the upper fork bridge.

9. Tighten the bolts to the following torque
   a. Upper fork bridge bolts: 7-9 ft.-lb. (9-13 N•m).
   b. Lower fork bridge bolts: 22-29 ft.-lb. (30-40 N•m).
   c. Caliper mounting bolts: 22-29 ft.-lb. (30-40 N•m).

10. Apply a light coat of grease to new O-ring seals and install them onto the air hose fittings (**Figure 27**). Install the air hose connector into the fork top cap/air valve assembly and tighten to 3-5 ft.-lb. (4-7 N•m). Install the air hose fitting first to the right-hand side fork cap and tighten to 3-5 ft.-lb. (4-7 N•m). Install the air hose to the left-hand side fork cap and tighten the fitting to 11-15 ft.-lb. (15-20 N•m).

NOTE
Hold onto the air hose connector (attached to the top fork cap/air hose assembly) with a wrench while tightening the air hose fitting.

11. Inflate the forks to the following air pressure:
   a. Model CB750K, C: 10-16 psi (0.7-1.1 kg/cm²).
   b. Model CB750F: 11-17 psi (0.8-1.2 kg/cm²).

Do not use compressed air; only use a small hand-operated air pump like the S & W Mini-Pump (**Figure 28**) or equivalent.

WARNING
Never use any type of compressed gas as an explosion may be lethal. Never heat the fork assembly with a torch or place it near an open flame or extreme heat as this will also result in an explosion.

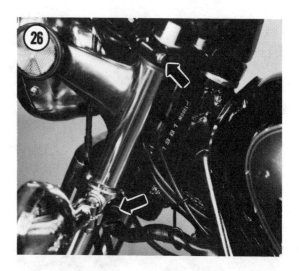

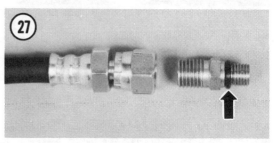

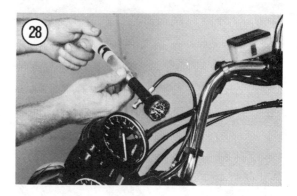

Disassembly/Assembly

Disassembly of this model front fork should be entrusted to a Honda dealer. In order to disassemble the fork the oil seal in the slider must be removed with special Honda tools and a hydraulic press.

Do not try to disassemble the fork tube from the slider with force as many internal components will be damaged. A considerable amount of money can be saved by removing the fork assemblies yourself and taking them to a Honda dealer for repair.

CHAPTER TEN

BRAKES

The brake system on the 1982 CB750K consists of a single disc on the front and a drum on the rear. On all other models there are dual discs on the front and a single disc on the rear. The caliper assemblies used on the 1981-1982 CB750F, the 1982 CB750C and the CB750K (front only) use dual pistons instead of a single piston as all other models do. Refer to **Table 2** for specifications and wear limits for the disc brake components.

During the 1982 model run, the CB750C and CB750K were equipped with two types of caliper assemblies. The differences between the 2 types are minimal and relate mainly to component specifications.

When referring to **Table 2** be sure to use the specifications for your specific model. Kokiko caliper assemblies are installed on bikes with the following frame serial numbers:

    a. CB750C: RC011-CM204182 through CM206708.

    b. CB750K: RC01E-CM301522 through CM303183.

Nisshin caliper assemblies are installed on bikes with the following frame serial numbers:

    a. CB750C: RC011-CM200003 through CM204181.

    b. CB750K: RC01E-CM300003 through CM301521.

    c. CB750F: All models.

BRAKE PAD REPLACEMENT
(1981-1982 CB750F, 1982 CB750C, 1982 CB750K)

There is no recommended mileage interval for changing the friction pads on the disc brake. Pad wear depends greatly on riding habits and conditions. The pads should be checked for wear every 600 miles (1,000 km) and replaced when the red line wear indicator reaches the edge of the brake disc. Always replace both pads (2 per disc) at the same time.

CAUTION
Watch the pads more closely when the red line approaches the disc. On some pads the red line is very close to the pad's metal backing plate. If pad wear is uneven the backing plate may come in contact with the disc and cause damage.

Refer to **Figure 29** for the front wheel and **Figure 30** for the rear wheel for this procedure.

1. Remove the screw securing the pin retainer on the backside of the caliper assembly and remove the pin retainer.
2. Remove the 2 pins (A, **Figure 31**) securing the pads in place; remove the pads and discard them.
3. Remove the caliper lower mounting bolt (B, **Figure 31**) and pivot the caliper up.

NOTE
Figure 31 is shown with the front wheel. The rear wheel configuration is basically the same.

4. Clean the pad recess and the end of the pistons with a soft brush. Do not use solvent, a wire brush or any hard tool which would damage the cylinders or pistons.
5. Carefully remove any rust or corrosion from the disc.

6. Lightly coat the end of the pistons and the backs of the new pads (*not the friction material*) with disc brake lubricant.

NOTE
When purchasing new pads, check with your dealer to make sure the friction compound of the new pad is compatible with the disc material. Remove any roughness from the backs of the new pads with a fine-cut file; blow them clean with compressed air.

7. When new pads are installed in the caliper the master cylinder brake fluid level will rise as the caliper pistons are repositioned. Clean the top of the master cylinder of all dirt and foreign matter. Remove the cap and diaphragm from the master cylinder and slowly push the caliper pistons into the caliper. Constantly check the reservoir to make sure brake fluid does not overflow. Remove fluid, if necessary, prior to it overflowing. The pistons should move freely. If they don't, and there is evidence of it sticking in the cylinder, the caliper should be removed and serviced as described under *Caliper Rebuilding* in this supplement.

8. Push the caliper in toward the disc to allow room for the new pads.

9. Install the inboard and outboard brake pads.

10. Install both pins securing the brake pads.

11. Install the pin retainer on the backside of the caliper and tighten the screw securely.

12. Repeat for the other caliper assembly.

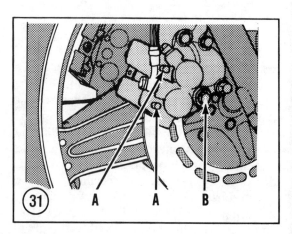

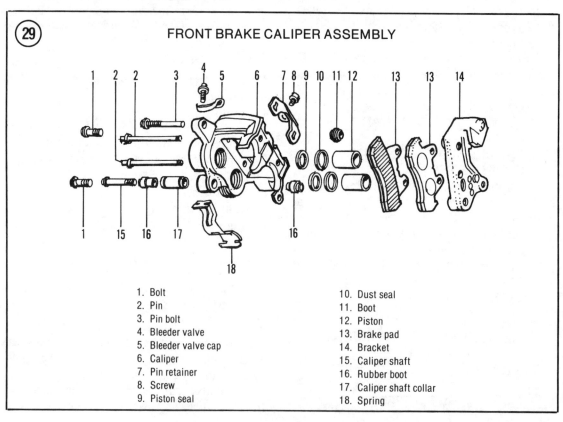

FRONT BRAKE CALIPER ASSEMBLY

1. Bolt	10. Dust seal
2. Pin	11. Boot
3. Pin bolt	12. Piston
4. Bleeder valve	13. Brake pad
5. Bleeder valve cap	14. Bracket
6. Caliper	15. Caliper shaft
7. Pin retainer	16. Rubber boot
8. Screw	17. Caliper shaft collar
9. Piston seal	18. Spring

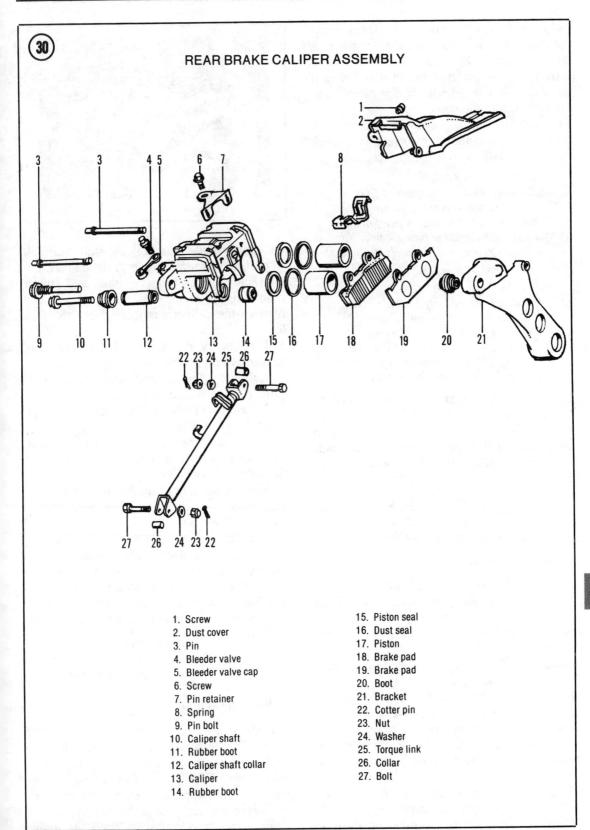

REAR BRAKE CALIPER ASSEMBLY

1. Screw
2. Dust cover
3. Pin
4. Bleeder valve
5. Bleeder valve cap
6. Screw
7. Pin retainer
8. Spring
9. Pin bolt
10. Caliper shaft
11. Rubber boot
12. Caliper shaft collar
13. Caliper
14. Rubber boot
15. Piston seal
16. Dust seal
17. Piston
18. Brake pad
19. Brake pad
20. Boot
21. Bracket
22. Cotter pin
23. Nut
24. Washer
25. Torque link
26. Collar
27. Bolt

12

13. Place a milk crate or wood blocks under the engine or frame so that the front wheel is off the ground. Spin the front wheel and activate the brake lever as many times as it takes to refill the cylinder in the caliper and correctly locate the pads.

14. Refill the master cylinder reservoir, if necessary, to maintain the correct fluid level. Install the diaphragm and top cap.

> *WARNING*
> *Use brake fluid clearly marked DOT 3 from a sealed container. Other types may vaporize and cause brake failure. Always use the same brand name; do not intermix as many brands are not compatible.*

> *WARNING*
> *Do not ride the motorcycle until you are sure the brake is operating correctly with full hydraulic advantage. If necessary, bleed the brake as described under **Bleeding the System** in Chapter Ten in the main body of this book.*

15. Bed the pads in gradually for the first 50 miles (80 km) by using only light pressure as much as possible. Immediate hard application will glaze the new friction pads and greatly reduce the effectiveness of the brake.

FRONT CALIPER
(1981-1982 CB750F,
1982 CB750C, 1982 CB750K)

Removal/Installation

Refer to **Figure 29** for this procedure.

It is not necessary to remove the front wheel in order to remove either or both caliper assemblies.

1. Remove the brake pads as described under *Brake Pad Replacement* in this supplement.

2. Remove the union bolt and 2 sealing washers attaching the brake hose to the caliper (A, **Figure 32**). To prevent the loss of brake fluid, cap the end of the brake hose and tie it up to the fork leg. Be sure to cap or tape the ends to prevent the entry of moisture and dirt.

3. Loosen the upper caliper shaft (B, **Figure 32**) and lower caliper mounting bolt (C, **Figure 32**) gradually in several steps. Push on

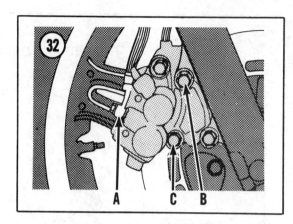

the caliper while loosening the shaft and bolt to push the pistons back into the caliper.

4. Remove the caliper shaft and lower mounting bolt securing the caliper and remove the caliper assembly from the fork leg.

5. If necessary, repeat Steps 1-4 for the other caliper assembly.

6. Lubricate the caliper shaft and lower caliper mounting bolt with silicone grease.

7. Install by reversing these removal steps, noting the following.

8. Make sure the rubber boots are still in place and correctly seated in the grooves in the caliper shaft collar.

9. Tighten the caliper shaft and caliper lower mounting bolt to the torque specification listed in **Table 3**.

10. Install the brake hose, with a sealing washer on each side of the fitting, onto the caliper. Install the union bolt and tighten to the torque specification listed in **Table 3**.

11. Bleed the brake as described in Chapter Ten in the main body of this book.

> *WARNING*
> *Do not ride the motorcycle until you are sure the brakes are operating properly.*

Caliper Rebuilding

If the caliper leaks, the caliper should be rebuilt. If the pistons stick in the cylinders, indicating severe wear or galling, the entire unit should be replaced. Rebuilding a leaky caliper requires special tools and experience.

Caliper service should be entrusted to a dealer, motorcycle repair shop or brake

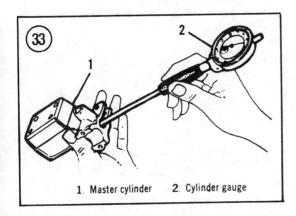

1. Master cylinder   2. Cylinder gauge

specialist. Considerable money can be saved by removing the caliper yourself and taking it in for repair.

FRONT MASTER CYLINDER
(1981-1982 CB750F, 1982 CB750C, 1982 CB750K)

Removal, installation, disassembly and assembly are the same as on previous models. Specifications are different and are covered in this inspection procedure and **Table 2**.

NOTE
The rear master cylinder is the same as on previous models.

Inspection

1. Clean all parts in denatured alcohol or fresh brake fluid. Inspect the cylinder bore and piston contact surfaces for signs of wear and damage. If either part is less than perfect, replace it.
2. Check the end of the piston for wear caused by the hand lever. Replace the piston if the secondary cup requires replacement.
3. Inspect the pivot hole in the hand lever. If worn or elongated it must be replaced.
4. Make sure the passages in the bottom of the brake fluid reservoir are clear. Check the reservoir cap and diaphragm for damage and deterioration. Replace if necessary.
5. Inspect the condition of the threads in the master cylinder body where the brake hose union bolt screws in. If the threads are damaged or partially stripped, replace the master cylinder body.

6. Check the hand lever pivot lug on the master cylinder body for cracks. Replace the master cylinder body if necessary.
7. Measure the cylinder bore (**Figure 33**). The cylinder bore must not exceed the dimension listed in **Table 2**. Replace the master cylinder assembly if it exceeds this dimension.
8. Measure the outside diameter of the piston. If the dimension is less than that listed in **Table 2** the piston must be replaced.

BRAKE DISC
FRONT AND REAR
(1981-1982 CB750F, 1982 CB750C)

Removal/Installation

1. Remove the front wheel as described under *Front Wheel Removal/Installation* in this supplement. Remove the rear wheel as described under *Rear Wheel Removal/Installation* in Chapter Nine in the main body of this book.

NOTE
Place a piece of wood in the calipers in place of the discs. This way, if the brake lever is inadvertently squeezed the pistons will not be forced out of the cylinder. If this does happen, the caliper might have to be disassembled to reseat the piston and the system will have to be bled. By using the wood, bleeding the system is not necessary when installing the wheel.

2A. On the front wheel, remove the speedometer gear housing. Remove the nuts on the right-hand side and remove the bolts from the left-hand side. Remove both discs and damping shims from the wheel.
2B. On the rear wheel, remove the nuts securing the brake disc to the rear hub and remove the disc.
3. Install by reversing these removal steps, noting the following.
4. On the front wheel, don't forget to install the damping shim between each disc and the wheel. Install the bolts from the left-hand side.
5. Tighten the bolts and nuts to 20-24 ft.-lb. (27-33 N•m) on both the front and rear wheel.

12

Inspection

It is not necessary to remove the disc from the wheel to inspect it. Small marks on the disc are not important, but scratches deep enough to snag a fingernail reduce braking effectiveness and increase brake pad wear. If these grooves are found, the disc should be replaced.

1. Measure the thickness of the disc at several locations around the disc with vernier calipers or a micrometer. The disc must be replaced if the thickness, in any area, is less than specified in **Table 2**.

2. Make sure the disc bolts and nuts are tight prior to running this check. Check the disc runout with a dial indicator as shown in **Figure 34**. Slowly rotate the wheel and watch the dial indicator. If the runout is 0.012 in. (0.3 mm) or greater the disc must be replaced.

3. Clean the disc of any rust or corrosion and wipe clean with lacquer thinner. Never use an oil-based solvent that may leave an oil residue on the disc.

Table 2 BRAKE SPECIFICATIONS

Item	Specification	Wear limit
Front master cylinder		
CB750C, CB750F		
Cylinder bore ID	15.870-15.913 mm	15.925 mm
	(0.6248-0.6265 in.)	(0.627 in.)
Piston OD	15.827-15.854 mm	15.815 mm
	(0.6231-0.6242 in.)	(0.6226 in.)
CB750K		
Cylinder bore ID	14.000-14.043 mm	14.055 mm
	(0.5512-0.5529 in.)	(0.553 in.)
Piston OD	13.957-13.984 mm	13.945 mm
	(0.5495-0.5506 in.)	(0.5490 in.)
Rear master cylinder		
Cylinder bore ID	14.000-14.043 mm	14.055 mm
	(0.5512-0.5529 in.)	(0.5533 in.)
Piston OD	13.957-13.984 mm	13.945 mm
	(0.5495-0.5506 in.)	(0.5490 in.)

(continued)

Table 2 BRAKE SPECIFICATIONS (continued)

Item	Specification	Wear limit
Front caliper		
Kokiko		
Cylinder bore ID	30.230-30.306 mm (1.1902-1.1931 in.)	30.316 mm (1.1935 in.)
Piston OD	30.150-30.200 mm (1.1870-1.1890 in.)	30.142 mm (1.1867 in.)
Nisshin		
Cylinder bore ID	30.230-30.280 mm (1.1902-1.1921 in.)	30.290 mm (1.1925 in.)
Piston OD	30.148-30.198 mm (1.1869-1.1889 in.)	30.140 mm (1.1866 in.)
Rear caliper		
Cylinder bore ID	27.000-27.050 mm (1.0630-1.0650 in.)	27.060 mm (1.0654 in.)
Piston OD	26.918-26.968 mm (1.0598-1.0617 in.)	26.910 mm (1.0594 in.)
Brake disc thickness		
Front		
CB750C, CB750F	4.9-5.1 mm (0.19-0.205 in.)	4.0 mm (0.16 in.)
CB750K	6.9-7.1 mm (0.27-0.28 in.)	6.0 mm (0.24 in.)
Rear	6.9-7.1 mm (0.27-0.28 in.)	6.0 mm (0.24 in.)
Disc runout	—	0.3 mm (0.12 in.)

Table 3 BRAKE TORQUE SPECIFICATIONS

Item	N•m	ft.-lb.
Brake hose union bolts	25-35	18-25
Caliper shaft nut—Kokiko	30-36	22-26
Caliper shaft—Nisshin	25-30	18-22
Caliper mounting bolt		
Kokiko	18-23	13-17
Nisshin	20-25	14-18
Brake disc mounting bolts and nuts	27-33	20-24

12

NOTES

INDEX

13

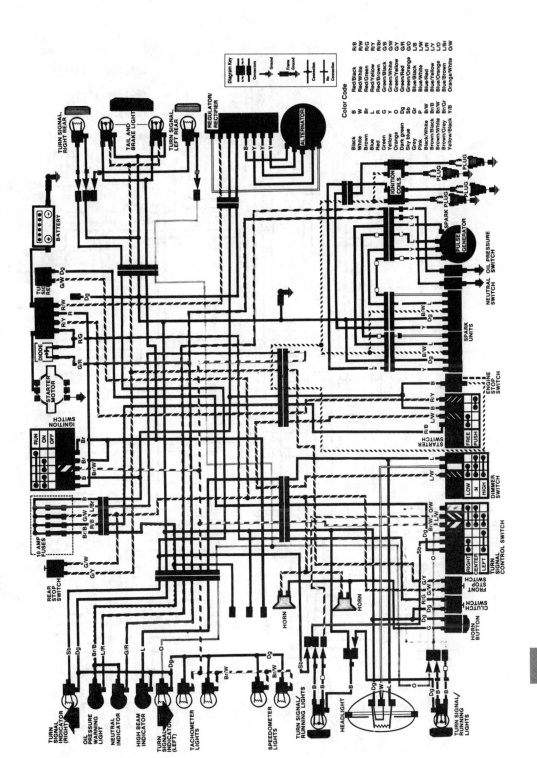

HONDA CB750F

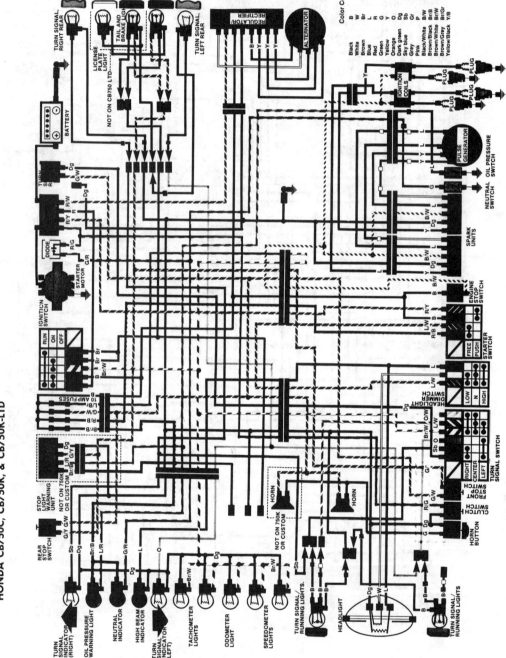

HONDA CB750C, CB750K, & CB750K-LTD

NOTES

NOTES

NOTES

NOTES

NOTES

NOTES

NOTES

MAINTENANCE LOG

Service Performed   **Mileage Reading**

Oil change (example)	2,836	5,782	8,601		